bbfal

CONTINGENCY THEORY

Rethinking the Boundaries of Social Thought

Gary Itzkowitz

University Press of America, Inc.
Lanham • New York • London

0389489

Copyright © 1996 by
University Press of America,® Inc.
4720 Boston Way
Lanham, Maryland 20706

3 Henrietta Street
London, WC2E 8LU England

Library of Congress Cataloging-in-Publication Data

Itzkowitz, Gary.
Contingency theory : rethinking the boundaries of social thought /
Gary Itzkowitz.
p.   cm.
Includes bibliographical references and index.
1. Sociology--Philosophy. I. Title.
HM24.I799   1996   301'.01 --dc20   96-20844   CIP

ISBN 0-7618-0442-0 (cloth: alk. ppr.)
ISBN 0-7618-0443-9 (pbk: alk. ppr.)

∞™The paper used in this publication meets the minimum
requirements of American National Standard for information
Sciences—Permanence of Paper for Printed Library Materials,
ANSI Z39.48—1984

For my son, Adam.

*He helped me remember the wonder of the stars
and teaches me every day about the wonder
of each human being.*

Acknowledgments

This book grew out of discussions I had fourteen years ago in a villa in Athens, Greece. Shortly after accepting a teaching position and arriving in Athens, I had the opportunity to meet a unique seeker of social truth, George Harvalias. Educated in several fields but holding no formal degrees, this eclectic intellectual inspired, promoted, and harassed my conceptions of social theory. Discipline not his strong suit, George would retort to every suggestion that he should write a book with, "You have the degree, you write it." Those discussions planted a seed that germinated and became this book. Many of my initial ideas have changed since then, but the source of the journey was George.

Other people have been good enough to discuss and help shape this book. I would like to thank the following individuals and groups in particular. First, the students at the University of Wisconsin - Stevens Point directly and indirectly added to my understanding of, and appreciation for, sociological theory. My colleagues in the Sociology Department at UW-SP always have been supportive and I am in their debt. I also wish to thank the University Professional Development Committee at UW-SP for two grants that enabled me to complete my work on this project. Finally, my sincere thanks to Sandra Wanserski and her staff for all the editorial and administrative help they provided.

***

Contents

Dedication
Preface

PART II: SEARCHING FOR CONTINGENT CLUES

PART III: CONCEIVING A NEW MODEL

Preface

This book makes a relatively simple suggestion for social theory. Theorists should abandon their protracted search for laws governing social order, and the relationship between social order and social action. Patterned after sixteenth-century scientific laws of physics, universal laws of social development have been inadequate to explain society. The mistaken search for social order is subject to growing condemnation among theorists. Some theorists conclude the normal state of social affairs is disorder, not order. However, the need to abandon overarching narratives does not leave postmodern conclusions as the only alternative. Society can be explained, but only when social development is considered unpredictable. Contingency is the term that best describes social outcomes, and implies social forms are neither pure happenstance or pre-determined. Instead, contingency asserts that explainable micro and macro social patterns do emerge in society, but interrelate in variable, and often unpredictable ways. The outcome can be social order, or deconstruction, or conflict.

The failure of most contemporary sociological theory rests in assumptions inherited and accepted from the past. Newton's mechanical universe suggested all physical reality is directly related, and that movement in one part of the physical universe instantaneously influences all other parts. Most early modern philosophers accepted this assumption and strained to match physics to society. The result was the emergence of empiricism, natural law, realism, and rationalism, each asserting how closely aligned it was with science. However, the classical sociologists realized that Newton's physical laws could not be directly applied to human society, and offered another model for explaining the social world. While each differed, Marx, Durkheim, and Weber all posited interaction between people as social, not natural, and social interaction became the cohesive feature of society in classical theory.

Replacing physical laws with social interaction was a immense step in the creation of sociology, but while science was no longer considered the perfect exemplar for society, the effort to explain social reality through universal laws remained. Consequently, classical theorists searched for a key to social development, and created persuasive rationales for their distinctive, all-encompassing arguments. Later, social theorists adopted one or another key, and created a fracture in social theory between those arguing for the primacy of social structures, and those arguing for the primacy of micro social actions.

The problem inherent in micro and macro searches for universal explanations is that large, tangible aspects of reality are removed from discussion. Abstract but logically coherent theories become the aim of universal narrations, even at the cost of presuming what is not empirically known or explored. Assumptions regarding gender relations, the relationship between people and nature, relations between the rich and poor, and social order as a societal goal were continually feigned by micro and macro theorists. These same assumptions have come under relentless attack and indictment in the contemporary era, notably by postmodernists, feminist theorists and ecological theorists. These indictments highlight how much concentrating on universal assumptions leaves in the dark, especially regarding the relationship between micro and macro social levels, and how power operates within both.

In part due to indictment theories, social theory has begun a process of self-criticism. Fractured micro and macro camps are no longer acceptable. Both micro and macro aspects of theory and reality must be taken into account in any contemporary sociology; unhappily, this is much easier said than done. While a consensus has emerged for the need to integrate theory, no new synthesis or paradigm has emerged. Instead, efforts to integrate social theory have made what I believe are three errors in construction.

1. Theories have merely attempted to expand micro principles to explain macro phenomena, or what I call ascending theories.

2. Theories have attempted to expand macro principles to explain micro phenomena, or what I call descending theories.

3. Theories view micro and macro phenomena as mutually fused, or what I call imploding theories.

The common error of contemporary integrated theories is their covert acceptance of a disastrous assumption inherited from early modern science: that time and space are contiguous. In brief, contemporary theorists presume micro and macro processes move along parallel time and space paths, an idea imported from Newton's mechanical universe, as well as western philosophy. Almost every major contemporary sociological theory assumes that micro and macro processes are immediately related. This book asserts they are not. Twentieth century science itself has shown this principle to be fundamentally flawed. Instead, micro and macro physical phenomena are now seen by science as autonomous; that is, micro and macro phenomena remain related, but only as an aftermath of autonomous developments in each level. Moreover, since neither level is seen as determining the other, the outcome of their relationship is necessarily contingent on the autonomous processes emerging in each.

Consequently, the basic premise of this work can be summarized as follows. The classical effort to emphasize social interaction was correct and must be reintroduced into contemporary efforts. However, micro and macro processes must be seen as autonomous, and the social interaction developing in each must be explored separately. In addition, the interests of those exercising social interaction must also be understood, both in relation to how interests are formed, and how they are applied. A recognition of these three simple ideas will enable theorists to overcome the long-standing bias toward finding universal laws of social order. The outgrowth of any analysis of social interaction as it is exercised within autonomous micro and macro processes must be considered contingent; comprehendible, but unpredictable according to universal laws.

Several predilections contained in this book require overt confessions. I have watched with frustration the examination of the micro/macro dichotomy that has absorbed sociological theory over the last decade or more. The source of this frustration rests in my belief that the micro/macro debate is, at its core, an expanded regurgitation of issues debated long ago. Nonetheless, recent proponents for micro/macro linkage discuss their efforts as if they provide a new opportunity for a theoretical future. As it is currently constructed, the micro/macro debate and suggested syntheses are one-way streets to dead ends, not avenues for advancement. Truly, new innovations in mainstream sociological theory have come to a standstill.

I also believe the micro/macro debate is inherently a conservative one: conservative politically, and conservative in its protection of current modes of sociological thought. One example is the near isolation in which theory is generated. Where the classical era plainly saw its debt and relation to other disciplines, including philosophy and science, contemporary social theory has become self-contained. After the classical era, sociological theory has progressively concerned itself with self-defined incestuous issues, and like in-breeding in nature, has given rise to curious theoretical offspring. Countless combinations of theories are endlessly offered at various levels of metatheory. What is common to almost all offerings is the scarcity of analysis of other fields, even when they shed light on theoretical issues and debates.

The prominent developments and discoveries of the twentieth century in science, intellectual thought, and society itself often appear immaterial in the contemporary work of the best-known and widely accepted sociological theorists. Those theories trying to incorporate, synthesize, or even dismiss mainstream frameworks, and correlate these views with empirical social reality, are dismissed or ignored. Post-modernism, feminist theory, and ecological theory are disregarded or intellectually spanked because they cannot be placed neatly into the micro/macro package of thought. This misses the essential effort these diverse theories have made at grappling with what mainstream contemporary theory has covertly accepted or ignored: the scientific and philosophical issues embedded in sociological inquiry, the importance of scientific discoveries of the twentieth century, and prejudices inherent in the application of theory to tangible events in the social world. While these indictment theories are criticized in this work, in many ways their "avant garde" approach is closer to classical traditions than current mainstream theories.

Part I of this work is a plea to rethink the boundaries of sociological theory. Chapter One will identify the underlying arguments that influenced the birth of sociological theory, including the philosophical and scientific issues directly influencing classical theorists. Chapter One also examines the divergent efforts of the classical sociological theorists as they grappled with those varied influences. Finally, Chapter One includes a brief description of the "fractured theories" that have emerged in the twentieth century.

Chapter Two will review the current trends in micro/macro theorizing, and explain the inadequacies of the three approaches cited above. Although not limited to these authors, Randall Collins will be used as an exemplar of ascending theories, Jeffrey Alexander will be used as an exemplar of descending theories, and Anthony Giddens will be used as an exemplar of imploding theories. This chapter shows that contemporary theorizing has not advanced classical efforts, as the scientific and philosophical influences giving rise to sociology have been submerged in arcane and socially irrelevant posturing.

Chapter Three will discuss the rise of the "indictment theories", which include post-modernism, feminist theory, and ecological theory. These theories both indict traditional theoretical frameworks, and call for theory to reassess its relationship with empirical reality. When seen in this light, indictment theories appear neither distant from classical forms of theorizing, nor as easily removed from current intellectual categories in social thought.

Part II of this book contains a multi-disciplinary search for instances where autonomy and contingency have crept into analyses. Chapter Four provides a general overview of scientific discoveries of the twentieth century, including the debates it has spawned within the philosophy of science. The theory of relativity, quantum mechanics, evolution, continental drift, chaos theory, and astro-physics are all examined. The aim of this chapter is two-fold: first, to show how new scientific discoveries and theories demolish the principles on which most sociological theory is based, and second, to illustrate how diverse sectors of the scientific community have come to accept micro and macro autonomy, as well as contingency.

Chapter Five reviews other disciplines recently imported into, or remaining outside, sociology that have incorporated at least some aspect of autonomy or contingency within their framework. While none of the work reviewed is explicitly a contingency theory, important lessons can be gleaned from the work of systems theorists, recent developments of NeoMarxism, and hermeneutics. One of the important clues gained is that social developments within or between micro and macro levels may be either consistent or inconsistent.

Chapter Six reviews the important work articulated within psychology and social psychology. These disciplines have always asserted micro independence, and while this is a step in the right direction, these theorists often completely detach micro activity from macro structures. Autonomy does not imply complete detachment. Rather, autonomy implies each level has its own history of development, and are related in variable ways. Nonetheless, psychology and social psychology offer ample clues to autonomous micro processes, including how individuals and groups formulate perceptions, and how individuals and groups interact.

Part III pursues a more formal analysis of contingency theory based on the arguments and ideas presented in the previous chapters. Chapter Seven explores autonomy and contingency at the micro level, and suggests individual and group processes are, themselves, autonomous and contingent, each creating social perceptions that variably influence each other. Chapter Eight examines autonomy and contingency at the macro level, and specifies four autonomous structures: political, economic, cultural, and ecological. Each is seen as autonomous from the others and related in contingent patterns. Chapter Nine investigates how the autonomous and contingent developments at micro and macro levels are themselves related. This chapter argues that neither level is determining, and social interaction and the exercise of power evident within micro and macro processes makes each distinctive. Consequently, the two levels may be consistent or inconsistent, may or may not be conflictual, and may or may not lead to fundamental social change. Finally, Chapter Ten organizes the conclusions of the previous chapters into a set of postulates for a contingency theory.

In order to realize the goals set for this work, several restrictions in scope were required. Discussions in both Part I and Part II are limited, in large part, to discussions that are germane to the development of a contingency theory. Other aspects of philosophical, sociological, or scientific frameworks are used as illustrations to show the implications of positions taken. Thus, the aim is not to provide a complete rendition of philosophical, sociological, or scientific arguments, but to isolate those issues and ideas relevant to the immediate purpose.

PART I

THE ILL-FATED MARRIAGE
OF MICRO AND MACRO LEVELS

Chapter One

The Courtship and Divorce

Contemporary efforts to integrate micro and macro phenomena are deeply rooted in western philosophical traditions. Western philosophy, itself, began by undermining older universal principles of knowledge and nature, and creating a new synthesis. Pre-Socratic philosophers questioned ancient mystical beliefs and symbols used to explain existence and nature. In turn, the classical Greeks explored how human knowledge is obtained, and why human knowledge is important. This compelling metaphysical question both shattered previous conceptions and set the parameters for generation after generation of future philosophers.

By the middle ages, philosophical responses to the Greek legacy became divided between nominalism and realism. In the struggle for acceptance, nominalist philosophy proved more salient. Its influence would be felt not only in the future social sciences, but in natural science as well. The nominalist proposal, based on objective descriptions of individual phenomena, became a critical assumption for the scientific method. From this basic set of assumptions, early classical scientists were drawn not to universal truths, but to objective descriptions of individual phenomena. Only when ample data on objects was collected and tested could more general principles be entertained. Moreover, the nominalist method allowed for new data to undermine old general principles.

Nevertheless, nominalism left a formidable obstacle for the early scientists: how to describe phenomena that was difficult, if not impossible, to directly observe. While the nominalist method was useful in detailing observable facts, astronomers and physicists needed to describe phenomena that was empirical, but not directly observable. The solution to this problem came from the use of mathematics. Mathematics allowed the early scientists to explain empirical data in an abstract way.

Copernicus used abstract mathematics to postulate the motion of the earth, and this dramatically transformed traditional notions of the earth as the center of a symmetrical universe, notions presumed from the time of Aristotle to the beginning of the sixteenth century. Kepler furthered the symmetrical collapse through the development of his three laws, but while Kepler's laws could be empirically confirmed, a causal explanation for their existence was omitted. It was Galileo who provided the link. He studied motion on earth by utilizing geometrical axioms, and this profound discovery meant physics could now become an exact, explanatory science. Through mathematics, scientists learned not only to describe unobservable phenomena, but to explain relationships between phenomena.

Galileo employed mathematical procedures to create partial proofs of reality; to prove his speculations, he was compelled to establish an experiment, and to do that, he had to select what he wanted to observe. In short, a hypothesis was needed. Understanding the need for an hypothesis pushed Galileo far beyond scientists of earlier centuries who simply observed phenomena. Observations allow one to collect data and even generalize about it, but hypotheses allow the empirical observer to test for cause and effect relationships.

Newton completed the synthesis of previous physicists, and in doing so, helped inspire new forms of intellectual thought. Through the development of his three laws of motion, combined with the law of gravity, Newton was able to complete both Galileo's project by explaining why the laws of motion on earth occurred, and also prove motion in the cosmos is relational to motion on earth. This astounding feat meant not only that the universe was observable, but a unity existed in the cosmos. Newton's ideas dominated science for centuries, but his influence went far beyond scientific circles. The notion of mechanistic and deterministic laws of nature governing the physical world was slowly absorbed into the general culture, and was a catalyst for philosophical thought.

Early Modern Philosophy

While science created new, universal explanations of nature, science was inadequate to explain subjective awareness. This left a crucial philosophical question to the early modern philosophers: to explain the duality between scientific, objective truth, and subjective interpretation.

Newton's mechanical explanation of the physical universe was every-one's starting point. With the mechanical universe as a catalyst, phi-losophers and social theorists could turn their attention to human issues and concerns. This acceptance of a mechanical, physical universe, and attention to human concerns within it, lasted for centuries. Only re-cently have classical scientific principles come under serious scrutiny. While early modern philosophers grappled with new arguments, they did so always within the realm of Newton's mechanical universe.

One philosophical school of thought, the empiricist school, ar-gued that the question of the relationship between subject and object, itself, was absurd. Any interrelationship between subject and object was meaningless since humans are directly and immediately aware of their surroundings only through the senses; reality is simply what it appears to be. What was common to the empiricist school was the de-sire to limit knowledge of the concrete world to observable, scientific discoveries. Subjective reflection, they thought, has no direct link to scientific reality. It follows, then, that empiricists rejected all religious doctrines which proposed universal laws. Instead, empiricists favored the growing discoveries of science. Moreover, to heighten the suprem-acy of science over religion, empiricists assailed reflection, the source of religious thought. In the contemporary sociological rhetoric, em-piricists rejected both macro explanations and micro reflections as un-scientific. What remained was the science of the physical senses and experience.

Empiricism, of course, was not the only explanation for how subjects and external objects relate. Another direction was taken by the philosophes during the Enlightenment. The philosophes strove to unify, not destroy, subjective reflection and external reality, not only to per-form a philosophical exercise, but to provide a mechanism to master and change the social world. The motive of change mandated that sub-jective reflection was important, and moreover, that reflection was possible through rational knowledge. Consequently and ironically, the philosophe justification for elevating reflection was exactly the same as the empiricist argument for rejecting reflection: the overarching power of scientific discoveries. According to the philosophe view, if the uni-verse was knowable through the discovery of physical laws, the same rational process could be applied to human society. Natural laws could now form the model to examine human society in a rational and rea-soned way. This natural rationality was translated into both natural rights of the individual, and a presumption that all forms of social or-ganization must conform to rational principles.

This use of reason was far different from empiricist representations of the previous century. Where empiricists confined knowledge to physical attributes and experiences, the philosophes believed human beings could rationally understand the social world, and convert it based on principles of scientific discovery. Thus people are granted power to create society. For example, Montesquieu believed laws were a reflection of people, and Rousseau believed people are logically prior to the state and engage in a social contract to initiate it.

Nevertheless, both the empiricists and philosophes, despite their recognition that individuals and macro patterns needed to be related, held firm to positions advocating the individual, either physical or thoughtful, as the starting point for any integration of micro and macro phenomena. While dissimilar in application, both sought to extend individual knowledge and connect subjective understanding to scientific explanations of reality. However, a critical difference remains: while empiricists allowed only for micro analysis, the philosophes assigned rational individuals the task of creating macro conditions. This process was seen by the philosophes as contiguous. That is, since individuals were seen as rational change agents, the micro activity and the macro conditions necessarily originate and develop along similar time paths.

The notion of micro and macro change within a contiguous time frame also finds its roots in classical science, where motion generates a concurrent relation between bodies. With this principle as their assumption, the philosophes believed micro thought and activity would concurrently shape social structures. This classical view of contemporaneous developments of micro and macro processes, although viewed in variable ways, remains endemic among most forms of contemporary theory. What is not often mentioned overtly by contemporary theories is that contiguous micro and macro development is an idea imported from the mechanical universe formulated centuries ago.

In contrast to the philosophes, another response to earlier thought developed in England. Rather than use rational reasoning as an attack on social institutions, these thinkers hoped to explain how social interaction provides a link to objective social conditions. The most important thinker of this genre was David Hume, and for purposes of this work, the key element of his work rests in its synthetic nature. Hume's synthesis was not aimed at integrating rational thought and scientific reality. Instead, his aim was to reject both sets of assumptions. This combined rejection enabled Hume to start anew.

Extending empiricist logic to what some believe is an extreme position, Hume argued that both subjective reflection and the use of science to test objective reality was an illusion. For Hume, perceptions gained from the physical senses could never be exact copies of objective reality, but rather are merely impressions of reality. Moreover, since ideas emanate from these same impressions, ideas are yet further detached from the realistic truth. Hume's skepticism, then, renounced not only the ability of humans to observe objective reality, but also subjective reflection.

Hume's skepticism does not preclude individual activity, however. Hume developed his theory based on experience, but it was an empiricism altered from earlier forms. Hume equated empiricism with individual experience, and this rendered universals based on scientific experimentation impotent; like subjective knowledge, science is reduced to probabilities based on impressions and ideas. Thus, Hume rejected both the empiricist equation of scientific facts with reality, and the philosophes' belief in the subjective, rational capability of understanding reality. Hume, however, did believe that when ideas and impressions are repeated over time, individuals come to expect their repetition and believe they understand what causes them. While always inexact and based on probabilities, it is on this foundation that individuals believe in cause and effect and take action. The task for the human sciences and the study of people, therefore, should be aimed not at uncovering scientific laws, but classifying what people experience and what they subjectively feel is practical and important.

Hume's own methodology for these classifications was based on an analysis of human interaction. When individuals draw inferences from observing two objects that are continuously "conjoined", the source of this inference is "custom". External customs, then, represent experiences useful for the individual, for without it, humans would be limited to knowledge obtained only from the physical senses, and with nothing to support reasoned conclusions. Consequently, both empiricist experience and rational thinking are included in Hume's arguments, but both must be attached to objects or events external to the individual.

But on what are these more extended attachments based? For Hume, external comparisons may be fruitfully analyzed on the basis of humanly and rationally created general rules. And if the rules are rational, so too is the state generating them, albeit mitigated through social custom. In short, subjective sympathies lie in the domain of the individual as they interact with others, but this interaction also promotes the objective process of comparisons, and comparisons are rooted in general laws developed by the extended society.

While Hume's system logically connects the individual with society, it must be remembered both the subjective beliefs based on repetitious cause and effect, as well as large scale rational laws are never equivalent to social or natural reality. The Humean skepticism remains. Thus relations between people are a matter of human interaction and what people "believe" is true and justified. Whether or not truth or justification actually exists in social relations is impossible to establish.

Hume's skepticism is an important development; it influenced both the philosophers who immediately followed him, and indirectly, issues of contemporary importance. An early critic of classical science, he cut humans and human society loose from scientific laws. What, however, would replace science as a logical model for society? Hume's answer was a modified form of rationalism and empiricism based on human interaction.

With the inclusion of Hume, several comments can be made about the philosophical linkage between micro and macro phenomena by the middle of the 18th century. The progression of science threatened the prior unifying, religious universals. The empiricists recognized this and limited their analysis to individual sense perception and experience, as they believed these were congruent to the physical laws of nature. The Philosphes introduced the notion of rationalism to allow for the prospect of micro and macro social integration. Since science proved rational thinking was possible, the Philosphes argued individuals were capable not only of connections with external objects, but of judging social institutions and relations between people. Those institutions found reasonable were to be accepted, and those unreasonable were to be rejected and replaced.

Hume, however, disowned both the empiricist and philosophe proposals. He argued that sense perception and rational thinking were not necessarily connected. This was a major blow to the ability to connect micro and macro phenomena. Hume replaced the senses and thought with social interaction as a unifying principle, but he insisted this was based on repetition, not reality.

Despite differences, a common thread does run through the empiricists, the philosophes, and Hume. All hoped to explain the development of society, and by the eighteenth century, new forms of human society, especially in Europe, were in need of explanation. How should these societies be organized, and what was the key to their social integration? Hume's explanation was rooted in social interaction, not the pure rationality of science as granted by the philosophes. However, like the philosophes, and the empiricists, Hume argued that micro and macro processes are inherently connected in time, and thus, must develop contiguously.

German idealism was formulated as yet another alternate answer to the problem of integrating the rational individual with the physical world, and indirectly, to provide a link between micro and macro phenomena. Immanuel Kant set out to bridge the gap between the subjective ego and experience, and objects. In *The Critique of Pure Reason,* Kant agreed with Hume that the limit of subjective analysis meant objects cannot be perfectly known. Nonetheless, objects do exist and make themselves known to the individual, even if imperfectly. Here Kant accepts a reformed notion of empiricism, where experience leads to knowledge, but not perfect knowledge of reality. Kant further argues that humans categorize and classify data from experiences and, in doing so, create something new. Objects, then, are knowable only as they are relate to classified categories of knowledge, albeit not the actual object itself. Here Kant also accepts a reformed notion of rationalism; simply thinking about reality is not equivalent to knowledge, because individuals add order to thought as reality is viewed within the context of preexisting classifications and categories. The object "in itself" exists and is essential for individual thought, but its reality is always just beyond the individual's grasp.

In brief, Kant's integration of micro and macro rests in the partial rejection and expansion of both empiricism and rationalism. He accepts humans as sensory, but suggests the senses cannot provide perfect knowledge. Kant also accepts rationalism, but suggests knowledge is categorized in ways that may not be a perfect replication of what is sensed. Thus, micro and macro phenomena may be integrated within the Kantian framework, but each required step contains a level of uncertainty about external reality, and must be qualified. In the end, each individual remains an individual.

Similar to Hume, then, Kant questions the symmetry between laws of natural science and human understanding, although Kant takes no pains to explicitly reject natural laws. But Kant is left with the problem of social integration. He provides a partial, and for him sufficient answer; humans may not know everything about their external world, but they can rationally comprehend enough to gain a basis for human life. That basis is the foundation for moral behavior.

Hegel is another German idealist who examined how subjective individuals acquire knowledge of objective reality. He made a distinction between information based on sense perception, and knowledge based on mental concepts of objects. To Hegel mental knowledge is conceptual knowledge. But Hegel was after more, for he also was interested in discovering an "absolute" knowledge that included both subject and object. For Hegel, history is the dialectical evolution of stages toward this absolute knowledge.

In short, Hegel's dialectic contains a dual synthesis toward absolute knowledge. Subjective thought is synthesized with the collective spirit, and both must integrated with the autonomous elements of nature. This pattern repeats itself as the autonomous spirit and nature form a continual synthesis on the path to absolute knowledge. Thought is not primarily subjective, according to Hegel. Instead, subjective thought is merely one autonomous element necessary to obtain absolute knowledge. As such, Hegel differs from Kant, who separated micro from macro but made only the micro intelligible. Hegel grants both micro and macro processes autonomy, and sees them as part of a continual synthesis.

Where Hume believed that social interaction led to general rules of society, and where Kant limited knowledge to the subjective individual, Hegel suggested society develops according to its own dialectical growth, and within this historical development, individuals both play only a specified role and are influenced by it. Thus Hegel has provided the first example of autonomy in social thought. He separates both micro and macro processes and separates both from natural processes. But this left Hegel with the problem of integration. How could this system be logically synthesized? His answer: since objects of the external world contain the same logic required of individuals when reasoning about their own experiences, individuals are inherently capable of reflecting on both subjective experiences and external objects. And thus, a link exists between subjective experience and the historical development of external objects. That link is natural reason. Thus, like other philosophers, Hegel accepts scientifically inspired notions of universal principles, but grants autonomy to the micro and macro elements. In order to integrate the two, he again proposed the scientific principle that both micro and macro developments are concurrent and follow the same logic, and as such, individuals can come to understand macro developments. In brief, the contemporaneous relationship between the spirit and nature allows individuals to be aware of history.

Before turning to other factors influencing the development of sociological thought, some discussion is necessary concerning the issues raised by scientific and philosophical thought. Three issues are critical in the philosophical discussions: the influence of, and human relation to, the physical universe; the importance of social integration; and the issue of time. Scientific ideas concerning the nature of the universe left an indelible mark on western philosophy. It set the parameters for analysis, even for Hume who disagreed with its universal laws. Consciously, or unconsciously, all western philosophers conceived a logic for society, a logic that is rational and discoverable. This is the legacy of the mechanical universe. It led philosophers to utilize scientific analogies to greater or lesser degrees, but all searched for logical analyses to explain human and social development.

This legacy also led philosophers to build logical connections to explain social integration, and unconsciously to set the parameters for the micro/macro debate in social theory. Other than the empiricists, who remained at the micro level of sense perception and experience, each of the philosophies took up the challenge. The philosophes believed micro and macro must be integrated through rational thinking because rational thought was inextricably tied to science. Hume constructed micro and macro processes, not through science, but through human interaction and the rational process it entailed. Kant limited knowledge to partial understanding, but suggested that enough external reality was included to provide a moral basis for social action. And Hegel logically connected the autonomous, but rational, elements of nature, and micro and macro processes within a coherent system. As will be discussed in Chapter 2, the modern effort at micro and macro synthesis are primarily a continuation of these efforts.

A final comment will also hint at issues essential to discussions in the chapters that follow. Because universal findings in classical science led to an exploration of social integration, each of the philosophers discussed viewed micro and macro processes as temporally aligned. That is, while micro and macro processes had variable influences given the different philosophical roles given, they were positioned within a closed system, each having a concurrent impact on the other. This too has roots in classical science. A fundamental postulate from Newton states that the gravitational pull of any object has an immediate and relational impact on any other object within a field. This is a primary basis for mechanical physics. All of the philosophers discussed, even when micro and macro processes were given a level of autonomy, absorbed the natural analogy into their frameworks. That is, each philosopher believed a change in either the micro or macro level leads to a corresponding and direct change in the other level. It will be argued in Chapters Four and Five that this is no longer an accepted belief by science. However, social theory, in all its contemporary forms, mistakenly continues to reaffirm this postulate.

The classical sociologists, Comte, Marx, Durkheim, and Weber have received great attention by sociologists. They are reviewed here with a specific purpose in mind: to uncover the techniques these authors employed to continue the debates of western philosophy. As such, this review will concentrate, primarily, on how the issues of physical science, social integration and temporal concepts are developed in their work.

Sociology Continues the Debate

Auguste Comte is generally given credit for producing the first works in sociological theory. Within his sociological studies, Comte gave primary status to the act of reasoning, but it is a rationalism far different from earlier philosophies. Reason, for Comte, was not to be used according to individual needs or desires, but to be employed only in the logical exploration of the macro development of society.

This positive methodology required an ontology where individuals, and even collective groups, must be observed only in relation to the external world. In turn, the external world is discoverable by humans through an awareness of the laws of nature. Thus, nature, society and individuals are all logically integrated and, in principle, discoverable if analyzed positively. Similar to Hegel, Comte's epistemological inquiry into how individuals are capable of grasping the positive method included the belief that the collective human mind progresses along with, and because of, the developmental stages of society. This logical positivist approach toward understanding the internal mechanisms of the social development could, for Comte, be accomplished through a combination of reason and observation.

Comte, therefore, accepted the empiricist notion that observations are critical to analysis, but he simultaneously placed observations within the context of a preexisting macro history. That is, observation alone is inadequate for social analysis, but observation specifically used to uncover the positive stages of society is a prerequisite and logical tool. Comte lodged a comparable criticism against rational thinking. A self-interested individual, no matter how rational, can never come to master the general development of humankind if thought is narrowed to individual concerns.

In the positive method, then, Comte searched for a synthesis between the power of general scientific laws and empiricism. His answer was to deductively accept natural laws of development as applied to human society (and found in his three stages of human development: theological-military, metaphysical-judicial, and science and industry), but inductively allow for the phenomena within those stages to become visible through observation and experience. Simultaneously, any exploration of the notion of cause is rejected as metaphysical by Comte. Description, not causal analysis, was to be the method of positivism, and since the stages of development were self-evident, their causes were irrelevant and individually problematic. Describing the internal mechanisms of the three stages was Comte's goal, but only within the context of the whole. Thus, while Comte allows for the independent and complex growth of structures of society, this growth remains integrated within the logic of the organic whole. These ideas, of course, would be the foundation of the sociological theory of functionalism.

The use of the organic analogy shows a clear connection between Comte's view of sociology and the relatively new science of biology (e.g. Comte, 1975 p. 163-181, 253-257). Biological inquiry revealed to Comte the necessity of understanding relational phenomena. In biology, phenomena are continually related to other phenomena within a given entity. Moreover, the totality must be grasped if the biological components are to be discerned. Biology also demonstrates that separate elements are not only relational but dependent on each other. The parts form an organic whole that must be synthetically related, and the proper method of grasping the organic whole is to compare one organism with another. The biological parallel and influence on Comte is obvious.

Where, then, does Comte stand in relation to the integration of micro and macro phenomena? Comte adopts aspects of Humean skepticism, especially Hume's exasperation with efforts to establish the scientific validity of cause and effect. It is on these grounds that empiricist views are eliminated by Comte. While individual interaction and self-interest are suggested by Hume to replace religious and natural law universals and link micro and macro levels, Comte disavowed human actions because he believed individuals are not capable of comprehending the stages of human development. Only those individuals employing the positive method could come to such an understanding.

Instead, Comte's integration rests in his duplication of an important development in German philosophy enabling individual knowledge of the stages of human development. While the Kantian rational individual is rejected, Comte accepted the more Hegelian notion that consciousness would conform to different historical stages; this made comprehension of the stages of macro development possible. This integrative link also allowed Comte to employ the positive method. Since consciousness and knowledge are external to rational thought, the need for a positive methodology now exists. Finally, Comte solidified his logic and made the micro/macro synthesis possible by claiming knowledge is knowable because it is a natural process and follows the laws of nature.

Of all the classical sociological theorists, Comte is most insistent that macro phenomena be autonomous. But in doing so, Comte's framework leaves no room for micro actors and actions. Consequently, Comte's work clearly separates micro and macro phenomena, but connects both to the overriding development of nature. Thus, despite their autonomy, micro and macro developments have no choice but to proceed in contiguous lockstep with the three stages of development. Although Comte's integration of micro and macro processes are the weakest of all the classical sociologists, and although he gives almost complete primacy to autonomous macro over micro processes, they do remain integrated. The positive method requires nothing less.

In contrast, Marx argued individuals are not subsumed by stages of social development, but that people have the capacity to act and make history. It is a history made, however, within the setting of what already exists. The human ability to make history within limits raises a fundamental question about human nature: how are people able to create their own history?

Marx, like the empiricists, believed physical senses are a necessary window to the outside world, but more than senses are required for human understanding (Marx, 1987 p. 104), and sensing an object is not the same as understanding its meaning (Marx, 1987 p.581). For Marx, physical senses and human powers and drives first interrelate with external objects before entering consciousness. Consequently, the development of human consciousness rests, in part, on the specific nature of objects available to people. Individual consciousness, then, emerges because individuals have both the capability to sense objects, and because objects have specific characteristics that are knowable to, and exert influence, on individuals.

Thus, Marx's view differs from Hume's skepticism and synthesis. Where Hume believes humans obtain imperfect knowledge of objects through repetitive acts and social interaction, Marx holds that people are not only capable of having knowledge of objects, but the objects also help define the individual. Marx was led, therefore, not toward social interaction as a synthesizing concept, but toward an understanding of the human knowledge of objects (Marx, 1987 p.106). This is precisely the point, where Marx parts company with Comte; predetermined natural stages of human development were replaced with a study of the interrelationship of people and objects in the struggle for survival.

This view of human consciousness was different from what most philosophers had historically argued. Marx rejects the Kantian limitation of rational knowledge as self-contained within individuals, and the importance empiricists placed on the physical properties of knowledge. Instead, Marx proposed it is illogical to conceive of consciousness apart from objects people need for survival since survival requires humans to relate to objects. Moreover, as humans must use objects to survive, consciousness and the specific objects used must be closely related (Marx, 1987 p. 110). Marx urged philosophers, therefore, to discontinue their concentration on the artificial division between people and objects and explore humans as they live their "real" lives.

Marx rebuked the notion of rational individuals with a second argument. He asserted rationalism artificially separates people into individual and isolated units and ignores the collective human ability to affect their surroundings. While consciousness first develops within the individual, consciousness could develop among large collective groups and lead to collective action. Allowing for the possibility of collective action was important for Marx, because it lifted the boundaries of human potential; humankind could now be seen as responsible for human history, a history that cannot be explained by emphasizing the individual alone. For Marx, therefore, history is humanly and collectively made within the context of existing natural and social objects.

Of all the previous attempts at integrating micro and macro, Hegal had the greatest influence on Marx. But while Marx accepted Hegel's concept of dialectics and the relational influence among various social and natural forces, Marx rejects Hegel's emphasis on absolute knowledge as the motivating force in history. Instead, Marx believed each mode of economic production contains a unique and temporal logic of development. An understanding of the formation of modes of production could only be established through an empirical investigation of human beings as they take social action to organize their labor.

Marx, then, like Hume, divorced the elements of natural reality from those of social reality. That is, Marx believed human society was not subject to natural, universal laws. However, human beings must relate, albeit autonomously, to nature in order to survive. Thus Marx does not oppose the notion of natural laws, but sees society as autonomous from it. This, it will be shown in Chapter Three, is a fundamental postulate of modern ecological theory.

Marx also viewed micro and macro social processes as autonomous. He does so, however, not through an analysis of subject/structure relationship, but by concentrating on the development of collectives in society. This allows him to establish more and less powerful groups, and moreover, explain how dominant groups maintain power over economic, political and cultural structures. These structures are not void of social action, and thus, Marx allows for micro action,

but the social activity taken within the context of capitalist structures is
dominated by one group: the ruling class. Moreover, the very actions of
the ruling class, always conducted within what Marx sees as a set of
contradictions within capitalist logic of their own making, ironically
provide the potential of social action by subservient groups, acting in
their own interests.

This means, then, that Marx allows for a modified autonomy between micro and macro processes. Structural development does contain
an independent influence on the micro level, albeit this autonomy is
itself structured by the dominant class. In turn, it is possible for the
receivers of the structural influences, the subservient class, to act on
those structures, but only when the capitalist logic grinds itself into a
contradictory halt. It follows, therefore, that Marx does allow for some
difference in the time paths between micro and macro processes. He
argued continuously, for example, that the micro act of revolution
could not occur until the macro processes of capitalist production fully
developed their inherent contradictions (e.g. Marx, 1973 p. 171-175).

Despite this autonomy, however, Marx's aim was to develop a
coherent, integrated, universal explanation of society. His effort to uncover the scientific laws of capitalist development carried with it the
classical scientific legacy of the enlightenment, and, as such, constrained not only the limits of social action, but the autonomy between
micro and macro levels. Within this framework, Marx had no other
choice but to see micro and macro time paths as generally contiguous,
where the micro and collective overthrow of the economic system becomes possible only when the macro contradictions are aligned with
micro material consciousness. Thus while Marx should be given more
credit for allowing social action than many reviewers allow, his effort
to uncover universal explanations of society influenced not only his
description of the political economy of capitalism and the social action
within it, and not only the relative autonomy between micro and macro
levels, but also his predictions concerning its present and future development, and the potential for its overthrow. His aim was to uncover
society much the same as earlier scientists uncovered the universe, and
his analysis of autonomy between micro and macro levels, social integration, and the issue of time all were affected.

Durkheim's synthesis between micro and macro phenomena differed greatly from Marx. The basic units of society, he maintained, are
the individuals. It is from individuals that groups, institutions, and society materialize. But, following Comte and influenced by biology,
Durkheim argued that individuality is not a solitary process occurring
only within the physical and mental growth of each person. Instead,

individuality is derived, in large part, from the collective activity of people as they interact with others and form society (Durkheim, 1973). This collective capacity prevails because human nature is a duality combining internal processes of individuals with external developments of society. Thus, it is the combination of internal and external environments which gives rise to the social individual and social collective.

This combination of individual and society contains several philosophical assumptions. Durkheim favored the empiricist priority placed on the physical senses, but merged that conviction with Hegel's and Comte's emphasis on historical development. Moreover, Durkheim acknowledged psychological development within individuals, but combined that viewpoint with biological notions of evolution. How, then, did Durkheim utilize these varied thoughts in forming a coherent theory? The unifying principle rests in the idea of social concepts.

To anchor the priority of social concepts, Durkheim adopted the Humean position that concepts and morality are social because they require human interaction; individuals alone cannot create social concepts or general moral values. And following Comte, Durkheim argued the interaction necessary to create social concepts, in part, is predicated on the use of words. In turn, the use of words implies social interaction between at least two people; while an individual may personalize words, or concepts, social classifications are required if categorization is to be intelligible. Thus, our human nature is a duality, composed of each person's unique physical and psychological traits, as well as external social concepts.

Durkheim, therefore, disagreed with two of the philosophical traditions previously discussed. He rejected both the empiricist argument that humans are reduced to physical senses, and the rationalist claim that reality is entirely conceptual. Durkheim, following Hume, asserted both explanations are incorrect because the physical senses and social concepts must be interrelated. However, while Durkheim believed individuals and conceptual knowledge are closely associated, he did not uphold a complete synthesis. Instead, he argued, they are distinct, and divided. Moreover, not only are individuals and concepts divided, but people confer a higher value to social concepts; social concepts are erected through collective activity, and people grant a higher status to collective thought and activity than to the individual (Durkheim, 1964). The source of these positive feelings toward collective concepts is a process "by which a plurality of individual consciousness enter in communion and are fused into a common consciousness."

Thus, humans have a double consciousness. The physical and mental state of the individual is the source of one form, and society, as represented by collective concepts and symbols, is the other. As humans engage in social actions through their interactions with the collective, the social concepts and structures they create become "emergent" and external from individuals. Since individuals grant superiority to collectively created social concepts and structures, a constraint is placed on individual acts and specific limitations and sanctions are imposed on individual behavior. These restraints do not necessarily imply unwilling compliance by individuals. Instead, as in human nature where individuals internalize social concepts, individuals also internalize the collective conscience. Consequently, individuals willingly self-regulate behavior according to the collectively created and superior social morality (Durkheim, 1965).

This premise--that individuals may willingly accept the collective conscience--is a highly unifying principle in Durkheim's work, and a distinguishing feature of his theory. Hume had rejected both rational thought and natural universals in favor of social interaction, but nevertheless turned to rational, although inexact, ideas of individuals to unify them with social customs and the state. Durkheim transcends the Humean synthesis by suggesting socially created concepts are willingly accepted by individuals because they readily grant superiority to those concepts. This process is the source of societal unification. Moreover, where Hegel limited the role of individuals to one element in the synthesis toward absolute knowledge, Durkheim asserts the responsibility for the development of social concepts rests squarely on the shoulders of individuals, even though they act collectively. Thus, the use of social concepts as a unifying concept allowed Durkheim to avoid ideas concerning the need for a strong authoritarian ruler, or limiting all action and thought to individuals.

In this light, Durkheim's views also differ from those of Kant. In the Kantian framework, the process of obtaining imperfect knowledge is more consequential than actual knowledge, but this necessarily reduced the unit of analysis to the level of the individual, and therefore, divided subjective values from external validity. Durkheim, however, disagreed with the Kantian formulation. He argued neither knowledge or values are derived from individuals. Rather, their origin is predicated on social organization. Moral and social concepts could not exist, Durkheim believed, without the prior development of society and the collective consciousness it created. In short, Durkheim replaced Kant's a priori of subjective, but inexact, knowledge with an a priori derived from the existence of social formations. Durkheim did not deny the existence of subjective thought, values, or validity. He simply attached their conceptual development to social formations, and in doing so made moral and social values superior to subjective morality.

In relation to issues important for this work, Durkheim, first, should be seen as closely aligning the development of society to the development of science. Durkheim's work, especially his notion that societies move from mechanical and simplistic forms of solidarity to organic and more complex forms, is directly influenced by the science of biology. His organic analogy fits perfectly with the previously developed ideas of evolutionary biology. While biology is surely different from the study of physics, both, at this point in their development, maintain a universal search for reality. Durkheim clearly adopts this premise.

Evolution also provided Durkheim some hints toward contingency. That is, in evolutionary theory there is no guarantee for species survival; they must successfully adapt to the environment. Durkheim argued humans must do the same, although there is no guarantee they will do so. Human social action, then, plays an important role, one that allows for some variability within the context of increasing complex collective structures.

Durkheim also sees a level of autonomy between individuals and collectives, but gives primacy to collectives, as individuals willingly grant superiority to their development. This modified form of autonomy also is at the root of Durkheim's integration between micro and macro processes. Since individuals collectively create social concepts and structures, Durkheim allows for micro responsibility for macro structures. Once created, however, the emergent structures now influence both individuals and collectivities. The micro/macro integration is further influenced by the developing complexity of society as it moves from mechanical to organic solidarity.

Finally, it also is evident that Durkheim allows for some separation of micro and macro processes into divergent time frames. Separate micro and macro time paths were not his hope, but he conceded the possibility. Since the growing complexity of social concepts and structures continually evolve and emerge, individuals are required to complement these developments or feel separated from them and suffer from anomie. Too much separation between individuals and society could lead to a general breakdown in society's ability to function. Thus, Durkheim desired a society where both micro and macro processes were contiguous, but warned of the danger if they were not.

In sum, with the effort to establish a universal explanation for the development of society, Durkheim was forced to choose a unifying element that could include both micro and macro processes, and relate that process to his beliefs in evolutionary development of general society. The unifying element was social concepts, and combined with his effort to develop universal and unifying explanations, Durkheim had little choice but to give primacy to evolutionary and structural influences over that of individuals.

Durkheim's work continues the search for general explanatory principles by the classical sociologists. However, not all would accept this as the goal for sociology. Weber's theories move in a different direction.

Weber focused his work on an analysis of social action, and believed sociology should do the same. Weber held sociology should be developed as a rational discipline, one which integrates and verifies purposeful actions taken by individuals. It was fruitless, Weber believed, to use philosophical inquiries of objective truth, or the physical senses, to explain social action. In contrast, human action should be perceived as qualitatively discrete from scientific phenomena. Humans are creative, thinking, purposive beings. These aspects of human nature could never, for Weber, be adequately described in the same way scientists described natural phenomena. Nevertheless, Weber (1964, p. 88-115) insisted the rationale and logic of science could be incorporated into the study of social action, just not in a deterministic way.

The appropriate methodology needed to recognize varied social actions was "interpretive." Its aim was to explain both the meaning of social action, as well as describe regular patterns of action. For Weber, the first step was to define social action.

Weber defined social actions as actions related to another individual or group. There are two implications to this belief. First, the subjective meaning of social action is the critical focus of Weber's attention. But second, subjective meanings must be attached to another individual or group external to the subject. Thus, external social objects, groups and conditions are components of the interpretive framework, because external factors have meaning for individuals engaging in social action. This meant, Weber argued (1964, p. 115-124), it was possible to objectively understand subjective human action.

A problem remains, however. While Weber believed social action is grounded in subjective meanings derived from a combination of subjective and objective influences, he also argued these influences may not be shared by all actors, even those for whom the action is directed. How, then, can causal relationships be constructed within this maze of social phenomena? Weber's answer was simple and clear: causal relationships between human actions were beyond comprehension. A relationship may be interpreted between the nature of a psychological state, the act of perception, and the meaning of an object. All three, in turn, may be related to socio-historical situation; this integration is temporal, void of predetermined developments, and beyond causal analysis (Weber, 1949).

It follows, then, that Weber does not believe the history of society could be revealed either through empiricist or positivist methodologies. Ideals, values and beliefs cannot be scientifically validated. They can, however, be analyzed. This is accomplished by separating means and ends. That is, if individual intent can be separated analytically from the actions taken to obtain a goal, a description of social action becomes possible. While the value or ideal of the intent is the subjective goal, and cannot be validated, the means utilized in social action may be scrutinized to test for consistency between goals and ends. Thus, a social scientist can show what means are available, what consequences may result, and even help clarify goals, but it cannot tell the individual what to do. Universal values do not exist; ideals can be analyzed, not judged.

Empirical reality, not generalized principles, is Weber's guiding principle for social research. The formulation of general principles are useful, but only when used as a catalyst for specific knowledge. Thus, research must conduct a "thought experiment" where a different outcome would have brought on a different set of circumstances. In this qualified fashion, restricted and influenced by the values of science and the researcher, causation can be entertained, but never universally proven.

The distinction between Weber and Durkheim is now apparent. Where Durkheim transformed Kant's subjective knowledge into social concepts as the critical explanatory tool, Weber follows Rickert and suggests social concepts and culture are merely values, which can be studied, but never proven valid. Moreover, where Durkheim conceives of the "whole" as a process of universal differentiation accurately reflecting objective reality, and the causal factor for other social phenomena, Weber's logic begins by stating the whole cannot be conceived, because the whole of social reality is beyond the scope of research. To accept Weber, one must accept that causal relationships of social phenomena is incomprehensible. Weber's aim was to explain subjective social action, and he understood the limitations imposed by his methodology; universal principles would have to give way to fragmented analysis and conclusions. The benefit in Durkheim's approach is the ability to explain external phenomena. However, the advantage in Weber's approach is the ability to explain "real" experiences. Other aspects of Weber's theory, including the study of the "regularities" of rationalization, forms of legitimate authority, social institutions, status and power, economics, and religion, all have these philosophical assumptions as a basis.

It is easy to see why most contemporary analyses of Weber posit his work in the tradition of Kant and neo-Kantians (e.g. Rose, 1981). There is good logic to suggest this proposition. Following Rickert, Weber accepted the Kantian notion that reality is too overwhelming and diffuse for subjective understanding. Individuals must categorize and classify information to grasp partial understanding of reality and obtain what Kant called transcendental knowledge.

Despite the influence of Kant, Weber's work shows repeated similarities to a source rarely mentioned in the literature: Hume. Similarities include:

1. Weber's specific arguments that no general laws or principles of social development are possible replicate Hume's more general skepticism;

2. the rejection of causal analysis is accepted by both theorists;

3. Weber's analysis of subjective selection of social action based on usage and custom follows Hume's own analysis of the role of custom;

4. Weber's use of the concept of ideal-types is similar to Hume's explanation of necessity and cause;

5. Weber's use of the concept of regularities is not dissimilar from Hume's use of social interaction and conditions;

6. Weber's exemplar of rationalization and the need for rationally based bureaucratic decisions parallels Hume's description of rationally created social rules for society;

7. And finally, both authors emphasized the role of social action in the development of their theories. Moreover, like Hume, Weber's analysis, although integrating micro and macro phenomena, fundamentally limits the ability for integration because description, not cause and effect, is the principle aim.

In relation to the issues outlined as critical for the investigations in this chapter, Weber uses some innovative theoretical ideas. First, Weber, like Marx, sees a clear division between natural phenomena and the development of society. However, Weber is willing to go much further than Marx in his condemnation of science and its method. All that is possible is a temporal description of collective regularities, where no value judgments are possible.

In concentrating on collective regularities, Weber includes a notion of autonomy between subjective, collective and external conditions, but any connections between them are beyond the scope of social analysis. While Weber believes individuals are rational, purposive social actors, subjective phenomena is impossible to articulate. Simultaneously, macro phenomena, such as normative values, are also beyond the judgment of social science. As a result, only a weak link is established between micro and macro processes in Weber's work. But this is of little concern to him. And since micro and macro integration are within the condemned parameters of causal analysis, so too are issues concerning the time paths each expresses. Nonetheless, despite the lack of attention Weber paid to issues of time as expressed in micro and macro development, if rational individuals take actions resulting in understandable regularities, it is sensible to assume Weber would view micro and macro processes as contiguous.

In summary, and except for Comte (who has relatively little contemporary influence) classical sociologists all explicitly incorporated the crucial theoretical issues of social integration, universal scientific principles, and temporal development between micro and macro levels. To explain social integration, all three theorists emphasized the notion of collectivities. All did so, I believe, to escape the choices inherited from western philosophy. Empiricist and philosophe dependence on natural law, Humean skepticism, Kantian subjective rationalism, and Hegelian primordial syntheses were not acceptable to Marx, Durkheim, and Weber. Each set out to explain the social, not natural, or purely subjective or holistic development. Necessarily, then, each considered collective social activity as having primary importance, even while believing a general explanation of social development was possible. This left a significant problem for all three theorists: how to reconcile the contingency of social life with the scientifically inspired aim of a general explanation of society? Since each classical sociologist rejected previous philosophical solutions, they needed to create their own. Marx chose political economy and power as the critical collective elements of integration, and found a unifying principle that both linked micro and macro processes, and allowed for a universal explanation of society. Durkheim chose differentiation and social concepts for unifying micro and macro, and this did not demand he sacrifice universal explanations. Weber chose to avoid unifying principles and causal analysis, but nonetheless provided large-scale explanations for forms of world religions and the transformation of feudalism into capitalism.

The effort to reconcile contingent social life and/or provide for universal and large-scale analysis of society led each theorist to grant relative autonomy to micro and macro phenomena. Rejecting scientific universalism and rationalism gave them little choice. Discarding natural explanations and unwilling to magnify the capacity of subjective thought, each needed to explain the mechanism binding the social system. The answer chosen was the social process itself. Within the social process, each could escape purely scientific and philosophical assumptions and directions, and could explore society for its own sake. By doing so, the classical theorists gave birth to sociological theory, but concentrating on the social process did not provide inherent principles of social development. The causal explanations of Marx and Durkheim, and the descriptions of regularities by Weber were created by dividing, to some degree, micro and macro processes. While each saw the level and form of autonomy differently, they each granted autonomy, then selected collective social action as a unifying principle.

Emerging as an essential argument in later chapters, the form of micro and macro autonomy chosen by the classical theorists was not true autonomy. That is, the classical struggle for universal and large scale explanations required that the autonomous levels be seen as necessarily unified. Marx believed individuals change in concert with structures, Durkheim argued micro and macro phenomena must be consistent to avoid anomie, and Weber argued for autonomy through his belief that anything below or beyond collectively created regularities, must be present, but is unknowable. In short, each believed micro and macro processes are mutually created in the temporal circumstances of their development. That is, each believed micro and macro levels are contemporaneous and contiguous. To believe otherwise, and to consider that micro and macro develop along separate time paths, would allow for true autonomy, but would destroy the classical effort at developing universal principles of social development.

Later in this work (see especially Chapter Five), the idea that micro and macro levels are contemporaneous, an idea originating in enlightenment science and universal explanations and passed down to the contemporary scene by the classical sociologists, is seen as a serious error. Briefly, viewing micro and macro processes as contemporaneous denies the ability to see these processes as moving along separate time paths, and ignores the temporal contradictions and/ or coherence that is generated. Separate time paths and a discussion of the dynamic relationship between micro and macro processes not only allow for inter- and intra-autonomy, but also allows for contingent results. By maintaining the search for universal explanations, and by ignoring the autonomous micro and macro time paths, classical theorists, as well as almost all contemporary social theorists, have misunderstood the contingent nature of society.

None of the above is meant to diminish the monumental advances of the classical theorists over previous frameworks. Sadly, contemporary theorists, particularly in the U.S., have failed to include much of what was so innovative in classical sociology. Above all else, the emphasis on collective social action as a unifying factor has been misplaced. The unifying influence of collectivities was a profound classical breakthrough in the development of social theory, and shattered the constraints of philosophical understanding. Instead of accepting the mantle from classical theory and further exploring the relationship between micro and macro levels, twentieth century social theory fractured into two camps. The first emphasized subjective individuals, and the second, universal structural explanations. While each school has intrinsic interest, their fracture offers little to an understanding of the relationship between micro and macro levels. As such, only a brief look at this work follows.

Fractured Theories

This chapter outlines the importance of social integration, the link between micro and macro phenomena, and issues of time throughout the history of scientific, philosophical, and early sociological thought. While each of the classical sociologists differed in relation to each of these influences, they all responded to them nonetheless. All directly confronted these theoretical obstacles. As more contemporary theories developed, however, they tended to rupture, rather than search for a synthesis.

Social Darwinism, for example, developed through the works of Spencer, Ward, and Sumner to have a powerful influence early in the twentieth century. Based on the science of biology, and loosely on the work of Comte, social Darwinism extolled competition and the survival of the fittest as an exemplar for society. In this way, society would evolve into an ever higher order. Viewed as a natural development requiring little conscious or proactive efforts by individuals, a synthesis between micro and macro became unnecessary.

The interaction school, based at the University of Chicago, argued for the primacy of micro social interaction. Following the work of Simmel, such theorists as Thomas, Park, Cooley, and Mead all argued for this focus. Interaction, while not divorced from the social context, must nevertheless be understood in terms of individual consciousness, the concept of self, and social role. While this approach maintains a "social" characteristic in that micro phenomena is based on the interaction of individuals with others (e.g. Mead's "social act" and Blumer's "joint interaction"), it ignores much of the concern of the classical sociologists. In one way or another, the classical theorists had either provided a model of micro and macro synthesis or specifically rejected a synthetic possibility, but with the interactionist school, the concentration is on micro phenomena to the exclusion of macro.

The opposite trend can be seen from the rise of structural functionalism to dominance in American sociology. Again based on Comte, biological theories, and Durkheim, structural functionalist theorists such as Parsons, particularly in his later works, focused almost exclusively on the functions of macro structures and their interrelationships. Moreover, structural functions were perceived as necessary to provide an equilibrium and social order. Stability and orderly change were emphasized as necessary components of all modern societies. In this case, structural analysis included little discussion of micro phenomena. The opportunity for synthesis, therefore, was made impossible.

In response to macro dominance, other micro theories emerged. Exchange theory based largely on the principles of behaviorist psychology, and expounded by Homans, aimed at an explanation of behavior rooted entirely at the micro level. The exchange emphasis on the process of rewards and costs as a catalyst for individual behavior is a prime example of this tendency. While Blau later attempted to apply exchange theory principles to more macro structures, he concluded functionalist assumptions were necessary to explain macro processes.

Other micro theories also developed in response to the dominance of structural functionalism. Phenomenological sociology, based on its philosophical counterpart, aimed at raising consciousness as the centerpoint of analysis. An analysis of consciousness was key to comprehending actions of both individuals and their interactions with others, and thus, subjective construction of reality was pivotal. Ethnomethodology, aimed at similar goals, concentrates on the ordinary activities of individuals, but rather than the phenomenological concern for consciousness, ethnomethodolgists are concerned with the actual activities individuals engage in.

While each of these micro and macro inquiries have uncovered highly useful arguments and empirical realities, by the 1970s their legacy was to fracture social theory, and create a double-barreled criticism aimed at each respective approach. The structural theorists argued continuously that micro theories did not, and could not, adequately account for structures in their analysis. Moreover, structural theorists argued that to accept micro theory was to deny the very existence and influence of large scale structures, a cornerstone of modern society. To ignore cultural, political, and economic structures, as well as other social institutions and complex organizations, was to deny modernity.

For their part, micro theorists argued vehemently that structural analysis did not, and could not, include individual behavior within the structural frameworks. To analyze social action and not include the micro phenomena of consciousness--rationality--the social construction of reality and conditions of behavior was pure structural folly.

This work alleges that the rupture created in fractured theories is a mistake of the highest order. The cost is not born by theory alone. The fracture of theory has made it nearly impossible to apply theory to the empirical world. Contemporary applications of theory have generally heightened the mistake by accepting one or another set of theoretical assumptions before conducting research. The only route out of this sociological cul de sac is to search for ways to integrate theory. This has been the central effort of theorists over the last decade. The emergence of integrated theories as the principle problematic in sociological theory is an important correction. Nevertheless, recent examinations of the micro/macro dichotomy are frustrating. The source of this frustration is that the micro/macro debate cannot move forward because of an obstruction in its core. That obstruction rests primarily with the acceptance of previously stated assumptions. After accepting a theoretical set of assumptions, many integrative authors simply expand suppositions of a particular perspective, and then proclaim a synthesis. These efforts aim more at gaining dominance over other perspectives than integrating micro and macro levels.

One reason contemporary theorizing has not advanced classical efforts is that the scientific and philosophical influences giving rise to sociology have been submerged beyond recognition. Those theories that try to liberate what the mainstream has submerged often are dismissed out of hand. Not surprisingly, the major indictments of both fractured theories and current attempts at micro/macro synthesis come from perspectives that have not been accepted by mainstream social thought. The indictment theories of postmodernism, feminist theory, and ecological theory are discussed in Chapter Three. First, the discussion turns to the ineffective efforts to synthesize micro and macro processes.

Chapter Two

Attempts at Reconciliation

Over the last decade, sociological theory has paid considerable attention to linking micro and macro theory. The emphasis on linkage has changed recent theorizing, in ways not likely overturned in the near future. The traditional fractured approach has been demolished. Neither micro rationale for individual action as wholly responsible for creating structures, nor macro rationale for structures dominating individuals, are tenable any longer. In place of fracture, sociology now aims at including micro and macro aspects of reality, and this realization is shared by almost all contemporary theorists.

The consensus for integration, however, has not led to a successful synthesis or new paradigm. Instead, efforts to integrate social theory have made, I believe, three errors in construction.

1. Theories have merely expanded micro principles to explain macro phenomena, and are designated in this work as ascendant theories.

2. Theories have merely expanded macro principles to explain micro phenomena, and are designated as descendent theories.

3. Theories view micro and macro phenomena as mutually initiated, and are designated as implosion theories.

The three current forms of micro/macro integration do not advance beyond the philosophical issues and sociological approaches discussed in Chapter One. The issues of empiricism, rationalism, and universal explanations remain. Moreover, the classical sociological efforts to explain social integration and micro and macro processes are not advanced. Instead, micro/macro integrationists seem most impressed with the worst aspects of fractured theories, and thus rarely discuss philosophical issues or the classical attempt to overcome them. These micro/macro linkages are loftily characterized as new opportunities for a theoretical future. They are not. If sociological theory maintains the three errors described above, creeping irrelevancy will result and the discipline may be prone to continual academic attack.

The failure of current efforts rests primarily with maintaining previously stated assumptions. After accepting a set of fractured assumptions a priori, authors attempt to expand the explanatory power of a particular perspective, and then proclaim a synthesis. Consequently, almost no new breakthroughs exist in mainstream sociological theory.

One common denominator is present in almost all contemporary attempts at synthetic analysis: the misrepresentation of temporal relationships between micro and macro levels. That is, theorists confuse time elements between micro processes (e.g. the social construction of reality) and the longer time frame of social institutions (e.g. higher education, and political and economic structures). This mistake originates in the pursuit of universal explanations for society. The enlightenment legacy, then, is alive and well in contemporary micro/macro theorists.

The dual errors of inheriting assumptions and misrepresenting temporal relationships are closely associated, and both are related to issues investigated by classical sociologists. As discussed in the last chapter, the classical theorists all tried to escape universal explanations of philosophy and science by emphasizing social integration and, in doing so, granted qualified autonomy to both micro and macro processes. Most contemporary theorists, however, have inherited fractured theoretical assumptions, not the work of classical theory, and continue the fractured practice of confining individual or conditional processes, or combining them in ways rendering it impossible to isolate their autonomous development. Consequently, integration is impeded and any application to empirical reality is not fully realized.

In contrast, Parts II and III of this work argue that micro and macro are distinct processes which variably integrate throughout history. Moreover, no set of micro or macro assumptions can explain the particular form of integration. Accordingly, the central task of an integrative framework must be to allow the relationship of the two processes to be uncovered. Acknowledging both micro and macro autonomy, then, is critical if theory is to be applied to social developments. Before these ideas can be fully explained, however, it is necessary to review current attempts at integration.

Micro Ascendant Theories

The impetus for sociological micro theory is to undo structural theory's objectivism which, micro theorists state, ignores the significance of the individual. In place of objectivism, traditional micro theory argued individuals and their actions are pivotal for the social world, and thus, society becomes intelligible only when phenomenal meanings and rational intentions of actors are discovered. In response, macro theorists leveled a basic criticism: the principle failure of micro theory rests in its inability to account for the creation and development of structures. In the structuralist view, micro theory either grants individuals more freedom and power to create, maintain, and change social structures than any empirical study would allow, or simply leaves the development of structures unexplained. When micro theories grant individuals rational, or phenomenal mastery over the production and reproduction of society, macro theorists would constantly condemn the exclusion of social contexts in which actions take place.

Ascendant micro theorists have recently sought to answer this criticism through the micro integration of structures. Despite the desire to account for structures, micro assumptions regarding individual primacy over structures remain, and this tempers the micro view of structural processes. In brief, structures are analyzed as contemporaneously created from micro social action. As such, structural history and the interplay between individuals and structural transitions is eliminated from ascendant theories.

One micro theorist who makes this mistake is Randall Collins. Collins (1987) seeks an empirically grounded explanation of micro and macro, but for him, social life is observable only if translated to the micro level. Macro structures consist of large numbers of people repeating actions in time and space. Any other description of structures may not correspond to aggregated micro encounters and are, therefore, "metaphorical." Structures never "do anything," only people can take actions. Thus, social change or a lack of change is due to, and occurs within, micro processes (Collins 1987, p. 195).

Consequently, Collins concentrates on integrating individuals with aggregate micro encounters to explain structures. To analyze the individual and aggregate relationships requires that he move beyond a purely micro level analysis of individual behavior. Traditional assumptions of micro theories such as phenomenology allowed only for analysis of the individual. Collins rejects this limiting view and installs the relationship between individuals and collective as a central focus. To delineate this relationship, he develops the notion of interaction ritual chains (IRC). IRCs are built from negotiations of conversation. Individual motivations and resources obtained from previous encounters are conversationally negotiated, and place individuals in positions of social membership. Individuals use previous encounters to further their social inclusion. The result is "emergent," not conditionally determined (Collins 1987, p. 195). Moreover, individuals are motivated to participate in conversations based on emotions, not cognitive decisions. Rational thinking is limited; individuals cannot cognitively "weigh complex decisions consciously."

Emotional energy and previous encounters, then, are two resources brought to a micro encounter, and to these Collins adds a third resource: social reputation. Social reputation is developed in a network of interactive conversations outside the control of the individual. In combination, these resources make conversations attractive or unattractive, and explain participation and possible conversational domination (Collins 1987, pp. 199-200).

Aggregate macro patterns emerge from this chain of interaction. Since different groups are characterized by typical, membership-identifying conversations, macro concepts, such as community, can be viewed as "various types of networks of repeated conversations among certain persons." These networks are the basis for ideology, culture and social systems extended over time (Collins 1987, p. 201).

Resources brought to conversations are central in Collins' theory, but they are not conditional. Resources are interactively enacted, often through struggle. For example, while the domination of property resources provides the "material setting" for interactions, the ability to mobilize resources from previous micro encounters is what leads to differences in power and stratification (Collins 1987, pp. 202-203). Indeed, the very power of nation-states, contained in their "geopolitical" relations, is based on the same micro principles of time, space and number; military and material relationships form social networks which create nation-states. The interactive power struggles contained within societies make up their "microexperiential reality" (Collins 1987, p. 197).

In summary, the integrative thread to such diverse aspects of social reality as a two-person conversation, social stratification and the formation of nations is the micro-generated IRC.

Collins' premise is that micro encounters are the only empirically valid reality. Structures exist only when they can be translated to a micro source. Empirical validity, however, is a problem for Collins' own assumptions, even within his own logic. The IRC is a creative application of many micro analytic suppositions. First, it concludes that interaction is typically a negotiation of conversation, and a wealth of empirical micro findings exists to support this reasoning. Second, conversations are chosen, in part, through emotional energy gained through previous encounters, but this claim has not been empirically established. In fact, the individual differences in emotional make-up and the physiological basis of emotions, particularly the relation of emotions to the brain, are not emphasized by Collins. Nevertheless, Collins relates emotions to other resources, which are then viewed as predictors of conversational participation and domination. These are fascinating ideas worth exploring, but since the source of emotions has not yet been established, no theory can use these suppositions and claim to be empirical.

Collins' approach, then, is a modified empiricism and rationalism. People's experiences remain a key feature, but they are no longer based on sense perception. People negotiate conversation, but non-rational emotions also play a role. In short, Collins combines a variety of fractured, micro theories in his analysis. This purely micro effort raises serious deficiencies in his analysis of social integration. The need to explain social integration is not dissimilar from the reason classical sociologists also moved in that direction. But where the classical theorists use social integration to replace universal scientific and philosophical assumptions, Collins uses social integration only to try and defeat macro criticisms of micro theory. Within this context, IRCs become networks of conversations, and power is enacted through the micro mobilization of resources, often through the appropriation of property. However, a theoretical and empirical question must be raised. Do patterns of property and stratification exist before individuals engage in micro encounters? Collins' answer is that if an IRC is repeated enough times over a wide area of social space, long-term macro patterns emerge. The inherent difficulty is that IRCs are both limited to the emotional lifespan of individuals, and extend over broad periods of time and space.

Whether one is born a noble or a serf should have an impact on micro encounters, not only because of individual micro encounters, but because of long-term IRCs. If this is true, the relational development of these processes needs explanation, even if analyzed strictly within a micro framework. If the property and stratification resources are due to micro encounters of previous generations, how are they passed on, and what is the relation between individual and collective IRCs?

Collins neither asks nor provides answers to these or similar questions, in large part because he insists all macro patterns must be translated to a micro source, and patterns of behavior and structures must not have conditional status. Thus, the relationships between individuals and patterns of behavior, and between interaction and structures are seen as contiguous; so much so that methods of explaining macro structures are rooted in conversations. If, however, macro patterns are not wholly recreated with each birth, then the study of autonomous micro and macro relationships patterns is a logical imperative.

The recognition of autonomous micro and macro patterns is especially integral to an analysis of nation-states. However, for Collins, national power is erected only from geopolitical, military and material networks, where power struggles are contiguously related to, and based on, IRCs. This proposal may aid in depicting present resources, but cannot reveal resource development, to which new individuals must relate. Even if IRCs are extended beyond Collins' intentions and are viewed as historical interaction patterns, individuals nonetheless, must form relationships with historically generated nation-states; existing social structures are not contemporaneously initiated by each individual, or network of individuals.

Collins also maintains aggregate data is inappropriate for study because aggregate data does not accurately reflect micro encounters. However, the reason macro data may not be a pure reflection of individual encounters is the empirical relationship is not contiguous. Social structures and patterns of behavior are related to, but not identical to, micro encounters. Because this is so does not mean macro conditions do not exist; rather, it means the micro encounters of the present are not the only explanatory source of collective action, social conditions, and social change. While micro theorists may well argue that action cannot be reduced from structures, Collins' notion that structures are myths is driven more by his theoretical assumptions than empirical reality.

Centuries ago, the empiricists and philosophes eliminated the need for autonomy because of their belief in the universal explanation of natural science. Collins eliminates autonomy between micro and macro because of accepted micro assumptions; in place of a universal science, Collins argues for the universality of encounters. All social activity and creations are derived from this source, and armed with this faithful assumption, no autonomous explanation is needed. And while differences between individuals and collectivities are discussed, in the end collectivities are merely aggregated encounters. To accept Collins requires throwing out both the concept and influence of structures, and the concept and influence of collectivities. It is difficult to discern how Collins' version of reality is more sensible than structural versions. It also is difficult to discern, therefore, how his framework advances social thought.

The confusion between the temporal development of structures and micro activity, and the distorted view of micro/macro synthesis is repeated by other micro theorists. While the integration of micro and macro might differ from Collins, acceptance of micro assumptions are repeated. Wippler and Lindenberg (1987), for example, do not view structures as myths, but claim a natural, human bias to understanding micro phenomena. In their view, structures are variable and always in flux. This creates a significant problem. Since boundary conditions of structures "differ widely and change considerably over time," some unchanging core aspect of society must be found to generate stability in sociological analysis." Stability is found in the primacy of the individual. But like Collins, Wippler and Lindenberg do not mean to reduce all analysis to the level of each individual. Instead, they argue that to fully understand individual behavior requires an acceptance of the influence of social conditions, but structural influence may be uncovered only within the individual (Wippler and Lindenberg 1987, p. 143-145). In other words, the reality of structures cannot be seen within the study of structures themselves, but are present and discoverable only at the micro level.

Like Collins, Wippler and Lindenberg's work supposes all social reality is exposed at the micro level. Once again, the micro level is selected because macro conditions are not knowable. This hearkens back to Kant, and the inability to grasp objects "in themselves." This position forced Kant to select a unifying element, and he chose moral behavior. Wippler and Lindenberg show their modern colors and choose psychology (e.g. Wippler and Lindenberg, 1987 p. 142). This choice is not made, however, on the basis of some undeniable empirical evidence, but because of philosophical and fractured theoretical assumptions. The question is, of course, why believe it?

Based on their choices and assumptions, Wippler and Lindenberg must necessarily view micro and macro relations as contiguous and contemporaneous. Once the two authors accept individuals as a priori to conditions, and structures as merely relative to micro processes, no other logical choice exists. If, however, fractured micro or macro assumptions are transcended, an alternative may be offered, where structures and individuals proceed along different paths of time. Here, structures exist when an individual is born, continue to develop through the time span of his or her life, and proceed after death. Limiting structural development to micro deductions means only present structures can be uncovered, and only as they are instantiated within the individual. This makes both the past and probable future of structures frivolous. Moreover, in Wippler and Lindenberg's version of ascendant theory, where the boundaries of structures are always changing, even the present development of structures become impossible to grasp.

Similar problems are evident in rational choice theory. While rational choice theorists now view the rational production of institutions as a major focus (Friedman and Hechter, 1990), the autonomous development of structures is unexplored. In Coleman's version (1990), emphasis on the individual is once again the theoretical starting point. Coleman decides to analyze individuals because of their empirical advantages over structures. Rational individuals are seen as acting purposely towards a goal, and maximizing their ability to gain an objective. Actors also use resources, and in doing so, create structures beyond the boundaries of single actors, even to the extent of granting authority and rights to others. Here again, the traditional criticism of micro theory is avoided by stating that rational choice theory may include aggregate groups.

Coleman also allows for differences between actors and groups; what might be in one group's interest can be gained at the expense of another group. In addition, structures can require individuals to move beyond single purposive action, and consider the interest of the collective, or even how the collective or group may oppose the interests of the individual. Nonetheless, the more macro processes may be revealed only when one assumes, and begins analysis, with rational choice actors.

However, the temporal problem remains. While Coleman clearly has a sense of history in his description of the modern rational choice actor (e.g. 1990 p. 531-43), the social context in which rational choice takes place is not examined. Even a discussion as to why the individual is a rational chooser is unsubstantiated. If one is to argue that society has developed from a form which included "natural actors" to one in which "corporate actors" are present, a discussion of the history of social structures that outdistance rational choices is required. Coleman is willing to include contemporary structures, and even accepts that structures may have certain constraining elements, but since micro assumptions mandate structures are contiguous to individuals, the historical and autonomous development of structures disappears from his discussion.

Thus while Coleman provides important theoretical room for structures, and grants some autonomy between individuals and collectives, his main focus is on the more empirically grounded rational choices of actors. But on what basis are rational actors more empirical? The only grounds available are philosophical and fractured theoretical assumptions. In contrast, one could examine the U.S. economy, for example, not only on the basis of rational choices, but through structural relations to other national economies, and even suggest this international relationship has some influence over individual rational choice. Saying, as Coleman does, that macro processes are difficult to uncover, so therefore ignore it, is an apparently weak argument.

Yet this micro assumption is repeated continually by micro integrationists. Fine (1990), for example, claims contemporary symbolic interactionism is "capable of addressing macro-sociological themes." Unlike the newly discovered appreciation that other micro theorists are developing for collective groups, the area of interpersonal relationships has long historical roots in symbolic interactionism (e.g. Blumer, 1939). A new generation of theorists attempt to extend interpersonal relationships to clarify macro structures. Nevertheless, when the aim is limited, as it is in the area of cultural studies, to clarifying how symbols are a function of interaction and how interaction becomes a consequence of symbolic display (Fine, 1990), then structural explanations are again eliminated. Moreover, the temporal problem facing other micro theorists is repeated by symbolic interactionists. Symbolic interaction, by definition, occurs in the present. Thus, the two autonomous time sequences of actors and structures is confused.

Similar problems emerge in contemporary exchange theory. Contemporary exchange theorists have suggested that their interests are inherently integrative. They study exchanges ranging from two actors, to organizations, and to nation-states. Thus, structures are perceived "as the interconnection of various positions in an exchange network (Cook et. al, 1990). This perspective, it is argued, can illuminate how structures emerge and how they change; repetitive exchanges result in patterned interactions and give rise to structures, and these structures may change if the pattern of exchange is altered. However, when viewed in this way, structures must be limited to the present forms of exchange which are its source. Once again, structures are not emphasized and the temporal problem is not sufficiently answered. Finally, Haferkamp (1987) sees macro structures as either rationally constructed social associations, or structures are resulting from action, but in either case, structures are not consciously understood by the acting subjects at the moment of genesis.

Thus, a common thread and problem exists among all ascending theories: in order to escape the macro criticism that micro theories are unable to explain structures, micro theorists have abandoned the traditional limit of theory aimed to explain each individual, and now argue that structures can be explained through an analysis of aggregate groups. But the aggregate group, a primary focus of most ascendant theorists, is not equivalent to the collectivities as seen by the classical sociologists. Classical theorists chose the concept of autonomous social collectivities to unify autonomous micro and macro levels. Ascendant theories, however, fail to see autonomous levels, or the need to unify them. This is reminiscent of the unresolvable debate between empiricists and the philosophes. Empiricism is more empirical, but philosophe rationalism allows for the construction of society. Arguments can fly back and forth, as they do in micro theory, but who is to say which perspective more accurately reflects reality? Only philosophical assumptions can direct you. Moreover, at least empiricism and rationalism of centuries ago was based on a broader concept that was concretely arguable: the mechanical universe. The assumptions of universal science and the question of which perspective more closely matched those assumptions could be debated. Ascendant theorists, in contrast, simply endorse the fractured assumption of the primacy of individuals. One is either a believer or a heretic. This is not to deny that ascendant theories allow more flexibility in discussing structures than their fractured predecessors. While this modification has allowed ascendant theorists to talk about issues previously reserved for structural analysis, such as power and social institutions, the micro bias remains. Fractured assumptions cannot foster theoretical growth.

Two issues emerge from this discussion. First, a culturally idealized conception of individual power is expressed in micro integrative efforts. In order for individuals or groups to pro-actively shape, or understand society, they must place individuals and groups in a democratic form of government that allows freedom of thought, choice, and action. Within this theoretical and ideological setting, power differentials are reduced to Collins' micro encounters leading to mobilization of resources, Wippler and Lindenberg's recognition of power by individuals, and Coleman's maximizing ability to carry out goals. These theoretical positions are possible only within a democratic framework, where structures become unimportant since individuals have, or struggle to have, freedom to express their micro predilections.

However, whether within the sphere of "western democracies" or in areas external to them, the proposition of relatively free proactive individuals is an presumption of leviathan proportions. Following this prescription, a study of poverty in Brazil, for example, would not include a discussion of international and national political and economic conditions. The fact that these structural conditions have been developing over centuries and have recently undergone significant changes could not be a feature of analysis. This would seem an obvious and serious omission.

The problems evident in ascendant assumptions should not imply that micro integrative theories should be ignored. On the contrary, micro theory has much to offer, often in areas unexplored by macro theory. Micro theorists are correct that micro processes are not determined by normative or instrumental structures. Interaction, psychology, physiology, emotions, morality, and the social construction of reality are critical in understanding social action, whether or not the action is rational, or based on objective reality. Each, and many combinations of these processes are fruitful in explaining individual development, whether as processes of internalization or as spring-boards for individual perceptions or behavior. However, if theory is to be integrated, the micro notion that patterns of behavior and structures are merely reducible to micro encounters, and that macro theory and research is mythological, must be eliminated.

To escape from this fractured cage it is necessary to temporally distinguish between actions and structures, and analytically uncover their dynamic relationship. The classical sociologists did just that. While not sufficient, it was a necessary step. Any thinker, not yet a fervent believer in a particular fractured faith, might ask him or herself a simple question. Is the ascendant approach to micro/macro synthesizing a move forward from classical efforts to solve the underlying philosophical issues that are sociology's heritage? Unless one is a true micro believer, expressing a liturgy filled with faith in the primacy of the individual, it seems reasonable to see what other fractured religions have to offer. A discussion of the descendent scripture follows.

Macro Descendent Theories

Macro theorists have long asserted that societies are unique because structures and social systems differ and change over time, not because people act. Theoretical analysis, then, should begin at the macro level, where actions are often presumed structurally constrained or encouraged. Micro critics of structural analysis have long and powerfully argued that macro inquiries miscalculate individual acts as predetermined by emergent conditions. Jeffrey Alexander is one macro theorist who has tried to answer this criticism.

Alexander (1987) contends theory must synthesize the "problem" of action and order, and that macro theories must include micro elements to successfully uncover empirical descriptions of reality. Micro and macro are "homologous." Each contains "variables and parameters of different levels of different size," all placed in an interactive system (Alexander 1987, p. 315).

Using this framework, Alexander explores the process of action. First, based on phenomenological insights, individuals interpret and become knowledgeable of actions because they occur within a known frame of reference, but each new action is different, as actors creatively attach new actions to past points of reference (Alexander, 1987 pp. 299-301).

Added to this "interpretation" by actors is "strategization." The elements of time, energy and knowledge encourage a cost benefit analysis of effort, as actors seek the shortest path to a goal. Effort, therefore, has a conditional influence; conditions constrain interpretation and strategy as individuals select courses of action (Alexander, 1987 pp. 302-303). Consequently, non-rational interpretation and rational strategization are synthesized with the objective world. Actions produce environments and environments constrain action (Alexander, 1987 p. 303).

Turning to an explanation of these environments, Alexander refers to Parsons (1937) and utilizes his three system model of social system-culture-personality. The three systems provide an order for action (Alexander, 1987 p. 304). The social system provides actors with "real objects," physical, natural and human (such as the division of labor, political institutions, groups, roles). These objects are ordered and form the backdrop in which actors interpret and strategize (Alexander, 1987 pp. 303-304). Cultural systems include symbolic naming and analoging of objects based on interpretation, as well as values. Values mediate between social systems and micro processes by providing social meaning to order as actors shape economic, political and social integration processes and define their commitment to these objects (Alexander, 1987 p.308).

Culture also contains other, more "dynamic" elements where the equilibrium problems of social systems are "culturally translated" and "symbolically reconstructed." Conflicts or threats to the social system, for example, are viewed as "profane" or "polluting" and removed by isolating or ritualizing order. The rituals are not determined by the form of threat or by established cultural forms; they are invented in creative ways and may lead to new cultural forms within the boundaries of interpretation and strategization (Alexander, 1987 p. 309).

The third environment, the personality system, is an unconscious, emotional element to which action also must be integrated. Personalities, however, are not wholly due to individual processes: they develop in relation to both social objects and what is considered deviant or conformist. Moreover, changing objects necessitate personality changes. Thus, while personalities are related to objects, cultural forms depend on the order developed in personalities (Alexander, 1987 pp. 310-311). Each of the three systems, then, provide an order in which action takes place.

Alexander further argues the capacity to carry out action has changed historically as rational social systems become differentiated, and culture and personality must allow for more adaptation. Modern personalities, for example, develop the capacity for "depersonalization and control", and the "splitting" between public and private spheres. This is the basis for modern interpretation and strategy (Alexander, 1987 pp. 310-312). Although emotional experience in uneven periods of modernization can predispose individuals to "unstable" micro processes and actions, even unstable action is in relation to existing environments (Alexander, 1987 p. 312).

Finally, social control in modern societies is necessary to "maintain psychological, social and interpretative consistency" because modern rationality is more open to action than traditional societies. Modern societies live in more complex and differentially changing environments. Modern action, therefore, requires rationality (Alexander, 1987 pp. 312-314).

The main goal of Alexander's integrative effort is to reinterpret Parsonian functionalism. While Alexander rejects the notion that macro structures are myths or non-empirical, and argues persuasively that actions can be discerned only in relation to social contexts, he nevertheless argues micro processes are significant in their own right, and clearly attests to action as a result of micro as well as macro environments. Moreover, while the goal of social integration is maintained, it is not assumed.

Using Alexander's synthesis as a model for integration, however, raises a question. Does the use of Parsons's three-system model accurately reflect the nature of social reality? The underlying principle shaping the three-system model is the principle of differentiation. While Alexander allows for variance and change within the differentiation process, differentiation remains the key and continually comes into play in Alexander's application of the three systems. Even the integration of actions and environments, where actions are synthesized to non-determining social environments, is, itself, referenced to differentiation. Alexander views the micro and macro processes as autonomous, and potentially conflictual, but always in relation to differentiation, even when the micro integration with environments creates unstable societies. Thus, what Alexander calls "dynamic elements" of culture are theoretically allowed, but only as problems of equilibrium within the development of differentiation.

Even when Alexander explicitly formulates different forms of structural and micro integrations, which can include variation and either conflict or consensus, the relationship to differentiation remains. The three integrative possibilities he offers (Alexander, 1988 pp. 154-155) include: harmony between social and cultural systems, where groups may be different but not in conflict; conflicts on the social system level combined with an integrated cultural system, where groups may develop antagonisms but not inherent conflict; and fundamental conflict in both social and cultural systems, where inherent conflicts emerge between groups and their beliefs. However, even the last and most conflictual example of social and cultural conflict cited by Alexander tends to occur "where traditional and modernizing cultures are carried by vigorous and contentious social groups" (Alexander, 1988 p. 159). In short, although structures are given more variability, and conflict plays a more important role in neo-functionalism as compared to traditional functionalism, differentiation is still given primacy over the individual.

Consequently, Alexander's theory requires acceptance of differentiation as the motive force of history; equilibrium as a general, although not always attainable system goal; and social integration as a social process whereby the two can be related, although not always successfully. Within these assumptions, micro and macro are viewed as different levels of order within the same social system. Although conflict and variation are introduced, Parsons' three-system model is related a priori to differentiation and modernization. Differentiation, however, is not an historical imperative. Colomy (1990a, 1990b), another neo-functionalist, argues traditional differentiation must be transcended within the neo-functionalism project. Differentiation must become more empirical, and allow for analysis of groups, conflict and power. He too suggests societies may or may not adopt the process of differentiation, and functional parts may or may not be in conflict.

Nevertheless, and even when micro and macro levels are granted some level of autonomy, if the general development of society is essential in comprehending the roots of actions, neo-functionalism has put itself squarely into a theoretical box from which it cannot answer the traditional micro criticism: structures are not able to determine individual action. Despite the new flexibility, and despite allowance for "considerable variation in the amount of differentiation both within and between societies" (Colomy, 1990b p. 470), differentiation remains the central theoretical assumption and necessarily dominates micro reac-

to the even more macro differentiation process. Luhmann (1982, 1987), who makes precisely this mistake, suggests the differentiation process has become so complex that success or failure in the selection process, is itself dependent on the functional attributes offered.

An alternate example of descendent integration can be found in network theory. For example, Burt (1982), like neo-functionalists, gives more flexibility to actors, but nevertheless, posits actions in relation to already existing structures. Social structures (found both at the micro and macro levels) influence choices made by actors (again conceived as either micro or macro). Thus, actions are a consequence "of actors pursuing their interests to the limit of their ability where both interests and ability are patterned by social structure." While actions can modify structural constraints, there is little doubt structures are the primary controlling interest.

Here again is the temporal problem, and once again it emerges from the inability to isolate actions and structures, and grant them autonomy. Consequently, the possibility that either inconsistency or integration exists between the two levels remains unexplored. The degree of micro and macro integration must be empirically established; therefore, searching for social order must not be the starting point of analysis, no matter how much flexibility is granted in the process. Instead, micro and macro reality must be viewed as distinct processes which integrate in unique and variable ways, each having the capacity to make order or disorder of the social system.

One integrative, and descendent, school of thought attempting to include issues of conflict is Neo-Marxism. Two main schools emerged in the later half of the twentieth century, which although different, express the descendent error. One school, Marxist poststructuralism, led by Althusser (1979), maintained that the later "scientific" Marx must take precedence over his earlier philosophical writings. In the poststructuralist view, society should be seen as a compilation of layers and structures, each independent and each containing its own dynamic and contradictions. This "decentered" approach rejected overarching explanations of development and crisis, and instead claimed a confluence of individual contradictions and changes would bring about general change. Thus, ideology, the superstructure, independent political practice, and the state (Poulantzas, 1978) are all seen as separate entities with a separate logic for development.

Poststructuralist Marxism sought a new Marxist politics for Europe and was erected in reaction to "economist" visions of Marx practiced in the Soviet Union and communist parties of Europe during the mid-twentieth century (Anderson, 1984; Antonio, 1990). Nonetheless, poststructuralism descendently destroys integration between individuals and structures. In the structuralist framework, structures are so complicated and diverse, only localized understanding of political action becomes possible. More importantly for the present discussion, autonomous levels of micro and macro also become unintelligible.

Once history becomes a compilation of isolated responses to individual structures, macro history is beyond comprehension. Althusser (1979, pp. 117-128) expresses this point explicitly. While structuralists acknowledge the existence of logic in each level of structure and, following Marx, structures are seen as determined by economics in the "last instance", the confluence of structures remain analytically independent. History, then, becomes a series of individual events and acts. This means structural Marxism accepts economics as a motive force in history, but history can be understood only as combinations of activities within structures.

Poststructuralism, then, rejects autonomy from two directions simultaneously. First, the confluence of structural circumstances that bring change are both micro and macro. Consequently, change in necessarily contiguous, and autonomy is destroyed. Second, poststructuralism must appoint some assumption as a unifying thread. Where neofunctionalism chose differentiation, poststructuralism selects omnipresent structures. These structures exist everywhere, even at the micro level, but whether micro or macro, structures exhibit constraining power. But why do structures exist? Poststructuralism falls back on a vague recognition of Marx's material primacy. Poststructuralist assumptions, then, intermingle Marx's material primacy with a doctrine of omnipresent structures. Nonetheless, both presumptions are beyond discovery because the structural matrix is so decentered, it is generally beyond explanation. Thus micro and macro processes not only are related in a maze of contiguous structures, they can never, in any case, be comprehended.

Another direction within neo-Marxism is suggested by Critical Marxists. While the emphasis is different, the failure to separate the two levels of social reality into autonomous regions is repeated. A common idea linking this school is that a ruling economic elite has created a cultural hegemony that corresponds to elite interests. With both economic and cultural control, the elite manipulate social ideas to gain popular acceptance in the face of conflicting self-interests. The emphasis on cultural hegemony represents a shift from classical Marxism's emphasis on economic structures and posits cultural domination as the linchpin of modern capitalism. Critical Marxists believe only a revolution in the cultural realm can be the catalyst for societal change.

These positions are best expressed in the work of Habermas. Where Marx emphasized the experiences of work (see Chapter One), Habermas is concerned with the cultural activity of communicative action, a fundamental feature of human beings intentionally distorted by the cultural elite (Habermas, 1987). In order to emphasize communication, Habermas changes the Marxist distinction between base and superstructure and replaces it with a distinction between labor and interaction. This allows Habermas to argue that forms of interaction dominate modern labor, and transformed it into a "purposive-rational" logic of labor (Antonio, 1990). Thus interaction becomes the analytic focus, and can be mutually beneficial if people recognize that mutual, cooperative understanding allows for the attainment of goals. This interaction potential, however, is precisely what has been distorted by elites in modern society. As long as communication is obstructed by the use of power, and as long as that power is currently aimed to encourage distorted versions of truth and reality, communicative action is suppressed.

Habermas (1989) also considers the process of communicative action within a micro/macro integration. At the micro level, communicative action arises within the "life-world", where interaction occurs and actors come to resolution and understanding. But actors also carry out communication within the context of a rationalized system, where structures emerge, grow in power, and negatively influence the potential for the life-world, communicative process. The elite's systematic "colonization" of the life-world turns micro communication into a more rationalized, and less communicative, process. The hope for the future is to decouple systemic domination through progressive social movements.

Critical theory, then, maintains the repetition of the temporal mistake common to all descendent theories. Here, culturally dominated communication and action is assumed. On this basis, only a movement organized as a frontal attack against such domination has the hope of ending hegemonic control. Thus, where Marx chose material power of the dominant class and the collective response to structural contradictions as the unifying thread between micro and macro processes, Habermas selects the cultural power and the communicative response to such domination as his unifying mechanism. Even within the field of Marxism, how is one to choose between the newest rage -- studies of culture -- and the traditional emphasis on economic structures?

An even-tempered review, however, might conclude that both have valuable insights. Since both Marx and Habermas developed the potential for micro activity on macro conditions, if economics and culture are explored in autonomous relation to each other, a fruitful analysis may emerge. Moreover, if both are seen as autonomous from micro processes, not as dominating them, then the inconsistencies or congruencies between them may be uncovered.

If this more open-ended proposal were applied to Habermas' framework, and the dynamic between the life-world and structural levels was seen as autonomous, new critical avenues for social action would appear. First, if micro autonomy were allowed, the fatalistic cultural hegemony in the life-world would become a process where micro communication and actions have more potential to affect change and challenge structural inconsistencies and power relations. Second, if structures are viewed autonomously, internal structural inconsistencies are made apparent, and thus, inconsistencies and power relations are more easily understood and acted upon. Consequently, permitting autonomy within and between micro and macro processes portrays general inconsistencies and power relations at both levels, and the "critical" hope for change may become more plausible.

Given the descendent bias of his theory, however, Habermas has no choice but to exclude autonomy. As long as cultural structures theoretically dominate micro processes of modern communication, then the two levels must be analytically conjoined. In this scenario, micro and macro are contiguously related and the temporal autonomy between the two is lost. As in other ascendant and descendent theories, critical theory makes assumptions, fixes primacy, and micro/macro relations follow accordingly.

This critique of descendent integration, however, is not to imply these efforts are lacking significance. Structures are not properly explained by micro processes, and people cannot shape structures as they please, even by repeating patterns of action. While structures may not instrumentally or normatively determine individual, group or collective action, structures are autonomously related to action. The development of structures are, therefore, as worthy of sociological inquiry as micro processes. If social theory is to be integrated, however, the descendent view of macro and micro reality as different pieces of a puzzle, each simultaneously developing and reflecting the other, but integrated on the basis of macro assumptions of system development, must be rejected.

Theories of Implosion

Theories of implosion are a third example of integrative theories failing to account for the autonomy and time differences between micro and macro phenomena. Where ascendant theories suggest structures develop as a contemporaneous result of micro phenomena, and where descendent theories suggest micro processes develop as a contemporaneous result of macro phenomena, implosion theories argue that micro and macro processes are simultaneously instantiated at each level. As such, autonomy and the unique histories of the two levels is omitted.

Perhaps the most widely read theory of implosion is the work of Anthony Giddens. In *The Constitution of Society*, Giddens (1984) contends social theory is concerned with actions and its relation to institutions. The two are integrated through the duality of micro and macro, where forms of action reproduced over time and space develop structural properties, and structures have properties that bind actions "across varying spans of time and space" (Giddens 1984, p. 17).

Giddens first analyzes micro processes and argues that individual acts contain unconscious motivations. Trust and a sense of security are needed to reduce anxiety in social interaction, and if obtained, allow for a practical, conscious knowledge of positive encounters. Individuals gain trust and security through the continuity and predictability of routine encounters, made possible because actions tend to develop patterns in various time-space regions (Giddens, 1984 pp. 60-121). Routine, then, allows actions to be familiar, and regionalism allows larger social systems to be variably differentiated by time and space (Giddens 1984 pp. 130-139).

Between the individual and social system lie institutional structures, which are mediating forces; they enable and constrain actions through the use of institutional rules and resources. While structures, therefore, are related to action, they also can be related to social systems as combinations of regional rule-resource sets of institutions. However, since social systems include many time-space regions, the various combinations of institutional rule-resource sets may extend beyond the control of many individuals; "they may stretch away in time and space and actors may reify social relations." Individuals do not, therefore, create whole societies; they remake them within the time-space of specific institutional structures (Giddens 1984 p. 171). Moreover, the only way to fruitfully analyze social systems and all the combinations of routines, regionalism and structural rules and resources, is to view them as suspended in time and space. In this way, symbolic dominating and legitimizing acts can be studied in relation to corresponding institutions (Giddens, 1984 pp. 28-37).

Individuals, then, have knowledge of, reproduce, and act upon institutional rules and resources. This is the basis of social patterns and integration (Giddens, 1984 pp. 17-25). Thus, institutions, not social systems, are central to research.

Giddens' view of social change corresponds to these principles. Knowledgeable actors are integrated with intersocietal systems and structures, loosely and variably grouped into episodes in world time. Change occurs as power, which is generated in and through the domination of resources in many institutions, is variably combined to generate a momentum toward new, often contradictory, social forms. The degree of change is related to the form of rules and resources. Traditional societies had less change because rules and resources were existential and based on kinship and tradition. Modern societies, however, have highly developed states and many institutions, which lead to struggles over rules and resources (Giddens, 1984 pp. 193-199). It is at the junction of the rules and resources of institutional structures, then, where the individual and social systems meet, and where action is enacted and constrained.

As with all implosion theorists, Giddens' theory includes troubling theoretical constructs. First, does the resolution of unconscious anxiety lead to rational knowledge? This supposition is empirically questionable. Since the nature of the unconscious is a source of much debate, its relation to rational knowledge is highly tenuous. Moreover, Giddens argues rational knowledge is made possible through routine interaction. While routine may describe a generally stable society, one undergoing change would necessarily have regions that question, destroy and replace routines. If this is so, it is unclear how unconscious anxieties would be resolved to allow interaction to take place. Nevertheless, Giddens claims secure and trusting individuals then develop rational and practical knowledge of structural rules and resources, which then mediate between actions and social systems. Again, this assumption may be more appropriately applied to a stable society; Giddens' synthesis of anxiety, routine, knowledge, and structures is possible only in a social system in relative harmony.

While Giddens does allow for interactive responses to institutional rules and resources, and change through new forms of domination, the source of new domination is restricted to internal momentum generated from interaction. Any relationship, then, between social system change and change within regionalized structures remains unexplored because it is outside the boundaries of anxiety, routine, knowledge, and social institutions. Giddens simply has no theoretical outlet to explain this dynamic. Since social systems are reified and beyond individual control, individuals can directly affect time and space specific institutions, but not social systems. The various regional combinations of institutional structures, make change at the system level practically unintelligible, except as abstract notions. Moreover, if Giddens included societal change within his framework, it would destroy the idea that interaction occurs through routine and regionalism, because system level developments would change the equation in which routine, regions and institutional structures develop.

Consequently, Giddens' theory requires an a priori acceptance that social systems and their change are beyond empirical reach. For Giddens, only interaction recreates and changes structures and only the institutional momentum of these combined forces yields contradiction and change at the societal level. Societal change, therefore, is made necessarily too complicated to comprehend.

But this need not be the case. Giddens clearly recognizes the problem of macro and micro realities. Unlike ascendant theorists, he was not prepared to describe all structures as the result of subjective actors. And unlike descendent theorists, he was not prepared to explain individual activity as constrained action. Giddens was left with two choices: accept the autonomy of the two levels, or choose implosion. Unfortunately, he chose the latter. Structuration theory envisions individuals and institutional structures as contiguous and mutually constitutive. Each are instantiated in the other.

However, contiguous micro and macro instantiation is what led to Giddens' difficulty in explaining social systems. How can individuals become instantiated with broad systemic structures? In accepting the principle that individuals and structures must be contiguously constituted, Giddens was forced to conclude systemic structures are beyond individual comprehension. This is the implosion bias and error. No logical imperative exists to discount knowledge of macro structures. Moreover, even if empirical evidence would suggest that individuals find it difficult to gain practical knowledge of macro structures, no logical imperative exists that such structures, therefore, do not exist.

As with other micro/macro synthesizers, Giddens' philosophical choices and emphasis on social integration set the parameters for his theoretical constructs. Importantly, Giddens abandons fractured explanations of society. He does so, however, not because he recognizes the inadequacy of placing social integration as the fundamental, a priori subject of social analysis, but because of limitations he sees within fractured explanations of social integration. Any element more macro

than institutions becomes a messy theoretical issue for Giddens, unpredictable and difficult to integrate. His choice, then, is to ignore these
aspects. But another conclusion can be made from Giddens' starting
point: while it is admittedly difficult to integrate micro and macro phenomena, sometimes extremely so, this is because micro and macro
levels move along two time paths and may be inconsistent and contradictory. Whether or not this is the case requires investigation, but in
Giddens' version of implosion, such investigations are outlawed. The
emphasis is on social integration, and implosion theories demand this
be so.

While Giddens does allow for limited autonomy between institutions and micro activity, and even suggests each exists in different
realms of time and space, by maintaining the social integration paradigm, he defines autonomy within the context of contiguous instantiation, and does not allow micro and macro processes to be separate
entities. Moreover, instantiation implies individuals are, primarily, ra-
tional-practical people, creating practical knowledge, routines and institutions. Even though each of these processes also influences
individuals, this is still a heavy load for rationalism to carry. It is reminiscent of the Philosphes' claim that rational people will understand
and reform society. But the philosophe belief was grounded in what
they believed to be the universal truths of science. What are Giddens'
beliefs based on? Not on philosophical or scientific universals, or on
fractured assumptions. What is left is Giddens' faith that his theory accurately reflects society. But empirical social reality often appears irrational, and lacks routine. Reading any daily newspaper will inevitably
provide some evidence for the irrationality and less-than-routine characteristics of society. Moreover, some people grasp and utilize institutional rules and resources in different ways, at different levels of
power, and sometimes appear impractical as they do so. All of this requires investigation, not theoretical assumptions.

This issue raises another point. Many of the theories discussed in
the first two chapters include various pictures of reality. It seems this
has always been the case in social thought. It is a mistake. Instead, theory should be constructed as the best possible model for uncovering
reality. In this way, theories could be constantly improved, reformed,
even overthrown. Theoretical validity would be proven to the extent
that it corresponds to empirical research. Again, however, this will be
possible only if inconsistencies and contradictions are given the same
theoretical standing as social integration, and in turn, the only theoretical avenue for allowing inconsistencies and contradictions is to grant
autonomy to micro and macro levels.

The implosion errors are made by two other theorists, Laclau and Mouffe (1985). Laclau and Mouffe are sometimes accurately referred to as postmodernists, but in this section, areas of their work representing implosion will be highlighted. The two authors theorize from a Neo-Marxist position, but like Habermas, Laclau and Mouffe concentrate on the cultural hegemony found in society. And like Habermas, they place hegemony as distinct from the traditional categories of Marxism. "In fact, it [hegemony] introduces a logic of the social which is incompatible with those categories." Instead, cultural hegemony is viewed as autonomous.

Laclau and Mouffe define autonomy in the following way: While people endeavor to establish relations between various social elements, and the elements are "articulated" into "moments", any resulting social formation is never unified either through individual actions or a priori structures. In fact, the common feature in articulated formations is the dispersion of relations at both levels. Only through recognizing disparate acts and conditions can any formulation be understood. Thus, "all identity is relational and all relations have a necessary character... Everything is so necessary in that modification of the whole and of the details reciprocally condition one another" (Laclau and Mouffe, 1985 p. 106).

Nothing social can exist outside these dispersed, reciprocal relationships. Moreover, relationships are possible only as differences are articulated within formations, and since formations are necessarily emergent, no structured reality can pre-determine their development. Thus formations are contingent, not pre-determined either by actors or structural necessity.

Laclau and Mouffe dispute the Kantian division between thought and external reality, and like Marx, they aspire to reduce the distance between the two. But unlike Marx, Laclau and Mouffe are uncomfortable with the notion of external objectivity. Their response is to conceive social formations as a result of contingent articulation between micro and macro processes. But their work is also a response to descendent Marxism, where the cultural domination of individuals is highlighted. In place of objective cultural domination, Laclau and Mouffe argue for dispersion, as institutions, rituals and practices maintain a contingent role. This theory, then, is the mirror image of Giddens'. Where Giddens accepts practicality and routine, LaClau and Mouffe accept dispersion and contingency. Both, however, come to the same conclusion. Whether it is Giddens' mutual interaction between individuals and institutions, or LaClau and Mouffe's reciprocal relationships between details and the whole, both view micro and macro phenomena as contiguous, and mutually responsible for their combined development.

In LaClau and Mouffe's case, with both objective and subjective assumptions eliminated, fractured theory's limitations are overcome. However, by replacing fractured assumptions with an assumption of dispersion, the ability to discuss autonomous macro structures is destroyed. Even though they allow for autonomy, and entertain the notion of macro contingency, their postmodern ideas implode micro and macro processes to the point where contingency becomes a decentered assumption, rather than social reality. It is in this light that Laclau and Mouffe proclaim that "society is not a valid object of discourse."

Another well-known example of implosion is found in the work of Bourdieu (1989). He too condenses micro and macro processes into areas that are contiguous and co-existent. For Bourdieu, two primary concepts describing and explaining social life are "habitus" and "field." Habitus are mental structures developed in relation to the social world. But this is not a purely individual process. Instead, habitus is conceived as a dual process of construction and internalization of social structures. Thus habitus is a dialectical process, one that Bourdieu describes as "constructivist structuralism or of structuralist constructivism..." (1989, p. 14). The mediating factor between habitus and social structures is practice; practice is necessary for the creation of habitus and the formation of social structures.

Bourdieu does not conceive of habitus or social structures as determining factors, however. In part, this is because social structures develop within "fields", where a multitude of practices, habitus and other fields interact, often in struggle with one another. This is a dynamic, not static process, characterized by relational, not determining factors (Bourdieu, 1989 p. 15-16.). Objective relations are located between positions of the field, and may include economic, cultural, social and symbolic capital, and individuals work both with the volume and location of their capital. Thus, "...social science must take as its object both this reality and the perception of this reality, the perspectives, the points of view which, by virtue of their position in objective social space, agents have on this reality" (Bourdieu, 1989 p. 18).

Though a creative effort to describe the dynamic between structures and individuals is employed by Bourdieu, evidence of implosion abounds. While there are times when he seems to recognize the need to analytically separate micro and macro processes (Wacquant, 1989 p. 33.), Bourdieu nonetheless maintains the mutual effect that habitus and fields -- individuals and structures -- have on one another. A field is a configuration or network of objective relations, whose limits, however, are not predetermined, and are subject to active struggle by agents, who act in relation to their habitus, which is shaped by field. Such is the implosion of Bourdieu.

The autonomous development of micro and macro over different time paths cannot be conceived within such a theoretical framework. Whenever micro and macro processes are seen as contiguously constitutive, then implosion is at work. This does not mean implosion theories have no value. Perhaps more than descendent and ascendant theories, implosion theories help articulate the dynamic relationship between the two levels. By rejecting either micro or macro fractured assumptions, implosion theorists are directed towards relational development. This is a major step forward. However, as long as the two levels are imploded, the analysis will be limited to the present relationship of the two levels, and not the historical and autonomous development of each. Without autonomy, meaningful factors in understanding both levels are lost.

The generalized critiques leveled at fractured micro and macro theory, then, have not been adequately overcome by the three theoretical frameworks described in this chapter. Descendent theories maintain a position of structural domination in the "last instance", while ascendant theories maintain the reverse through the primacy of the individual. The common problem between them is they fail to grasp what the other has shown: micro activity develops autonomously from macro activity, which has its own history of development. Maintaining micro and macro assumptions as a legacy from the century-long fracture of theories has excluded a simple conclusion: micro and macro processes develop along two time paths which necessarily requires they be viewed autonomously.

Implosion theories are aimed at correcting the bias of accepting either micro or macro assumptions. This is accomplished, however, by accepting their own implosion bias: micro and macro levels are mutually and contiguously instantiated. Consequently, the implosion bias also leads to a misunderstanding of the temporal difference between micro and macro processes. Instead of complete autonomy, implosion theorists are logically forced to limit any consideration of macro structures. Any structure beyond rational and practical knowledge and/or participation must logically be eliminated. The result is that large scale phenomena (e.g. political-economic developments) are necessarily removed from discussion and discovery, as is collective influence over their development.

Micro/macro synthetic efforts, then, have not repaired the damage done by the fracture of social theories in the twentieth century. As long as ascendant, descendent and implosion assumptions are carried on, no improvement will occur. Moreover, by remaining within the fractured box of issues, social theories have lost the very advance of the classical sociologists. The notion of autonomy and the importance of collectivities are largely missing in the current debate. The fruit of ascendant, descendent and implosion theories should be picked clean when any of their ideas seem fertile, but if theory is to be fundamentally advanced, the fractured assumptions and limited reform of those assumptions, which are the roots of these theories, should be plowed under.

The question remaining, then, is how can micro and macro theory be integrated, while maintaining the integrity of practical and empirical findings of the last century? While a more thorough discussion of this topic will be covered in Part III, some preliminary remarks are in order.

Toward an Integrative Approach

The insights and issues emerging from ascendant, descendent, and implosion theories should be consolidated. First, ascendant theories variably use rationalism to explain behavior that maximizes needs and desires. This rational process is used to define social life. While not all social life is viewed as rational, non-rational and even anti-social behavior are defined in comparison to the rational. In micro versions of rational choice and exchange theory, the macro is researched only as aggregate individual choices. In more contemporary ascendant efforts, rationalism is combined with a hybrid of empiricism. Although differing in the social mechanism selected, all ascendant theories share the belief that common everyday experiences, either mental, communicative, or physical, posit social action as empirical phenomenon. But this seems to raise a contradictory position. If actions are subjective, no connection to "social" aspects of life is necessary; pure rationalism would seem a prescription for anarchy. How, then, does social integration or change develop? The ascendant theories skirt this dilemma by asserting faith in assorted integrative devices. Each elected device, however, appears as convincing as another. Ascendant theorists have no choice but to pick at least one faithful assumption, for without it rational choice would make the very definition of social mute. It is one thing to say actors subjectively evaluate and act on social conditions; it is quite another to say aggregate actors cohesively create social conditions continually, and in a form that can be derived from cumulative actions.

What is missing in contemporary rationalism was found by the classical sociologists: collectivities. Collective groups were classically endowed with some degree of autonomy from individuals. The more modern trend is to acknowledge that individuals act within collectives, but to define collectives merely as aggregated individuals. Contemporary ascendant efforts are a step backward, not forward, in the explanation of social integration. How individuals are related to collectives is rarely discussed by contemporary rationalists, and when it is, it is explained away on the basis of theoretical assumptions. The autonomy between individuals and collectives, first introduced by classical sociologists, is left detached from contemporary efforts.

The classical assertion of autonomy, however, must itself be transcended. In classical theory, collective groups were inserted to connect various predetermined versions of social order. Instead, collective groups should be viewed in relation to individuals, not equivalent to aggregate groups of individuals, and not predisposed to socially integrate society. Granting real autonomy between individuals and groups requires the relationship between the two be dynamic and unpredictable, sometimes generating social cohesion, and sometimes generating inconsistencies and contradictions between inter and intra groups and individuals. Let the empirical findings of research of a particular society in a particular place be the guide to what the dynamic relationship is, not predetermined relations created as a tool to prove a priori theoretical assumptions. Unfortunately, none of the theories discussed in this chapter allow for this dynamic.

The failure to allow for the dynamic relationship between individuals and groups points to another general weakness in ascendant (and many implosion) applications of rationalism: the failure to adequately account for power in society. A pluralistic, democratic bias appears in most ascendant theories, and denies groups or classes the ability to gain power over others, or to shape social conditions. Why is it conceivable that all actors are able to access resources, and even conceivable that some actors have more access than others, but inconceivable that some actors use superior access to shape the social life of others? Certainly, this is at least plausible, and as such, the history of the social conditions and how they have been used is a necessary area of inquiry. An analysis of power, and the instruments of its use, would not outlaw the concept of human rationality, but would promote the exploration of social conditions as equally important.

The ascendant emphasis on modern rationality, then, invites serious omissions. On the one hand, rational thought implies knowledge and/or interaction is practical, and shared through forms of thought and/or interaction, but the origin of those shared forms is not explored. Instead, only immediate subjective or social circumstances which give rise to rational thinking are uncovered, but the social context which facilitates rational thought, and power relations that give rise to the social context, are given short shrift.

The opposite mistake is made by descendent theorists who ignore the autonomy of subjective actors by explaining social action as reduced from structures, either economic, political, cultural, or from differentiation. This form of analysis does contend structural universals are separate from human action, but only structures are allowed autonomy. While descendent theorists are modern enough to insist subjective appearances and knowledge are not equivalent to social conditions, they nonetheless, uphold social conditions as the catalyst for subjective thought and action. Descendent theories, then, collapse subjective differences. In its contemporary descendent form, social actions respond to social positions created by social conditions. Yet even here, a form of rationalism still exists. While conditions influence subjective thought and action, individuals are still perceived to act rationally within that context, no matter the degree of flexibility permitted. But on what basis should these constructs be believed? On what grounds are either rationalist micro or macro explanations deemed adequate? The answer seems to be that theorists want to explain social integration and order. Is that enough?

A third alternative is provided by implosion theorists. Implosion theorists reject pure rationalism and its division between subject and object. Moreover, it rejects the idealistic vision of macro structures propagated by descendent theorists. In their place, implosion theorists use a social form of realism, where individuals are fully capable of knowing external objects and the social world. But all implosion theorists fully understand the limits to their realism: if individuals must be capable of knowing the external world, then the external world must be narrowed to what is subjectively knowable. Consequently, only specific institutions, "fields" or micro/macro formations are practically knowable. In this case, structural formations, change, and power become inexplicable.

These weaknesses of ascendant, descendent and implosion theories are precisely where the indictment theories of postmodernism, feminist theory and ecological theory have launched their most powerful criticism. These issues are discussed in more detail in the next chapter. Nonetheless, some preliminary points are called for here, as well as some suggestions for solving these problems are explored in Part III.

Micro sociologists have shown people are creative, active individuals, not determined by structures. At the same time, macro sociologists have shown structures and patterns of behavior are autonomous and have a relationship to action. Enough theoretical and empirical research exists to convince theoretically flexible sociologists that both perspectives have produced valuable insights, and that no set of theoretical postulates can prove a determining quality. The role of integrated theory, therefore, must be to allow for the existence of micro and macro reality, grasp how these distinct processes are related, but above all transcend the limitations of the current micro/macro debate they spawned. This can be accomplished only by allowing micro and macro autonomy, and by recognizing they are variably integrated over time.

The two notions of autonomy and dual time paths carry several implications. First, the philosophical issues of reality and knowledge may be analyzed in a new way. While Kant was correct that all reality cannot be subjectively known "in itself", all reality is potentially knowable. That is, not all individuals will know everything, but all reality is discoverable. As conscious individuals, humans come to understand the external world through their own reflection on external objects, but not all objects appear to all individuals. Thus knowledge is neither a priori to the individual, available to all, or structurally determined. Rather, subjective perception is derived through the partial relationship between individuals and the reality they encounter. Further, differences exist between individuals and groups and the actions and interactions taken are autonomous entities. This is due to a variety of reasons, but power differentials are a common feature. While the full implication of this idea will be explored in Part III, a brief example will be illustrative.

Modern social development in the third world provides a useful example. Third world development is empirically inexplicable unless conditions, both internal and external, are accounted for. The history of colonialism, neo-colonialism and the contemporary developments and changes in structural and social relations highlight the conditional presence. Indeed, the development of the third world nation-state, for the most part artificially designed by foreign powers regardless of previous cultural boundaries, is a prime example. While attention to the use of social resources must be paid, it is also true that people are born into these sets of social conditions. Conditional development does have a logic and momentum of its own. These conditions are characterized by a different time path from micro processes.

This is not to argue that conditions determine micro processes and action; micro processes are autonomous from conditions. Moreover, the reaction to, the reproduction of, and the creative actions upon these conditions are variable and due to micro activities. Thus, current conditional development was neither inevitable, nor necessarily permanent.

Allowing for and variably establishing the relationship between micro and macro levels of reality is, therefore, a necessary first step for an integrative theory. Next, it will be necessary to establish the internal relationships of elements existing within both conditions and micro processes.

On the micro level, the autonomous, yet related, integration between individuals and collectivities requires delineation. The causes of individual acts are complex. However, micro theories have a long and rich history which highlight much of the micro process. Micro processes include individual development of psychology, physiology, interaction, and the social construction of reality. What develops is unique and individual. However, individuals perceive, define, and rationalize themselves at more than the individual or small group level. In the modern world, a relationship to collectivities is also available and demanded, in some form, at larger group, organizational, ethnic, political, ecological, and economic levels, as well as in established behavior patterns. The relationship between individuals and collectivities combines in what might be called a social perception system. In each region, country and area, this perception system interrelates differently.

Consequently, social acts are an outcome of both micro relations with other immediate individuals, and relationships formed with modern collectivities. The theoretical concept of social action, therefore, must include acts that result after, not merely prior to, the integration of social perception.

Although social actions may differ among individuals and collectivities, and may also result in unintended consequences, they are empirically discoverable. This discovery requires utilization of a variety of qualitative and quantitative research applicable to the micro level. However, which elements of individual and collective processes are central to particular research inquiries must remain an open empirical question. Giddens, Collins, and Alexander all provide alternative explanations of micro processes worthy of empirical application.

Micro processes and action do not occur in a vacuum, however. Alexander correctly points out that social environments are related to social perception, but conditions also must be empirically validated and internally integrated. Extending the third world example will be illustrative.

Economic gain was a primary catalyst for colonialism, and the impact of colonialism on culture, politics and patterns of behavior has forever changed third world societies. In the more recent era, the economic domination of third world countries continues to wield enormous influences. Western-influenced economic growth has led to obtuse internal economic structures, whereby development is geared toward export, and economic growth benefits only a few indigenous upper class people and foreign companies. Broadly based economic development and generally high standards of living are non-existent. In turn, the few who benefit from this form of development have the greatest influence over political structures. They act, with outside aid, according to those interests. In turn, institutions and patterns of behavior are changed.

These economic structures do not determine other conditions, however. For instance, the growth of liberation theology in religious institutions has developed partially as a result of the church's own history and internal development (both macro and micro), but also as a response to economic developments. Moreover, neither the religious establishment nor those who control economic structures rejoice in the growth of liberation theology. In short, religious structures are autonomous from economic structures. Relative autonomy also exists among other conditional processes, such as ecological and political structures. Consequently, economic structures must not be seen as determining other conditional processes. Instead, the variable relationships between macro structures must be uncovered, but without any predispositions gleaned from theoretical assumptions.

These variable and developing conditions of the modern world constitute a second distinct process of social reality, and can be empirically established using macro methods of survey research, aggregate data analysis, and political economy, etc. Macro conditions, however, must then be seen in relation to individual and collective processes. What follows is a more complete picture of social reality. Capitalist, socialist, democratic or authoritarian societies, each containing concurrent structures and patterns of behavior, as well as micro processes, form intra and interrelationships. It is through the integration of these distinct processes that modern societies can be explained.

Although perception and conditional systems are distinct and variable, it is possible to empirically establish their integration. However, this requires that neither a micro or macro set of theoretical assumptions are accepted either as determining, or requiring, adaptation to a universal principle of development. Micro and macro theory and research show in combination that either has the potential to dominate the relationship formed. Again, this only can be shown empirically.

Moreover, analyzing the distinct, but related developments of micro and macro processes will move beyond static descriptions and toward explanations of social action, social movements and change, for it is within this integration that social action emerges. Specifically, integrative approaches should explore whether social perception systems are generally consistent with or opposed to conditional developments. For instance, if people through individual and collective processes relate to the behavioral and structural conditions of a social formation (e.g. capitalism), and encounter and/or expect economic growth, a high standard of living, and individual freedoms, etc., the social perception of whether these exist, or are possible, is critical to whether social acts will or will not reproduce the status quo. This is so even if the perception is incorrect.

Consequently, if conditional changes, or a lack of change, appears consistent with the development of social perception, the likelihood of significant social change is reduced. Conversely, if conditional change, or a lack of change, is inconsistent with social perception development, then actions can potentially create change at the micro and/or macro level. Thus, micro and macro processes are hardly a permanent phenomena. Only a modern society in a perfect state of reproduction can expect all elements to remain stable. The reality is that societies are almost never in perfect reproduction, and actions continually rise to the forefront and bring change at all levels. The form and result of actions, moreover, will always be colored by the particular form of micro and macro integration.

Thus, while social change is predictable if explored empirically through integrative theory, no universal law of social change can be pre-determined. Change can be in any direction, especially political change. All racial, ethnic gender, class, and age groups develop through the autonomous process of individual and collective social perception related to macro conditions. Simultaneously, conditional development is in sync or opposed to developed perceptions. And actions are the result of the integration of the two processes. Consequently, the civil rights, women's, environmental, nationalist, community based, the new right, and class-based social actions and movements in the U.S., for example, can be explained through an integrative analysis.

In summary, intra and interlevels of reality are related, yet autonomous. Integrative sociologists can escape the limitations of theoretical assumptions by viewing micro and macro as distinct processes over time and empirically uncovering their relationship. To uncover whether inter or intraelements of micro or macro reality dominate, are at odds, or in a perfect state of reproduction, requires research based on such an integrative approach. Consequently, it is necessary that ascendant, descendent, and implosion theories be abandoned.

Conclusions

Based on the above, a preparatory set of integrative principles follows:

1. While micro and macro processes are distinct, their development is relational. Neither micro or macro, however, has a priori determining qualities.

2. People are born into pre-existing patterns of social behavior and structures. Each individual and collective process establishes a relationship to social conditions grounded on his/her social perception, which is autonomous and creative. This integration gives rise to actions. Actions are not, therefore isolated from the conditions into which people are born, nor do present aggregate actions equal conditions. Conversely, actions are not solely the result of conditions.

3. While conditional development inherently is related to social actions, not all, or even a majority of, people need take action in relation to a particular conditional development. A socially powerful group, class, or some other collectivity may provide the action link, even when many disagree or are unaware of conditions due to their own perceptions. The source of that power, and the scope of potential action does not rest on resources alone, but on the particular development of the micro and macro integration.

4. There is no logical imperative to limit conditional development. The formalization and development of conditions should not be not restricted in number or size and may occur at the national or international level.

5. At any point in history, the conditions and perceptions that are reproduced, or changed, differ. Why they are different, how they

develop, and what actions might result cannot be answered by
universal theoretical laws; it is necessarily an empirical question.

6. The history of societies provides evidence that inter and intrarela-
    tions of micro and macro processes are uneven. One, or a combi-
    nation of elements may dominate, but this does not necessarily
    preclude other elements from moving to the social forefront; the
    form of integration is continually recreated. Although always
    unique, the causes and results of integration can be empirically
    validated, and as such, predictions are possible.

7. It follows, that if micro and macro are relatively autonomous,
    each may be studied in isolation, but only the relationship be-
    tween the two can provide an explanation of social change.

8. It further follows that if diverse people develop creatively and act
    upon, reproduce, and change patterns of social behavior and
    structures, and if conditions have a momentum of their own
    which variably influences perceptions, and if the source of social
    action is in the form of integration between these two processes,
    social theory must be integrated.

Chapter Three

Indictments of the Offspring

Postmodernism, feminist theory, and ecological theory have provided indispensable critiques of both fractured theories, and the ascendant, descendent and implosion theories discussed in the last chapter. Each critique differs in its premise and implications, but all share an intrinsic belief that modern theory, as presently constructed, is destitute; unifying theories founded on middle-age scientific reality has led to a dead end, and the traditional theoretical emphasis on social integration must be transcended. While the indictment theories are at their strongest when criticizing, the replacements they suggest have serious shortcomings. A discussion of these theories and their common denominator follows.

Postmodernism

The nucleus of varied postmodern arguments is that a theoretically derived order is impossible. Postmodernists view the world as contingent and chaotic. Within this framework, scientific truth is nonsensical, institutional structures dissolve, and macro narratives become "stories." The prime reason for this "deconstruction" is that multiple interpretations are initiated by a multitude of people. Postmodernists castigate macro narratives for missing this essential point, and covertly applying internal and a priori assumptions. Modern macro descriptions are classified as inherent to a specific time and geographic location, and imbued with a series of unstated, but theoretically influencing ideas. These influencing ideas include the supremacy of Western industrialized society, and the a priori acceptance of science as the appropriate method for understanding the social world (Nicholson, 1989). In place of these characteristic attributes of modern social science, post-modernists see the social world as a series of independent, localized events.

The postmodern, localized vision is considered politically pro-gressive and inclusive. One of the important errors of metanarratives is their failure to see the diverse social movements developed over the last twenty-five years. The anti-war, environmental, civil rights, women's rights, and anti-nuclear movements all shared a more local flavor and construction. None of them fit neatly into mainstream con-structions, and their development caught all theories by surprise (Richardson, 1991).

Postmodernists, then, reject the modern vision of science, phi-losophy, and society as it developed from its roots in the Enlighten-ment. Since the early scientists, theorists have asserted the world knowable and controllable through a rationally ordered scientific method. By the late 18th and early 19th century, when political and economic turmoil were commonplace, rational science underwent re-form but not fundamental change; the progressive era promised society could change for the better through rational thinking. This promise has never been universally accepted. In different ways Nietzsche and Hei-degger, and members of the Frankfurt School including Adorno and Horkheimer, challenged major modernist beliefs. After World War II, however, the positivist interpretation of modernism remained dominant in both science and social science. Within positivism, sweeping and rational explanations of social and scientific matter reigned supreme.

In dissent of the positivist metanarrative, postmodernists use a two-pronged explanation of the development of science. On the one hand, technological advancements have, for postmodernists, signifi-cantly gone astray. The human and environmental damage through technological warfare and economic development is self-evident. On the other hand, postmodernists direct attention to scientific discoveries of twentieth-century science which shows natural reality to be discon-tinuous, catastrophic, and paradoxical. These newer developments in science are categorically ignored within metanarratives. However, since new frontiers in science are the center of discussion in Chapter Four, here the main focus is on the limitations of social scientific theo-ries, and it is here that postmodernism levels its harshest attacks.

Through a series of books, Foucault (e.g. 1965, 1970, 1972, 1977) has relentlessly argued power is localized, not a macro function as in normative theories, or a reflection of the mode of production as in Marxism. Whether existing in a prison, hospital, or academic depart-ment within a university, power is executed locally within its own process. As such, the power process is neglected by overarching theories aimed at explanations of generalized patterns. By contrast, postmodernists believe reality resides within the experiences of the location, and is revealed through a combination of the situational logic and subjective negotiations in which the location is made sense of, articulated, and struggled over. The locale, therefore, becomes the setting for political acts (Nicholson, 1989 p. 8-13).

Lyotard (1984) extends the same logic and suggests language is a key contributor to localized situations. He argues language is expressed in countless forms, all dependent on local situations and processes. Language, then, can never be used to represent a universal truth or even a prevailing concept. At most, language can be only poetic and metamorphical. Here, Lyotard attacks the structuralism of Levi-Strauss, who uses language as a universal structure to examine all cultures. Lyotard, by contrast, argues language is used and understood in so many unique ways that it cannot be a universal common denominator between people. The limit of language is subjective; it is through language the subject is constituted, and beyond the individualized text nothing can be said, literally or figuratively.

Lyotard asserts the legitimation of individuals is not found within grand narrative descriptions of normative, structural processes which beget consciousness, but resides instead within the multiple, local discourses of individuals within their various locales. Moreover, individual discourse is itself rooted within multiple situations and practices, and this makes social identities inordinately complex and beyond social scientific description (Fraser and Nicholson, 1990 p. 22-25).

Derrida (1987) takes Lyotard one step further and suggests the contingent nature of language may be shown through a process of deconstruction. Writers or speakers, write or speak through the catalyst of their own individual history. Since individual histories and situations are different, each person brings a discrete perspective to the words written or spoken. This has at least two important implications. First, an individual writer or speaker cannot provide a universal truth in his description of some event or social structure, but only a unique understanding of it. And second, each reader or listener is subject to the same limitations. The outcome is a series of intersections between individual histories that extend beyond any definitions of words. In short, the interplay between sender and receiver is wholly contingent on situational histories.

Within postmodern thought, predictability and logic -- the hallmarks of rational scientific method -- are impossible to conjure. Moreover, postmodernism is perceived concretely, not just analytically; fragmentation, not predictability, is characteristic of the post-modern society. Postmodern social actors react to immediate, local situations, not long-term normative values or goals, or stratified inequities. In this framework, the past and future is irrelevant. All that remains is the contingent, localized present.

The local process cannot be predetermined from existing patterns, nor can they be abstracted from them. The classical mistake of scientific method, and repeated by modern social scientists, is that assumptions can never be proved merely by collecting evidence. If one changes the assumptions, then what is proved and assumed logical also changes (Frank, 1989 p.392-405). General theories, therefore, become metaphysical exercises based on ideological beliefs. As such, empirical validation of theoretical logic cannot be "scientifically" proven; it is merely ideologically proven.

It is a mistake, however, to see postmodernism as an attack only on macro social theory. At the micro level other serious mistakes are performed. Micro theory frequently suggests individuals are able to make sense of the world through a combination of intentional, or rational understanding of external signifiers. In postmodernism, symbolic understanding also is destroyed; the relationship between the sign and subjective individual becomes arbitrary (Ashley, 1990). The textual discourse is merely the individualized intersection of multiple subjective and situational histories. As such, the "logic" of micro analysis is made moot. Without a clearly defined subject, on what basis could micro theory proceed?

Postmodernists do not see the double rejection of micro and macro theory as debilitating. On the contrary, once universal truths about individuals or structures are abandoned, new and more fluid possibilities are opened, and moreover, overcoming intractable debates between micro and macro metanarratives may be addressed. As long as a priori micro or macro truths are the starting point for theories of society, any synthesis between the two schools is necessarily impossible (Seidman, 1991). When theoretical assumptions are replaced with a concentration on localized processes, the theory of postmodernism shows its more democratic possibilities. It is the failure to posit the locale of temporal and spatial events that lead metanarratives to analyze what was local and transform their findings into universal postulates (Seidman, 1991 p 140).

Postmodernists, then, can philosophically be termed antirationalists. Rather than seeing history and society as an expression of causal explanations, postmodernists adopt an antirationalist position and see all social phenomena as a series of processes which cannot be understood according to preset patterns, static analyses, or abstracted from the actual event itself. Moreover, this means subjects, which are a part of the process, have no means to control or alter the process. Although social or political order is not entirely eliminated in postmodernism, such order is merely seen as temporary phenomena within the context of the local processional.

Postmodernists, then, subscribe to antirationalism, where order is possible but not expected. They reject irrationalism, where order is inconceivable (Schwab, 1989 p. xiv-xvi). Postmodernism also attacks the traditional concern of metaphysics: how do individuals gain an understanding of objective reality? For postmodernists, objective reality simply does not exist, nor does a universal history as accepted by superstitious academicians (Schwab, 1989 p. xv-xvii).

At its core, then, postmodernism is a criticism. However, the quintessential criticism has itself been criticized. One area of concern is the depiction of social reality as fragmented and chaotic. What has led postmodernists to make such a generalized statement? While postmodernists would surely raise issue with any narrative that explores this topic, the belief in a chaotic state of affairs cannot be abstracted out of thin air. This greatly weakens the postmodern agenda. It appears self-serving to exclaim postmodernists know enough to challenge current thinking on society, but no one can ever know enough to suggest a replacement.

Second, are postmodernists correct when they argue that modern social theory has been inadequate to explain the contemporary state of social affairs? While the contemporary era is certainly changed, and creates distinct problems for many previously held assumptions, on what basis are we to conclude theories are incapable of new explanations? Moreover, on what basis are we to conclude a new metanarrative will necessarily be inadequate? Postmodernists claim that neither new revisions or entirely new metatheories will yield correctives because the effort for metaexplanation is itself a false and impossible desire. According to many postmodernists, even the words we hear or read cannot be shared beyond local events. But even if this is correct, does this mean the postmodern depiction of social reality is the correct one, that it matches reality, that it is easier to discover than macro or micro phenomena (Antonio, 1990)? Indeed, when limiting theoretical investigation (as many postmodernists would) to individually constructed and received discourse, how does one proceed at all (Lemert, 1990 p 242-243)? If reality is so individualized, postmodernism would seem to call an end to all theory, including itself.

By contrast, neo-Marxists, for example, have argued that while Marx may be in need of revision, much of the traditional Marxist framework is able to describe contemporary societies within a metatheoretical framework To accomplish this, Neo-Marxists employ various combinations of cultural domination and alienation, and/or modern developments in the method of Marxist political economy (e.g. Harvey, 1990; Callincos, 1990; Antonio, 1990). Indeed, in their view, postmodernism is an abstract, conservative movement that excuses individual desires without any discussion of positive social movements (Callincos, 1990 p. 112-16; Best, 1989). Some feminist theorists (e. g. Lovibond, 1990) and others (e.g. Alexander, 1991) have raised much the same issue. Postmodernism is seen by these authors as eliminating the possibility of large-scale corrections to societal inequities. In this account, postmodernism ends the struggle for macro-oriented change. In postmodern hands, then, the familiar environmental call to action "think globally and act locally" is changed to "speak, write, hear, and read locally, and then act locally." Critics claim this is a prescription for the elite, however defined, to go unchallenged (Boyne, 1990 p. 36-37).

Other more micro-oriented theorists raise additional objections. Postmodernism aims its focus on discourse, and this shifts the focus of micro analysis from rational consciousness and intentions to the signifying activities of individuals. Why is this deemed the appropriate level of local analysis? The choice of language as a central component must be justified, but postmodernism refuses precisely this kind of justification. Again a contradiction emerges between the basis of postmodern critique of metanarratives, and their own process of selecting what is to be analyzed (Benhabib, 1989).

Finally, the most renowned criticism of postmodernism has come from Habermas (1985). He accepts the postmodernism critique of Enlightenment philosophies, but finds fault with the postmodern replacement. Habermas too has problems with Enlightenment thinking, although instead of replacement, he counsels that its emphasis on liberation be continued to its logical conclusion.

Postmodern issues have roots in age-old philosophical debates. In fact, when viewed from that perspective, the abstract positions expressed by various postmodern theorists, and the uproar they engender, become lucid. Two forms of philosophical rejection of the Enlightenment currently exist. The first is based on Kant's framework. Kant rejected the Philosphes' emphasis on rational explanations of society, and replaced it with an emphasis on subjective thought. While individuals categorize and classify external information, the natural and social worlds are never perfectly known; external objects are reduced in Kantian philosophy to the level of appearances. It is on this basis that, for Kant, individuals may never come to know external objects "in themselves." Nonetheless, Kant maintained individuals are capable of knowing a great deal, enough so they may lead moral lives. Postmodernists reject Kant because his analysis still maintains a belief individuals can be creative and knowing social actors. For postmodernists, Kant modified Enlightenment thinking, but did not break clean through.

Linguistic philosophy is the second school that rejects the Enlightenment framework. Wittgenstein (1953) also dismisses Kant, and his belief that subjective knowledge can be cumulated toward moral values. For Wittgenstein, words and sentences are required for categorization, but words and sentences have discrete and varied subjective uses. The variations are so extensive that widespread acceptance is impossible. Thus both the idea that words and language are derived from culture, and that subjective consciousness may be generalized from theories, must be rejected. Obviously, postmodernism forges its own views on the principles of this second critique.

These issues also are closely related to the philosophical and practical problem of relativism. In brief, relativism asserts no one idea or social formation is, a priori, better than another, especially since only those in the immediate context have intimate knowledge of that setting. Relativism is not a new notion, nor is it confined to sociology. Anthropologists, such as Boas, have long invoked relativism to argue that a fair impression of other cultures is possible only if other cultures are revered. In short, no hierarchy of cultures should exist, and exporting cultural judgments, such as the Enlightenment version of progress, must be abandoned.

Relativism has also been applied to science. Barnes (1974) suggests relativism in science will end the domination of specific scientific paradigms and enhance attaining goals. Finally, relativism is also a springboard for an attack on traditional philosophical inquiry. Dewey, Wittgenstein, Quine, Sellars, Davidson and Rorty all have launched relativist arguments against the epistemological search for a set of rules governing human knowledge (Hollis and Lukes, 1982 p. 2-5). It is easy to see why postmodernism found much in concert with relativism.

Relativism, however, suggests two contradictory concepts simultaneously. On the one hand, relativism implies social foundations to subjective thought do exist, or, as in the postmodern adaptation, social foundations to locales exist. But why do social foundations exist only at the locale? The reason seems to be that relativists and many postmodernists wish to avoid total irrationalism, and need to accept some basis for knowing. But the same arguments used to dispense macro universals also apply to subjective thought and local contexts. Why postmodernists accept the one and not the other is never made clear. Nonetheless, relativism and postmodernism proceed by eliminating one half of Kant, but accepting the other half; a priori subjective knowledge is eliminated, but the use of subjective categories and classifications to make sense out of the external world is accepted. Subjective categories, moreover, result from individual histories, not universal ideas. Thus, relativists believe that individuals are their own interpreters of the external world, but nothing general may be said of the interpretations. Many postmodernists extend this argument to its logical conclusion and assert the external world does not even exist.

The practical implication of these positions is to make humankind philosophically, socially and politically impotent. While the individual is capable of creating a philosophy, a social life, and subjective politics, the possibility of organizing any of these categories is eliminated. Thus, philosophies, social and political organizations, etc., are not only safe from critique, but according to some, are figments of overactive imaginations. The only difference between slavery, democratic capitalism, socialism, etc., is subjective classifications derived from specific locales. Instead of liberating local politics, the ironic outgrowth of postmodern thinking may be to ensure the status quo, no matter its form.

Despite these criticisms, postmodernism is a legitimate warning of overstatements found in both micro and macro theory, and the various attempts at their synthesis. The postmodern core critique is well taken: on what basis do theorists presume theoretical assumptions? Can the basis be merely ego, ethno, and cultural centrism? If so, and as long as metatheoretical assumptions are maintained, the ability of social theory to describe and explain contemporary events and society will be lost. Perhaps postmodernism is a call for the end of theory.

But another possibility exists. To uncover it requires an acceptance of the postmodern critique, but not its theoretical replacement. The postmodern criticism is that the theoretical efforts to explain social integration and order are misplaced, impossible to accomplish, and do not reflect modern reality. If one grants postmodernists this point, a significant concept is unleashed: contingency.

Contingency implies the development of society can never be predicted as inevitable through a set of theoretical assumptions. Social integration, therefore, cannot be assumed, and should not be a main focus of social analysis. The postmodern reality, with all of its fragmentation and diversity, is a contingent possibility. Thus, macro and descendent assumptions of social conditions, and micro and ascendant assumptions both must be rejected, especially when aimed at explaining social integration and coherence. And so too must the implosion instantiation that leads to coherent and practical systems. Contingency means other alternative realities, including the postmodern one must be accepted as possible.

The postmodern criticism, then, which raises the issue of contingency is well taken. However, accepting contingency means the postmodern replacement for traditional theory must, itself, be rejected. Postmodern deconstruction is simply a possibility, not a universal principle. No logical imperative exists to have deconstruction replace social cohesion as the primary theoretical assumption. It seems reasonable that either choice is possible. But postmodernism narrows possibilities by outlawing investigations of macro phenomena. This notion, itself, must be rejected, and then so too must postmodern deconstruction as an a priori postulate.

Without micro and macro assumptions, how can relativism be avoided? The answer, I believe, is to allow for the autonomous existence of both levels, as they develop along distinct paths of time. This allows for contingent relationships to emerge within and between the levels. Before a full exploration of time paths and contingency can be developed, however, the autonomy between micro and macro processes needs further explanation. Feminist theory deals directly with that issue, all the while launching its own indictment of mainstream contemporary theory.

Feminist Theory

Like postmodernism, feminist theory disowns many claims of traditional social analysis. Unlike postmodernism, however, feminist theory aspires to clarify social reality. The motive is to observe women's social position, and to change inequities found there. Perhaps the fundamental idea emerging from feminist theory is the concept of the situated actor (Lengermann and Niebrugge-Brantley, 1990). To digest the import of situated actors demands that traditional methods of social science be abandoned. In feminist theory, the situated actor constructs social reality from various vantage points, and since each actor is situated differently, various vantage points emerge. Truth, therefore, is not conditionally objective, but is a combination of various points of reference. Consequently, the age-old philosophical question of "how can people come to know reality" is misplaced. For feminist theorists, there is more than one reality (Spender, 1980). The same principle holds for natural scientists. The science they uncover may well be valid and true, but does not contain universal truth (Nicholson, 1990). Rather it is a truth that reflects the particular vantage point of the questions and methods used by the researcher.

In the social sciences, the problem is made more acute when the object of study is people. How researchers perceive people does not reflect the true nature of subjects, but rather the vantage point the researcher imposes on those studied. Truth, therefore, rests within various vantage points, as each individual absorbs only partial aspects of reality. Consequently, only equitable interactions between individuals can yield a comprehensive recognition of the social world, and since equality does not exist in modern society, what is portrayed as truth is merely cultural and institutional expressions of power. Institutionally expressed truth is ideology, not fact (Smith, 1990a).

Employing feminist methodology requires that the "standpoint" of subjects be taken into account (Smith, 1987; Harding, 1990). Subjects of research are conceived as knowers and actors. Thus researchers must come to understand subjects in their everyday life, in their locales. This requires that individuals be transformed from objects of research to active participants. Subjects must be encouraged to exercise the right to speak for themselves (Smith, 1987).

Allowing subjects to speak for themselves is rarely allowed in sociological research. Often, research questions are developed and asked by researchers, and require subjects to answer within specified parameters. Researchers then analyze answers, and formulate statements about the subjects. Obviously this process needs little input from the subject, especially when the aim is to make generalized statements about generalized patterns. Feminist sociologists argue that patterns emerging from this form of research infers more about the researcher than either the subject or truth. However, the variety of individual perceptions and experiences raises several methodological problems for gender analysis.

1.   If individual vantage points are a combination of family, religious, gender, race, class, and geographic location, etc. (Hill, 1992; Connel, 1992), how is it possible to make any sociological statements at all?

2. If theorists elevate gender over other elements of the situated actor, does feminist analysis, itself, become a repressive theory (Di Stefeno, 1990; Flax, 1990)?

3. Since gender studies also include an analysis of macro phenomena to understand women's social position, what is the mechanism that integrates both subject and institutions, and micro and macro (Harding, 1990)?

In addition, at the micro level, at least two problems arise as researchers examine individuals. First, how are feminist researchers assured that individual vantage points "authentically" reflect reality? Second, how can researchers be confident they accurately represent the subject's standpoint? To answer these problems, feminist researchers often "privilege" some subjective accounts over others. They do so because the dominant version of truth is already well established, and it becomes necessary to recognize subordinate accounts to comprehend the full reality (Smith, 1987; Lengermann and Niebrugge-Brantley, 1990). In this way, feminist theory allows subjects to speak for themselves, eliminates the problem of authenticity by assuming truth is really a combination of all truths, and encourages the study of women as a subordinate group separate from the dominant culture.

Obviously, feminist theory carries some assumptions about the social world. The primary assumption is that power is not equally distributed, and power influences theory, methods, and portrayals of truth. Defining power and truth in this form directly challenges most positivist, and "western" democratic presumptions of societal development and interaction, and demands that voices of subordinates be heard. Moreover, feminist theory requires that new theories and methods be explored to correct the inequity (Fraser and Nicholson, 1990).

The feminist theory and methodology, then, differs from the overt relativism of postmodernism. While the locale is of primary importance, so too are macro relations, particularly as they relate to gender. Localized power as described by Foucault, for example, would eliminate investigations into the institutionalization of male power, the aim of many gender analyses (Bordo, 1990). Relativism would ignore the macro exploration needed by feminist theory to establish the context in which vantage points emerge. Simultaneously, feminist theory differs from positivist doctrine, characterized especially by functional analysis. While macro conditions are accepted as legitimate areas of inquiry, the situated actor also must be taken into consideration (Lenergerman and Niebrugge-Brantley, 1990).

Similar dichotomies and issues between situated actors and social contexts have emerged within African-American thought (e.g. West, 1993). Within the last decade, a debate has crystallized over the concept of Afrocentricity. This concept implies that African people must no longer be considered objects of alien paradigms, but rather must be seen as active subjects (Asante, 1980). Africa, not Eurocentric ideology and values, must become the center of knowledge of Afro-Americans. As with feminist theory, the intent is to bring academic and practical problems together as the everyday existence of African-Americans is explored. However, critics of Afrocentricity suggest that while the intent may be noble, Afrocentricity both understates the complexity of African and African-American origins and diversity (e.g. Dyson, 1993 p. xvii-xxii), and elevates Afrocentricity to mythical heights. Practical actions are extraordinarily hard, if not impossible, to conceive within this context (Muwakkil, 1990).

Consequently, African-American and feminist theory both share an underlying problem: how does the situated actor relate to macro phenomena that, in turn, influences individual vantage points? Put in different words, how can micro and macro be integrated? Feminist theory has developed a variety of answers. Lengermann and Niebrugge-Brantley (1990, p. 329-30) present four strategies.

The first is a strategy of aggregation. In this scenario, aggregated accounts of situated actors are accumulated. As Smith (1987) suggests, this can lead to an understanding of both micro and macro levels. A second strategy is to use accounts of situated actors to prove or disprove macro feminist concepts. Here, macro validity can be tested through corresponding micro accounts. A third strategy is to combine researchers and subjects in a coordinated effort to uncover social reality. This approach allows research to uncover subjective and macro phenomena simultaneously. A fourth approach separates micro and macro phenomena to explore interrelations, but within that separation the actors perceptions and experiences must always be integrated into the macro account.

Smith (1987, 1990b) combines the first three of these approaches. She prompts researchers to begin with individuals and understand their real relationships and practices. This can be accomplished only by allowing individuals to speak for themselves. Second, researchers employ individual perceptions to establish how subjects coordinate activities with others, and how these activities change over time. Third, individuals may also express how macro levels influence their behavior, and express how levels are coordinated and conflictual. These three steps are the path to macro analysis, but unlike macro theories, the

analysis is grounded on something real: people's experiences and perceptions, not a macro-oriented fable. Moreover, theory itself becomes
dynamic as its assumptions are corrected by empirical vantage points.

Fraser and Nicholson (1990) also attempt to integrate the various
strains within feminist theory. They accept the conclusion of some
feminists and postmodernists that universal explanations are to be
abandoned. They do not conclude, however, that all macro analysis be
deserted. Instead, a contingency theory emerges. Theory may be historical and cultural, but it must not be universalistic. Comparative
analysis would search for differences and change, rather than trying to
find universal laws that explain all social reality.

Lastly, Ring (1992) also accepts contingency as an important aspect to her theory, but then adds conflict, and develops what she calls a
minimalist dialectics. Ring argues that individuals form a relationship
both with nature and the past. Thus she sees subject and object as di-
chotomous and, moreover, in conflict. Conflict occurs as individuals
come to understand their natural and social environment, and relate to
environments in non-determined ways. The process is continuous, and
conflicts may not fully resolve themselves. Minimalist dialectics, then,
is interested in the process of interaction between subject and object.
Thus a focus exists "upon interaction in a limited time frame, rather
than a grander historical sweep." Minimalist dialectics rejects assumptions concerning origins and outcomes.

What assessment can be made from the various insights and
methods of feminist theory? First, of all the contemporary theories discussed in this work, feminist theory is by far the most integrative. Unlike descendent theories, feminist social inquiry allows ample room at
the subjective level, and indeed, centers the actor as a defining characteristic. Unlike ascendant theories, feminist theories realize macro
conditions help shape gender relations and influence the situated actor.
And unlike implosion theories, some feminist theorists recognize micro
and macro processes as autonomous.

These positions culminate in a repudiation of fractured micro and
macro assumptions. At the macro level, functionalist-inspired theories
are renounced because women cannot be placed in compartmentalized
roles and functions according to accepted assumptions. The perception
of roles and functions have more to do with power in society, especially male-dominated power, than some function that culture plays in
the spectrum of action and order. And while some elements of Marxist
theory are maintained, especially the notion of value driven theory and
research, the limiting view of power and inequality as predominantly
economic also is abandoned. The mistakes of macro theory are made

most clear, argue feminist theorists, by the ignorance of, and lack of explanation for, women's inequality.

Feminist theory also requires a censure of micro sociological theory. Micro theory is based largely on the notion of rational and intentional individuals who pursue objects or shared meanings, or goals. This implies an equal opportunity society with shared power, a proposition that feminist theorists argue is inconsistent with many women's lives.

Unlike contemporary sociological theory, feminist theory directly participates in questions of philosophy, especially questions of representations and knowledge of reality. In philosophy, the main proponent that representations of reality are possible was empiricism, which emphasized experiences and the physical senses, and the main proponents of knowledge and rationality was expressed in different forms by the philosophes and Kant. In either case the individual and/or society were viewed as intelligible. Opposed to rationalism in this form, and replacing it with a conditional primacy of their own were Hegel, Marx and the Frankfurt school. Finally, following Nietzsche and Heidegger, postmodernists claim the epistemological question is non-sensical.

While some theorists can be found in each of the three approaches, feminist sociology appears uncomfortable with the dominance of any one of these epistemologies. Some feminist theories (e.g. Friedan, 1991) originated from the rationalist school and argue that all people are equally rational. Thus it is unfair to exclude any particular group. Others maintain an antirationalist position and argue the differences in gender are to be accepted and women accommodated. And yet others (e.g. Benhabib, 1990; Haraway, 1991) move clearly in a postmodern direction. Finally, others, (e.g. Fraser and Nicholson, 1990) see the need for some confluence of approaches.

The explanation for why feminist theory comprises multiple proposals is rooted in the effort to analyze both the situated actor, and macro social conditions. However, each of the proposals adopted are deficient for reasons previously given. In their place, feminist theory should validate the autonomous and contingent nature of micro and macro processes. Doing so would not deter either theorists who concentrate on the situated actor, or those who explore the macro conditions of gender relations and discrimination.

However, autonomy and contingency does require that the integrative efforts of feminist theorists, such as Smith, be transcended. Micro analyses of situated actors alone cannot uncover macro processes because they exist in different time paths. Autonomy does not deny the fundamental truth that situated actors must be considered, or the truth

that situated actors are more than mere reflections of theoretical assumptions. However, theories implying macro levels may be eventually
exposed from purely micro perceptions and experiences are mistaken.
First, the methodological problem of showing how such situations can
inductively, and accurately, reflect reality exists. Second, and more
important for this work, such attempts require a contemporaneous
viewpoint, where macro conditions are reflected in the same time
frame as micro processes. This approach would vastly limit the power
of macro studies over time, which are necessary to uncover such issues
as the history of gender relations.

Fraser and Nicholson raise the idea of contingency and autonomy,
but do not recognize the dynamic relationship between micro and
macro, and have not developed a formal theoretical framework. Such a
framework would need to include another concept used by feminist
theorists, the concept of power. Power, however, as currently used to
privilege certain subjective accounts over others, is misplaced. Rather,
power should be contingently investigated as it develops between individuals and groups, and how groups use that power in relation to
autonomous macro structures. This combination of factors combines
what is best about feminist theory, the classical sociologists, and the
concepts of autonomy and contingency. That is, both situated actors
and power relationships are developed, and the notion of collectivities
are also included, all of which is made discoverable by unlocking the
autonomous and contingent relationships between micro and macro
levels.

Even these considerations may not be adequate for transcending
the current level of theorizing, however. Additional concerns are raised
within ecological theory.

Ecological Theory

Like many social theories discussed in this work, ecological theory is based on scientific principles and discoveries. In this case, the
work of environmental scientists is stressed. One principle idea of environmental science is the concept of ecosystems. An ecosystem contains
all of the organisms and physical objects within a given geographic
location, both living and non-living. Deserts, farms, cities and forests
all fit under the rubric of an ecosystem. Energy allows for the formation of an ecosystem, and its maintenance or change. Energy is the motive force for both life on earth and for the universe, and while energy
comes in many forms (e.g. light, heat, chemical, electrical, kinetic, nu-

clear, etc.) each form is transferable into the other. Moreover, once transformed, no new net amount of energy is created or lost (the first law of thermodynamics). Since many living organisms within an ecosystem cannot create their own food internally, they are dependent on the transformation of energy for survival.

While the first law of thermodynamics suggests the total amount of energy in the universe never diminishes, the second law of thermodynamics states a natural tendency exists for energy to dissipate and become disorganized. When building a fire, for example, the energy is intense at its source but spreads out and becomes less organized as heat enters the air. Consequently, the quantity of energy remains throughout the process, but the form has changed.

The same transferal occurs between, as well as within, ecosystems. This allows energy and corresponding nutrients and materials to flow back and forth. At the beginning of the earth's history, the rate of transfer between ecosystems was relatively high, but in more recent times the process has become more stable. This stability is what allows for life itself. Nevertheless, change is omnipresent, and some ecosystems and organisms are more adaptable than others. Environmental scientists emphasize the age of an ecosystem as a relevant factor in adaptability. The more mature an ecosystem, the less tolerant it is of change. Thus a newly developing ecosystem is more adaptable than an ancient forest. Moreover, the more simplified an ecosystem, the less it is able to withstand change. For example, land transformed into farms is more easily destroyed than wetlands, and cities are more vulnerable to pollution than rainforests. Moreover, since the earth itself has become a more stable and mature ecosystem, it too is less adaptable than it once was.

While general principles concerning the stability of ecosystems are possible, it is impossible to determine how an ecosystem will react to the endless varieties of change. The interactions are so complicated that cause and effect principles cannot be applied. Moreover, even if changes could be determined, and then repaired, it would still be impossible to repeat the original patterns of stability.

Using these environmental facts as a foundation, ecological theorists establish a set of principles encompassing not only natural development, but the relationship between nature and people. In the last three decades, ecological theory has launched a full scale theoretical search. Robyn Eckersley (1992) suggests that ecological theory has evolved through three main phases: participation, survival, and emancipation. The participation phase involved recognizing the damage wrought onto the environment, and the need to more equitably and

inclusively make decisions concerning its condition. Thus, participation meant more democratic decision-making and planning of the environment. The second survival phase culminated into a consensus of the global environmental crisis and its threat to human existence. During this phase, self-interest for short-term benefits was acknowledged as leading to common environmental destruction. In this context, individualism, private property, free markets, and representative democracy all were questioned.

The most recent phase, emancipation, asserts science and technology is neither the answer to human well-being, nor can it "fix" the environmental disaster at hand. This phase, moreover, calls for a reevaluation of "western" culture and politics. The aim is to question the economic, political and cultural values of industrialized societies, including unending economic development, consumerism, and hierarchical designs of economic, gender, and environmental systems (Eckersley, 1992 p. 8-22).

Many of these ideas have fermented into "Green" politics, a growing force in Europe, but less influential in the United States. The Green political agenda opposes industrialization in its conservative, liberal and socialist forms. It rejects individualism, laissez faire economics, and authoritarianism. Any political system allowing the powerful to protect and promote unfettered economic growth is faulted. According to the Greens, all industrialized political and cultural systems, moreover, are criticized for incorporating Enlightenment attitudes designed to overcome material scarcity through technological innovation. The environmental crisis shows the inadequacy of these fundamental beliefs.

Many, but not all, ecological theorists indicate an ecocentric approach is needed to correct flaws in current environmental conceptions. Ecocentrism places the human relation to nature a priori to political and social arrangements. Humans are not viewed as evolutionary royalty, and as such, must gain a keener awareness and compassion for living and nonliving elements of ecosystems. Environmental crises are caused by human self-centeredness and perceived importance. Solutions range from a deep reduction in the human population, to protection of biological diversity, even at a cost to human beings (Eckersley, 1992 p. 26-29).

A synthesized approach to ecological theories and issues, then, would include the following ideas.

1.   All natural developments are related to all other natural developments; nothing is created, maintained or changed in isolation.

2.   The general ecosystem of the earth is finite and has limited natural resources.

3.   Social and economic problems arise with continued industrial growth; the capacity to service unbridled growth, with its concurrent need for raw materials and assimilation of waste, is limited.

4.   Not everything humanly possible should be done; science and technology is a double-edged sword, offering promises of never ending development, while threatening the environment that provides for human existence (Fritsch, 1979; Spretnak, 1991).

Ecological theorists suggest that a major reason for the current environmental problems is the contradiction between cultural values promulgated by industrialized societies, and the limitations inherent within the state of the environment. Individualism and economic self-interest discourage a global, and often even a local, concern for the environment. What appears to be in self-interest in the short-run, in the long run can be disastrous (Porritt, 1985; Rifkin, 1989).

Ecological theorists, then, share with postmodernists and feminist theorists a general distrust for the mechanical view of science and the earth, where humankind controls and manipulates nature for its own ends. Like the literary trends of romanticism and transcendentalism, ecologists argue for an independent respect for nature apart from human considerations. Modern cultural values, however, do not encourage mutual respect for nature, or the unpredictability it engenders. Instead, industrial values encourage a rational cost benefit analysis of nature, within the context of a technological canon where environmental problems can always be corrected. This faith is contrary to the organic and unpredictable facts of the ecological environment (Spretnak, 1991; Pepper, 1984).

The critical factor in overcoming harmful environmental values, is a change in individual consciousness. Following phenomenological ideas, most ecologists argue the world and nature are constructions of subjective individuals. This is as true for the scientist who purports to know cause and effect relationships as it is the individual seeking a deeper understanding of ecosystems. In short, subjective individuals need to overcome cultural filters and understand the reality of nature (Pepper, 1984).

However, like feminist theory, ecological theory also demands micro processes be related to macro events. However, the ecological

emphasis is not on social conditions, but on natural processes. Ecologists deny the postmodern concern for local and unconnected events, and maintain life itself is inconceivable without natural processes existing in the universe. Moreover, once interrelationships are appreciated as a common feature of the universe and human life, human beings must necessarily be tied to natural development, and to one another (Spretnak, 1991 p.17-20).

What, then, are the prospects for a fundamental change in environmental values? The historical relationship between humans and nature shows an ascending disregard for the environment. In pre-industrial society, the development of agriculture, patterns of hunting, and the construction of rudimentary dams foreshadowed more serious developments later. This early period saw agriculture merely scratch the earth's surface, hunting generate limited influence on various species, and dams developed only for milling grain and limited other uses. By 1850, however, technological and economic appetites were relatively enormous and would continue to grow at exponential rates. Scientific knowledge and the practical uses of technology merged into a single powerful force, not only in the realm of commerce, but within the culture (De Bell, 1970).

Once merged, science and technology, coupled with the rise of democratic capitalist societies, reinforced cultural values of human dominance over nature. These ideas were grounded in the philosophical arguments of many thinkers. Bacon laid the groundwork for human dominance as he established a connection to a perfectly working machine; Descartes popularized mathematical power as a precise instrument to measure natural phenomena; Newton founded the mechanical universe; and Smith believed economics followed natural laws.

Religion also played an important role. Where paganism and Asian religions counseled a harmony with nature, the Judeo-Christian belief system placed humans in God's image, and clearly God was above nature. Where natural objects embodied their own spirit in antiquity, the modern view placed a single supernatural spirit as preeminent over nature. People, by transference, also came to see nature as inferior. It is against this legacy that ecologists try to change people's minds.

The ecological belief that a change in cultural values is key to changed perceptions of nature was refuted by Marx and Marxists. Marx argued that a direct and permanent relationship exists between humans and nature through the process of labor. As discussed in Chapter 1, the form of work is variable, but developed within capitalism as a means of dominance by those in control of the economic system. Consequently,

Marx would view the ecological hope to overcome cultural values toward nature as idealist; the power of the capitalist mode of production which generates such values first must be overcome. Ecological theorists respond, however, that Marx and Marxists too often glorified technology and economic development, albeit in a more equitable form. This mistake led to misinterpretations concerning the relationship of humans to nature. In Marxism, human relations remain more important than the relationship between humans and nature. As such, ecological theory argues that the Marxist critique is incapable of understanding the process and importance of nature.

Several theoretical issues, then, are raised by ecologists. First, the traditional concern with social order seems at odds with nature. Rather than order, the laws of thermodynamics and entropy suggest that increasing disorder is a central part of natural development. Moreover, disorder may be as true for micro as it is for macro processes. The micro dependence of rational choice and/or intentions may not reflect the biological, or even mental process of human beings. This issue is discussed further in Chapter Four.

Second, ecological theory apparently questions the traditional sociological dichotomy between subject and object. Since human beings are themselves natural beings, and are dependent on nature for survival, the connection between humans and nature becomes self-evident. This raises the possibility that the appropriate relationship is not subject/object, but subject/object/nature. In this case, while all three are interrelated, objects (material and normative) play mediating roles between subjective perception and material survival, and nature. This means perception is not solely subjective, and social objects and values are not solely external; both are related through natural existence. Moreover, since nature itself is potentially disorderly, the cohesiveness of relationships between subject, objects and nature is contingent.

In this light, ecological theorists are mistaken when they claim these interrelated processes are dependent only on natural phenomena. All three combine in a continually contingent process, where any of the subject/object/nature elements become internally or externally cohesive or contradictory. Once again, the most practical way to unearth the contingent relationships within this trichotomy is to allow for and uncover their autonomous development.

The mainstream ecological mission of changed social values, then, is inadequate to forestall the environmental destruction they predict. Similar to feminist discussions of situated actors and macro conditions, ecological theory critically discusses subjective values and the macro institutions that alter value development. The aim is to change attitudes and actions at both levels as they relate to nature. While the contemporary environmental movement has succeeded in changing, to some degree, subjective thought and institutional actions, it underestimates the autonomy of macro processes and the use of power. On this score, Marx was right: a limited argument for a change in cultural values will be ineffective for environmental gains. If macro processes were granted autonomy and contingency, ecologists would see the shortcoming of a purely value-laden argument.

Similar concerns may be raised at the micro level. Again, ecological theorists are wrong to restrict debate only to moral and ethical relationships to nature. Micro psychological, spiritual, and rational perceptions are not always related to nature, and even when they are, subjective values are expressed across a large panorama of subjective and social dynamics. Here, ecologists underestimated the autonomous development of micro processes. Subjective thought and action are not merely responses to macro conditions, no matter how powerfully cultural values, such as economic development, are promulgated.

Again, the theoretical and logical extension of environmental concerns leads to autonomy and contingency, but now altered to include a third level for the natural environment. That is, micro and macro processes should be seen as autonomous and contingent, but both should be seen in relation to the autonomous and contingent development of nature. The concepts of autonomy and contingency would allow for much of the current work in ecological theory, including the subjective perspective of value creation, the conditional influence of cultural structures, and the relationship between both and nature. Moreover, within the context of autonomy and contingency, ecologists may be in a better position to uncover and articulate a more effective course of action.

Despite the shortcomings outlined above, the ecological indictment is worthy of consideration. Not only does it share a critical view of western science and thought with other indictment theories, but corrects the scarcity of concern for nature and its relation to social development. Ecological theory makes clear the perilous omission of nature from social theory, especially since it is the prime source for sustaining life. The issue of contingent natural development, and its implications, and relationship for micro and macro processes will be more fully addressed in the next chapter.

Conclusions

The three indictment theories share a common criticism of traditional social theory. All three reject rational thought and universal principles uncovered through classical social and scientific method. Postmodernism defines locale, not social order, as the focal point of theoretical and empirical investigations. Feminist theory places situated actors as a central concept, and points out the obtuse nature of theory when assumptions deny their inclusion. And ecological theory highlights how theoretical and scientific assumptions have led to both a misunderstanding of natural developments, and the relationship between nature and social development.

The indictment theories also share a reluctance to replace assumptions with a set of their own. Contingency plays a significant role in each of the indictments. Postmodernism sees the locale as containing a multitude of factors and events that defy logical and universal explanations. No set of presumed variables can predict events. Feminist theory, however, suggests more than one reality, and as such, general depictions purvey theoretical aims, rather than objective description. Once again, predictability is drastically reduced. Ecological theory includes contingency within its scientific approach to understanding natural change. Thermodynamics and entropy require nothing less. In brief, the predictability and logic residing in sociological theory is eliminated by the indictment theories. In place of social order and predictability, indictment theorists allow for a far greater degree of contingency than does any traditional or micro/macro synthetic theory.

Along with these common features, the three indictment theories also contain differences. Postmodernism is a strictly subjective micro approach to social analysis, characterized by symbolic interpretations of micro events. Feminist theory contains elements of both micro and macro to account for the full spectrum of differences based on gender. However, the two levels are not well integrated. Advocating situated actors, and simultaneously explaining macro-oriented influences on gender is a theoretical and methodological dilemma not yet settled by feminist theory. And while ecological theory is by definition concerned with structural phenomena, it analyzes subjective and cultural relationships to nature.

Despite differences, all three perspectives point to inherent problems in traditional and contemporary approaches in sociological theory. Each highlights social areas long neglected. Postmodernism demonstrates that the cause and aftermath of principal social movements have been excluded. Feminist theory asks why, throughout the course of its history, social theory has ignored gender issues, a fundamental element in society. Ecological theory targets both essential issues of human existence, as well as a powerful social movement over the past twenty years, and asks why theoretical models are inadequate to explain either. In short, each of the indictment theories raises social and theoretical questions that traditional theory disregards; unfortunately, being above these questions has relegated social theory to an obscure place on the fringe.

One source of obscurity is the timidity often expressed in social theory. Almost a phobia exists towards fundamental considerations. Instead, a rupture persists between theory and research, where little is asked of the researcher and research. The effect is that research often theoretically constructs its own questions for application. While nothing is inherently wrong, and much can be discovered using such an approach, no coherent body of knowledge can result. Research applications begin with their own assumptions, sometimes theoretically derived, and often not. The researcher proceeds to ask questions related to those assumptions, conduct statistical analysis on a computer, and prove or disprove the questions asked. These efforts mostly act to maintain beliefs about how the world looks, or uncover interesting, but often obscure, bits of social reality. By ignoring autonomy and contingency, and thereby ignoring fundamental social and political questions, contemporary sociology conserves the status quo. It asks little of itself, and it asks nothing of the individuals it studies. Above all, it asks nothing of the society as a whole. Paradoxically, if the social world is autonomous and contingent, a great deal should be asked of theorists, researchers, subjects, and the society.

If sociology is to become more relevant for society, avoid being the butt of jokes on late night television, avoid its name being bandied about as if it is the epitome of irrelevance, then its theories and empirical investigations must be pertinent to the social and political issues of the day, not abstractions of them. However, the indictment theories do not provide an adequate method for understanding these problems and issues. The expression "indictment theories" was chosen purposively. As a legal term, an indictment means enough evidence has been gathered to continue to a formal trial; in this case, enough accumulated evidence have been shown by postmodernism, feminist theory and ecological theory to bring social theory to a hearing. However, the replacements suggested by the indictment theories do not inherently point to a correction in social thought. That is the topic for discussion in Parts II and III. The first step in that effort is a discussion of an area long overdue for review by sociologists: the innovations of twentieth century science.

PART II

SEARCHING FOR
CONTINGENT CLUES

Chapter Four

Discoveries of Twentieth Century Science

Jonathan Piel (1991) proclaims scientific discoveries in the twentieth century are nothing short of astounding. Starting with Einstein's macro theory of relativity, through discoveries of micro quantum mechanics, and back again to macro theories of the origin of the universe, twentieth century discoveries in physics have been characterized as revolutionary. However, physics is not the only scientific discipline to unearth stunning discoveries: biology unlocked the fundamental elements of life, including the discovery of DNA, and has begun to grasp brain functions; geologists now postulate the development of earth's surface through the theory of continental drift; and while the progression of the computer can be traced to the needs of science, computerization now influences every aspect of scientific research. New developments in computer technology, especially the potential of computer chips created through optics and lasers, will vastly increase the speed and breadth of computer capabilities.

And yet, despite the enormous advances of twentieth century science, a troubling pattern has emerged. In its simplest form, science has been unable to accurately predict tomorrow's weather. More fundamentally, the analytic authority of science has been questioned. And while critics have always perceived an overconfidence in science, the newer criticisms arise from twentieth century science itself. In place of scientific laws, the emerging scientific paradigm is contingency. A brief tour of recent scientific discoveries, and problems that emerge, is in order.

Relativity

The fundamental postulate of Einstein's theory of relativity indicates laws of physics should apply to all freely moving objects, no matter their speed. To fathom the revolutionary magnitude of relativity requires knowledge of why nothing may be faster than the speed of light, that space-time is not flat, and that time and space is relative to position.

Nothing may move faster than the speed of light. This is so because the equivalence of energy and mass, where an object's energy is due to its motion, and its motion will add to its mass. However, increased mass decreases the energy available from speed, and thus, as an object accelerates toward the speed of light, its mass rises ever more quickly, requiring ever more energy. Consequently, an object can never reach the speed of light because an infinite level of mass and energy would be needed. Only light or other waves with no intrinsic mass can move at the speed of light.

Thus, relativity is at odds with the Newton's theory of gravity, which stated both that the gravitational force between objects is dependent only on the distance between them, and that gravitational attraction has infinite velocity. Newton believed, in other words, that gravitational pull of one object would instantaneously necessitate a change of position in the other. Relativity proved, however, that space-time was not flat as Newton had believed. Instead, space-time is curved relative to the distribution of mass and energy within it. In our solar system, the mass of the sun curves space-time. Thus, light, for instance, does not move along straight lines, but is curved. This explains why the moon looks larger on the horizon, but smaller overhead. The moon, of course, maintains its size, but at the horizon, the gravitational pull of the earth bends the light through which the moon is observed. The curvature of space-times means gravitational pull is not direct or instantaneous, but is relative to, and contingent on, the distribution of mass and energy present in the gravitational field.

The theory of relativity also changed conceptions of time. Relativity claims time appears slower near massive bodies such as planets. Varied time is due to a relation between the energy of light and its frequency; the higher the frequency the slower time should become. As light travels near bodies with a large mass, time should appear to slow down, because upward in the gravitational field, light loses energy, causing its frequency to decrease. Thus, to someone higher up in the gravitational field, it would appear everything below was taking longer to happen. This is the explanation for why an individual who travels in space and then returns, finds the time taken for space travel differs depending whether one escaped the gravitational field or remained on the earth's surface. In short, the space traveler ages at a different rate than those left on earth.

Thus, relativity proved the dynamic nature of space and time, and has changed our ideas of both. When a body moves or a force acts, it affects the curvature of space and time, and vice versa. While observers must agree on the absolute speed of light, different observers at different points in curved space-time need not agree on the distance the light has traveled. Thus, two observers moving relative to each other will assign different times and positions to the same event. What is revolutionary is that the observers, assigning different times and positions to the same event, are both correct! Relativity, then, put an end to Newtonian notions of absolute time.

The importance of the theory of relativity is at least two-fold. On the one hand, the theory explained the physical universe in more profound ways than previously understood. In brief, it allowed physics to become a more exact science. At the same time, relativity jolted the foundations of commonly understood concepts; time and space were no longer measurable through universal mathematical computations. Instead, time and space were now relative, and could be analyzed differently by different observers.

While these discoveries were remarkable in their refocusing of physics, they remained within the explanatory dictums of scientific endeavors. Einstein maintained science aims at uncovering simple and fundamental laws of nature. But another discovery of twentieth-century science shook the discipline at its roots, and has required science to lose its simplicity for all but the most macro of physical events. That discovery was quantum mechanics.

Quantum Mechanics

Where relativity contemplated the macro universe, quantum mechanics explored micro, sub-atomic matter, commonly referred to as particle matter. The problem with sub-atomic exploration is that absolute measurements are impossible. This, as Max Planck showed, is due to the relationship between the observer and the observed. When an observer tries to establish the position of a particle, the observer must make measurements of light waves. However, during measurement, the observer must shine at least one quantum of light on the particle under study. This is problematic because the particle under study is, itself, disturbed by the quantum of light, and in unpredictable ways. Moreover, the smaller the quantum particle, the more velocity its matter has, and the more unpredictable its movements.

Quantum phenomenon might be termed "schizophrenic", at times acting like waves and at other times like particles. As long as quantum phenomena are undisturbed and allowed to spread through space, waves develop, but as soon as they are measured, by viewing photons through slits or bouncing off of screens, the photons behave as particles (Horgan, 1992).

This dynamic obviously presented problems for scientific observation, and led to quantum mechanics, which no longer searched for well-defined positions or velocities, but instead aimed at description of quantum states of particle matter, a much less certain description. Consequently, prediction within quantum mechanics is based on probabilities, not definite measurements, and these probabilities, moreover, are aimed at various possible outcomes. The level of doubt inherent in such probabilities has become known as Heisenberg's uncertainty principle.

Where relativity maintained the effort to discover universal principles of nature, quantum mechanics destroys that possibility, at least on the micro level. Thus the historic scientific effort is challenged by quantum mechanics, not only because of the uncertainty of future universal theories, but because it creates a divide between the observer and the observed. If observation alters the object being measured, the entire scientific method is called into question. While quantum mechanics does not suggest science and its historic method are of no value, it does invite science to step down from the pedestal it traditionally has demanded.

As Prigogine and Stengers (1984) have suggested, since observers must be distinguished from objects under study, and measurement devices also influence those objects, then questions asked and instruments selected for observation must influence findings. Even then, findings can be based only on the probability of various outcomes. This explanation of quantum phenomena has been termed the Copenhagen interpretation, and is far removed both from assurances of Newton's mechanical universe, and the assumption that science can describe all reality.

More recently, some physicists have suggested the progress of science continues despite quantum mechanics. Bell has argued that quantum entities still exist in a particular time and place, only their behavior is subject to nonlocality. Others, such as Ghiradi, Weber, and Pearle have suggested that at the macro level, even quantum phenomena become combined into a single state system, observable and predictable. Yet others claim traditional views of science are destroyed by quantum reality. For example, and perhaps most incredibly, Everett concludes quantum entities are unpredictable because the universe splits and the course of action is not mandatory (Horgan, 1992).

Moreover, beyond relativity, quantum theory further destroys the idea of absolute time. The observer is left only with a subjective interpretation of the irreversibility of time. Since the velocity and position of particles cannot be definitely situated, it is impossible to differentiate, at least on the micro level, the past from the future.

Quantum theory, then, raises many questions within the philosophy of science, discussed in a later section. These questions include: is the micro a special case that does not disturb the search for universal macro phenomena; does the uncertainty of the micro field eliminate or require a synthesis between micro and macro; and since a detailed causal explanation is ruled out by quantum mechanics, is it necessary to rule out the possibility of scientific discovery entirely?

Questions raised about the utility of science have sources other than relativity and quantum mechanics, however. One example is found in new developments in biology and the theory of evolution.

Biology and Evolution

Early developments in biology and evolution, and their influence on classical sociologists, were discussed in an earlier chapter. Of course, the advance of the biology has continued into the present century. The discoveries of chromosomes and genes within cells, and later discoveries of DNA and RNA were monumental advances in the descriptions of life itself. Limitations of space preclude a full description of these discoveries. More germane to the direction of this chapter is the emerging debate about the origin of life, and the direction of evolutionary change. While the theories suggested in this section are far more debatable within the biological discipline than relativity or quantum mechanics are within physics, the debate continues the pattern of calling some of science's most precious beliefs into question.

In their book, *Blueprints: Solving the Mystery of Evolution,* Edey and Johanson (1990, p. 281-95) describe the current state of theories concerning the origins of life. From primitive bacteria fossils found in a 3.5 billion-year-old rock shield in Australia, they conclude life must have begun some 3.5 to 4 billion years ago. The question is, how?

At least three explanations are currently suggested. The first is promoted by Eigen. Based on attempts to create the building blocks of life in a test tube, he and his colleagues uncovered what they believe is a workable theory for the origin of life. Since basic elements of life are mutually dependent and could not be produced in chronological order apart from each other, Eigen concluded more than one mutually dependent element must have existed at life's origin. Eigen described this phenomena as a "feedback loop", where one element enhances another element and gives it evolutionary strength to maintain stability and stand out among the myriad of possibilities. Eigen call this process a "hypercircle", and has been given strength through additional experimentation and mathematical computations.

A second approach to explaining the origin of life is suggested by Cairns-Smith, who argues Eigen's hypercircle puts the cart before the horse. In his view, searching for the basic elements of life is too far along the evolutionary chain. Instead, the search for life must be found in a more simple substance. His answer is clay. Clay is widespread and has the inherent capability of producing crystals. Moreover, clay evolves; the formation of crystals is variable and each variation creates yet other variations. Eventually, basic elements of life, such as RNA or enzymes, settled into clay structures and replaced them as a dominant evolutionary organism.

A third approach suggests that spores or amino acids found on meteorites were exported to earth from space. While these two ideas do have some logic and support, they are not generally well accepted in the scientific community.

Whatever the alternatives, a common denominator is present. An element of chance is inherent in the process. In the hypercircle model, the elements necessary for life evolved from countless other possibilities. The stability and mutual enhancement of elements are not drawn from a predetermined path, but by a chance attraction within specific conditions. Consequently, slightly different conditions would have led to different combinations of elements that would also have been mutually dependent and enhancing. Thus, unless one wishes to attribute this phenomena to the a divine plan of God, the origin of life appears accidental. Similar conclusions must be drawn for the theory of life developing from clay, and certainly the same applies to life being exported to earth from space.

The chance development of life, and eventually of human beings, is not limited life's origins. Evidence is mounting that each step of evolution contains contingency. In his book, *Wonderful Life: The Burgess Shale and the Nature of History* (1989), Stephen Jay Gould argues the entire path of evolution is fraught with accidental happenstance. Until recently, most evolutionists followed Darwin's premise that as life exploded it became a crowded maze, and competition ensued. Eventually, a balance materializes, and evolutionary change slows.

Gould accepts this premise as a necessary, but insufficient, explanation of evolution. Evidence for the need to transcend Darwin exists in the influential fossil discoveries found in the Burgess Shale in the Canadian Rocky Mountains.

The Burgess Shale fossils represent life as it existed just after the "Cambrian explosion" when multicellular animal life first appeared and, with startling rapidity, grew in abundance some 570 million years ago. The Burgess discoveries, then, represent a time teeming with varieties of early life forms. Moreover, the Burgess discoveries were important because the soft part of the animals were preserved, a rare condition in paleontology.

The Burgess fossils raised two problems for previous thinking about the history of life. First, how could such a variety of life have emerged, and second, what were the conditions that allowed only some life forms to evolve? Gould suggests a straightforward answer to the first problem: if an immense variety of life exploded, the environment must have allowed for myriad forms of life. To answer the second question, however, required a reversal of previous thinking. Instead of a limited beginning, where multicellular life competed with and dominated previous forms of life, the enormity of multicellular life yields the conclusion that life forms became dominant because of specific conditions emerging by historical accident.

This process is what occurred in the Burgess Shale. A great variety of life was at first present, but later most life forms were decimated, and only particular forms remained. In short, multicellular life began with unlimited flexibility, but only a few survived. Nevertheless, the evidence indicates that previous to the decimation, all had an equal chance for survival. While it was not pure accident that the survivors remained, survival was "the product of massive historical contingency, and would probably never rise again," even if the Cambrian explosion were to repeat itself. Moreover, the Burgess Shale fossils suggests the survivors did not destroy competitors, nor can the competitors be seen as inferior.

Further, Gould argues for a new understanding of mass extinctions. Mass extinctions occur more often and are more rapid than we have traditionally understood. The changes in environmental conditions may be so devastating that organisms have no time to evolve through the process of natural selection. Moreover, survivors of mass extinctions have little in common with those organisms that previously experienced evolutionary success.

These ideas raise an intriguing question regarding human evolution: did human beings evolve through a process of natural selection, or because of historical contingency? While all researchers agree the Cambrian period was certainly filled with rapid growth, some paleontologists maintain the growth is still explainable through evolutionary models (e.g. Beardsley, 1992).

Nevertheless, theories related to the extinction of dinosaurs and the rise of humans gives further evidence of historical contingency. Sixty-five million years ago, life on earth underwent colossal change. Half of all plant and animal species disappeared. Among those that became extinct were the dinosaurs. Two theories of the mass extinction of dinosaurs are currently given. The first has been promoted by Walter Alvarez and Frank Asaro (1990). In their view, an enormous asteroid crashed into earth and set off a chain reaction of environmental disasters. The impact of the asteroid caused a series of "storms, tsunamis, cold and darkness, greenhouse warming, acid rains and global fires. When quiet returned at last, half the flora and fauna had become extinct. The history of the earth had taken a new and unexpected path." The fact that sediments taken from the Cretaceous-Tertiary boundary (the age at which dinosaurs became extinct) contain levels of iridium, and that impact-generated quartz crystals have been found from the same period, supplies evidence for the asteroid theory.

An alternative theory for the mass extinction has been argued by Courtillot (1990). He maintains dinosaur extinction was caused by massive volcanic eruptions within the area now claimed by Italy. It too presumes that enormous clouds of dust were generated, as well as chemical changes in the atmosphere. The ecological result was a changed environment in which numerous species of life, including the dinosaurs, could no longer exist.

In either case, the eventual influence on evolutionary processes is unmistakable. Rather than a slow gradual development of natural selection, environmental upheavals caused a sudden and dramatic turn in life processes. While the causes can be debated and eventually solved through more scientific research, the element of historical contingency cannot be ignored. Neither can speculation of what might have happened if mass extinctions did not take place.

Gould points out that mammals evolved roughly at the same time as dinosaurs and were dominated by them for 100 million years. Indeed, for roughly two thirds of their time on earth, mammals showed no progress against the dinosaurs The size of the mammal brain did not increase, nor did its strength. Only when dinosaurs became extinct, through historical contingency, did the human ancestors begin to emerge. No reason exists to believe that if dinosaurs had dominated mammals for 100 million years, they would not continue to do so for another 60 million. In short, the very existence of humans is dependent on historical happenstance.

The notion of contingency in science is found in other disciplines as well. One of the more interesting theories has developed within the area of geology.

Geology and Continental Drift

In 1912, a German scientist, Alfred Wegener, speculated separate areas of land on earth were once part of a single, gigantic landmass existing some 200 million years ago. Current land distributions are the outcome of an ancient splitting apart, a process that continues and is termed continental drift. While this theory was proposed early in the twentieth century, it was ignored for decades. However, recent scientific findings have brought the theory to the forefront of geologic research (Piel, 1991).

One important recent discovery found a deep ridge, first on the floor of the Atlantic, and then the Pacific and other oceans. Next, seafloor rocks were examined and determined to be of different ages; rocks closest to the ridges were younger than those further away, and both were younger than rocks resting on the surface of continents. This meant the ridges were made up of molten rock, and this, in turn, led scientists to believe the earth is made up of plates of various thickness, where ridges represent boundaries where the plates collide. Moreover, as plates transfigure, they have the capacity to transport surface areas. While scientists still debate the cause of the movement of the plates, there is now little doubt that the plates do in fact move (Piel, 1991, p. 8). This allows for an explanation not only of continent formation, but also for mountain ranges (Murphy and Nance, 1992).

Some geologists speculate the gradual movement and collisions of the earth's crust has influenced climatic conditions. The shift of the earth's plates has created plateaus both in the North American and Eurasian continents. In turn, this may alter the circulation patterns of the atmosphere, producing the 40-million year cooling trend of atmospheric temperature. Finally, some speculation exists that current continental shapes have not always prevailed; continental drift repeats itself, albeit with differing results, every several hundred million years (Piel, 1991, p. 9-10).

Once again, the implications of continental drift on the historical contingency thesis is apparent. Since the drift is variable, no law of science can predict its future. Moreover, if continental drift affects climate, alternate formations could affect, or eliminate, human life. Finally, if the process renews itself, even if over enormously long periods of time, the earth must be contingent in its own development. Must not human life and social development share contingency with the host planet?

All of the discussions of this chapter indicate the earth, and the evolution of living species within it, are variable and subject to historical contingency. This raises a similar, but even more perplexing idea. If this is true of earth, what of the universe? Is it possible the evolution of the universe is subject to the same flexibility found on earth? Much of the very recent work in cosmology leads to just such a conclusion.

Contingency in the Cosmos

Most modern astrophysicists have come to the conclusion that the origin of the universe began with a "big bang." However, this belief raises more questions than it answers. In his book, *A Brief History of Time*, Stephen Hawking (1988) explains the big bang theory and related issues and questions.

At the point of the big bang, the universe must have been infinitely small and infinitely hot. This allowed the particles present to escape gravitational attraction and to expand rapidly. Soon after, temperatures dropped and gravitational attraction reasserted itself. Gravity would assert itself in proportion to the density of matter present. Regions of higher density would start to collapse and the gravitational pull of other regions would encourage a rotational spin. The spin would increase until it was in balance with the gravitational force on it. Thus, rotational spin of regions is variable. Moreover, other regions would not spin at all, but become oval shaped and create internal stability through orbiting its center.

While this picture of the origin of the universe is backed by observational evidence, important questions remain. Why was the universe so hot at its origin; why does it remain so uniform; and why did it start out with the exact amount of expansion which allows for stability? The theory of relativity cannot answer these questions because it is a theory of the universe as it currently exists; explanations derived from relativity break down at the point of the big bang (Hawking, 1988 p. 121-22).

Hawking argues a key to unlocking these puzzling questions is found in a combination of quantum mechanics and gravity. First, according to quantum mechanics, particles have no discoverable past or present. As discussed earlier, this is because a particle-wave can only be ascertained by adding all the possible movements through a point and making probability judgments on its position. Thus, quantum mechanics is in opposition to classical theories of gravity which suggest the universe either began in a singularity as in the big bang theory, or has existed for an infinite amount of time. By contrast, quantum mechanics suggests a third possibility. The third possibility is that while space-time may be seen as finite and observable, the universe has no beginning or end (Hawking, 1988 p. 135-36), or may keep regenerating itself because of quantum fluctuations (Horgan, 1993).

This theory raises additional problems. In brief, "One therefore has a theory that seems to predict that certain quantities, such as the curvature of space-time are really infinite, yet these quantities can be observed and measured to be perfectly finite." Thus, the discovery of micro level quantum mechanics has transformed the macro questions asked by astrophysicists. Its aim remains to formulate a set of laws enabling the prediction of events, but now only up to a point: the point of the uncertainty principle.

The desire to establish a set of laws remains constant, however, and continues to influence the selection of questions asked. Hawking, for instance contends that what is so puzzling about quantum mechanics is that the universe is smooth and precisely shaped to allow for the development of life. However, even this assumption is now under question. Astronomers have long believed galaxies were evenly dispersed through space on the basis of gravitational attraction, and if plotted on a map would look like the smooth pattern Hawking hypothesized about. This belief was omnipresent, and astronomers never attempted the ponderous task of mapping the universe. In the mid-1980s, however, a group of astronomers, attempting only to catalog the number of galaxies present in the universe, made an astounding accidental discovery. Rather than in a random and smooth spread, galaxies were grouped atop the surface of gigantic bubbles. Since galaxies rested on the top of these bubbles, the internal space of the bubbles was a colossal void of space (Bartusiak, 1990).

Moreover, astronomers have now delved deeper into space and discovered a series of "great walls." The walls are separated by empty spaces as wide as 400 million light years apart. While only a tiny fraction of the universe has so far been mapped, these findings have important implications for thinking about the universe. Instead of conceiving the universe in rational terms, it is possible that rational explanation is, itself, impossible. If this is true, then the entire methodology of science may be called into question. While Hawking does not accept this hypothesis, he does raise the possibility and potential importance of this idea.

Hawking explains the universe may have formed chaotic boundaries. This implies the configuration of any region of space is probable; it was no more likely to take its present form than any other configuration. Moreover, recent work on the inflationary models (models based on an expanding universe) show the present state of the universe could have arisen from quite a large number of different original configurations at the big bang (Hawking, 1988 p. 123). Thus, both the initial state of the universe at the big bang, and the present form of galaxies that resulted, are a matter of historical contingency, what Hawking refers to a the wormhole theory, where space-time can tunnel into other universes or form "cul de sacs" of stability. Even more astounding, the inflationary model suggests the reason the universe appears so uniform and predictable is because the universe is colossal when compared to our microscopic comprehension of its size (Horgan, 1990). Consequently, what we currently observe as a stable universe may well contain instability far from our boundaries of knowing.

As if wormholes and inflationary theories are not enough to fathom, two other models of the universe require equal thought expansion. The many worlds theory suggests the possibility of a variety of parallel universes, and the many-histories theory claims the universe acted like a quantum particle at the big bang (Horgan, 1990). These depictions of the origin and development of the universe is similar to the description of the origins and development of life on earth. While there is logic to the development of the universe and for the evolution of life on earth, a level of contingency is also inherent. Three choices seem to be available to scientists if they are to deal with the notion of contingency.

First, both the universe and life on earth are all part of God's divine plan. Faith in this choice not only answers all of the questions raised by contingency, but puts an end for the need for science. Second, there is a discoverable universal logic to both the universe and life on earth. Both the first and second choices have been available for quite some time. But a new choice also exists. Its roots are in the very discoveries of science in the twentieth century, and encourages the proposition that no logical, universal explanation to the physical world exists. Some scientists have extended these ideas and contend the normal state of the physical world is chaotic. This is the basis of chaos theory, a set of beliefs continually gaining converts both within and outside of science.

Chaos and Contingency

Much of the early work in chaos was conducted by biologists. Issues such as the growth of isolated populations not overlapping future generations, the physiology of blood production, and the dynamics of biochemical relations, led biologists to consider the possibility that these events were in many ways random (Schaffer and Kot, 1986). Because it is common for biologists to measure physiological properties according to the function of time, incorporating chaotic relationships required biologists turn to mathematics (Glass, 1988). Four mathematical ideas play a role here: steady states, oscillation, chaos, and noise.

The mathematical concept of steady states implies a dynamic relationship has found a state of relative equilibrium. Many physiological analogies are available including blood sugar, blood gases, osmolarity, electrolytes, blood pressure, and pH. But the human body also contains a series of oscillations no less important for human life. The release of insulin, electrical activity in the cortex of the brain, the nervous system, and constrictions in peripheral blood vessels are all examples of necessary oscillations in the body (Glass, 1988 p. 4-6). The body contains, then, stationary, steady state systems as well as oscillating systems. Both are necessary for the successful continuation of the physical being, and both perform in relation to each other.

At times, however, these physiological systems cannot be characterized either as in a steady state, or as oscillating. This phenomenon is usually attributed to exterior conditions. For example, exercise, food intake, and periods of rest can influence blood pressure and insulin production. Moreover, changes in one physiological system can influence the others. However, even when exterior conditions are held constant, the physiological systems themselves sometimes act in variable ways. The electrical activity of the brain is a good example of this phenomena (Glass, 1988 p. 6).

Mathematics offers two techniques to consider irregularities. The first is the concept of noise, which refers to irregularities caused by chance exterior conditions. The second is chaos, which occurs even when there is an absence of noise. In chaos, future predictions are impossible because the chaos can be attributed neither to internal systems, nor the exterior environment (Glass, 1988 p.6).

Like quantum mechanics, chaos implies a level of uncertainty. Relationships between internal and external variables are muted by the inability to predict their future. While stability and oscillation are sometimes identifiable, at other times they are not. Chaos, however, does not imply total randomness. In fact, chaotic conditions are highly ordered, and even deterministic (Ranger-Moore, 1992). For example, using computer simulation, astronomers suggest the solar system is chaotic in behavior, but also has long term stability (Peterson, 1993a). Nevertheless, unpredictable irregularity does play a part. The notion of chaos is now becoming accepted in many disciplines and has relevance in electronics, optics, chemistry, and hydrodynamics (Schaffer and Kot, 1986). Moreover, chaos is being utilized in the fields of computers, ecology, astrophysics, and mathematics (Gleick, 1987), and in medical technology to increase the power of lasers, and stabilize erratic heart-beats (Ditto and Pecora, 1993).

In their book, *Order Out of Chaos*, Nobel prize winners Prigogine and Stengers, (1984) explain the fundamental problems that chaos presents for the traditions of science. In the nineteenth century, science revolved around the explanation of equilibrium states. Matter near equilibrium states behaves in predictable and universal ways. These notions, based on Newtonian principles, accepted positivist and rational paradigms, where cause and effect are connected to motion. Moreover, equilibrium states and motion were rationally explained through the theory of gravity and corresponding ideas of absolute time. As discussed earlier, Newtonian motion can be explained through the gravitational pull of objects, and their instantaneous influence on each other. Thus, mathematical calculations are possible in the Newtonian system, both for the past and the future. Quantum mechanics puts an end to this scientific ideology, however, and raises questions both about predictability and origins of systems (Prigogine and Stengers, 1984; see Chapter. 2). How, for instance, can the universe appear uniform when viewed from a great distance, but as "lumpy" waves upon closer inspection (Ruthen, 1992)? The lumpiness is caused by curved space-time, where large masses, like galaxies, and the immense gravitational pull of black holes, produce an effect roughly equivalent to a down quilt that has been punched randomly to create indentations (Peterson, 1993b).

The problems raised by quantum mechanics and more recent work in the area of chaos has led to new conceptualizations. While equilibrium states are not discounted in the new thinking, steady states are no longer accepted as normal. While matter near equilibrium states behaves in understandable ways, matter in "far from equilibrium states" is not only chaotic, but may generate new structures entirely on its own, a process known as biurfication. These new structures may, in turn, influence the original state of equilibrium. Prigogine and Stengers call these new structures, "dissipative" to emphasize the constructive nature of what are, at their essence, dissipative and chaotic processes.

The method to grasp the unique problems created from chaos is non-liner dynamics, where, put in simple terms, what happens on one side of the equation does not cause a proportional change on the other side of the equation (Peterson, 1993b). In short, balance is destroyed, and this precarious reality causes severe anxiety among mathematicians and scientists.

Moreover, the incidence of natural chaotic biurfication is higher than stability and equilibrium states, and this is as true for those natural systems which have boundary conditions, as it is for those open to the environment. Stability, then, can no longer be the aim of science. Fluctuations either in equilibrium states, and particularly in far-from-equilibrium states, can dramatically change the original configuration in unpredictable ways. Phenomena of this kind have been shown in hydrodynamics and fluid flow, as well as in the sub-atomic level, where chaos has been detected in energy levels of certain atomic systems, and even in wave patterns (Gutzwiller, 1992). Even more importantly, probability no longer is of use at this point because the future of both equilibrium and far-from-equilibrium states are beyond rational comprehension. The process of chaotic biurfication is creative and nonexplanatory (Prigogene and Stengers, 1984; see Chapter. 5).

Thus, when considering either micro physiological systems or macro ecosystems, chaos leads to the assumption that fluctuations, most probably in far-from-equilibrium states, begin a chain reaction at a variable, but precise moment, that is eventually integrated into a new equilibrium state. The process is ongoing, and unpredictable. Even more shattering, the very process of chaotic bifurcation becomes necessary for eventual stability in equilibrium systems. In other words, the equilibrium systems, which we more easily rationalize, are the result of chaotic processes within nonequilibrium systems. And what is more, while the equilibrium states may appear to be independently discrete, it is the separate and hidden nonequilibrium states which provide unity and coherence in the more stable states (Prigogine and Stengers, 1984; see Chapter. 6).

What conclusions can be drawn from the work conducted in chaos? Prigogine and Stengers have little trouble integrating these new findings and conceptions with reality. They conclude a new unity is emerging. In equilibrium states the traditional laws of physics and science still have utility, but the equilibrium states cannot be viewed in isolation from nonequilibrium states. This means vaunted beliefs such as the irreversibility of time now are questioned. But the irreversibility of time in nonequilibrium states is inherent only within its own boundaries and not for stable states. In brief, some processes reach equilibrium and some do not, and in either case, both predictable and nonpredictable processes help shape the eventual formation of the new state.

If this is true, some of the most heralded scientific laws must now be rejected. One example is scientific laws governing thermodynamics. The first law states energy and matter are constant. Energy, for instance, can change its form, but the total amount of energy after the change in form must equal the amount present before the change. So far, this is consistent with the ideas of quantum mechanics and chaos. However, problems arise with the second law of thermodynamics. It states that while the amount of energy must remain constant, the change in form must be in one direction, from usable to unusable and from ordered to unordered. But biurfication suggests something entirely different. In nonequilibrium states the disorder may well create a reaction leading to a new order and equilibrium.

Chaos theory, then, along with all of the issues raised in this brief description of scientific developments in the twentieth century, understandably has influenced the debates conducted within the philosophy of science. An overview of those discussions will also draw this analysis one step closer to the possible implications for sociological theory.

Issues in the Philosophy of Science

Current debates within the philosophy of science reflect many of the issues discussed in this and previous chapters. With mounting evidence, the attack on traditional forms of scientific thought and research has intensified within and outside of science. Philosophers of science have grappled with issues questioning the inductive method used by scientists, whether general theories are possible, and the future of science as a whole. A brief review of the development of these issues is illustrative of the need to account for autonomy and contingency.

From the time of Bacon's inductive method, science has been on a value-free quest. Kant built on Bacon's notions and formalized scientific endeavor as rational. The Vienna school of science in the 1920s and 1930s extended these ideas even further and, similar to Comte's approach to sociology, considered science a logical, positivist enterprise. Like Comte in sociology, the Vienna school's aim was to distinguish science from both religion and philosophy, and produce ahistorical and universal scientific research. However, as both indictment theorists and quantum mechanics suggest, research is influenced by the questions and activities of researchers. The same idea is suggested by philosophers of science.

The very discoveries of early scientists seem to highlight the researcher/research relationship. Kepler, for instance, asserted that planets orbit the sun with mathematical regularity, but his conclusion was not founded on collected data and inductive reasoning. Instead, he subjectively analyzed data and came to unique and creative conclusions (O'Hear, 1989 p. 22). Moreover, all scientific theories face the prospect of continuous challenge and overthrow. Many of the discoveries of twentieth century science have done just that. In short, the positivist school no longer has a theory with which it can be positive (Chalmers, 1990).

The temporal nature of scientific theories have led some to claim science accommodates reality no better than religion or mythology (Feyerabend, 1975). Others suggest scientific observations cannot be rational because they are theory-laden, or are merely reduced to the level of conversation (Rorty, 1980). In response to the continual overthrow of previous "facts," philosophers searched for more flexible methodologies for science. The aim was to step back from notions of universal truth in order to avoid relativist conclusions that science has no permanent application for reality. Lakatos (1978), for example, suggests universal theories in science remain relevant because at least they may be distinguished from irrational approaches.

Perhaps the most famous attempt to reestablish scientific rationality, but avoid problems exhibited by the inductive method, is found in the work of Karl Popper (1966). Popper views the inductive method, with its laborious step-by-step approach, as incongruous with actual activities of scientists. He argues science has continually developed rational and general theories far more often than the inductive method should allow. Consequently, Popper replaces induction with the notion of falsification, where science continuously attempts to falsify general theories, and progresses through these efforts.

Critics of Popper, however, specify science is not limited to generalization of reality, but also provides practical knowledge of natural phenomena (O'Hear, 1989; Chalmers, 1990). The practical use of falsification is much less clear once generalized theories are removed as the goal. Moreover, falsification requires a testing process, and tests use inductive methods. This leads to a circular argument, or what Collins (1985) calls the experimenter's regress, where an experiment is dependent on a theory, and the theory is dependent on accurate experiments, which are, again, dependent on an accurate theory.

In the real world of science, efforts to create general theories have continued, and so too have inductive efforts to prove the truth or falsity of generalizations. But current theories and proofs have not escaped the intrinsic quandary; science is filled with examples where general theories are accepted and empirically proven, only later to be tossed out with the development of new general theories. This led Thomas Kuhn to suggest science progresses on the basis of new paradigms of scientific thought, not through falsification. He claims falsification is not frequently employed by the scientific community, for if it were, older scientific theories would be more readily rejected. Instead, Kuhn argues that once a paradigm of scientific thought becomes entrenched, analytic techniques and data are created in a positivistic approach to reaffirm the theory.

For Kuhn, science progresses from one paradigm to the next for more than scientific reasons; social and psychological factors must also be accounted. Such factors might include the motivations of individual scientists, the political and economic factors influencing funding sources to one project over another, or power structures within the scientific community itself. Because science is subjectively and culturally influenced, Kuhn and others (e.g. Feyerabend, 1975) reject the scientific distinction between observation and theory. Observations are traditionally used to uphold or reject a theory, but if observations are, themselves, subjectively and culturally influenced, then observations are not proper falsifying mechanisms. They are, in short, historically contingent (Manicas, 1987 p. 259-61).

It is now generally accepted within the philosophy of science that the traditional connection between observation and theory has been muted, if not dismantled altogether. But an additional problem faces scientists and philosophers of science. While the connection between observation and theory is problematic, an even more difficult problem arises when the existence of unobservable phenomena is considered. Any theory of unobservable phenomena, such as gravity, runs the risk of "underdetermination." This issue is not wholly modern. Berkeley criticized Newton on precisely this point. In addition, Hume's and Weber's criticisms of causal analysis, and their statements that reality is reducible only to empirical regularities, also are germane. The situation becomes even more murky when unobservables can be explained through more than one theory.

The development of positivism in science during the early part of the twentieth century was a reaction to these very problems. According to positivism, if any theory is to be practical, it must, by definition, be observable and verifiable. By contrast, scientific realists, such as Popper, argue unobservables are possible to comprehend, albeit with evidence that must necessarily be indirect. In this view, if a theory explains data more profoundly than any other framework -- what is called "the inference to the best explanation" -- then good reason exists to accept the theory. The general problem remains, however: theories based on inference to the best explanation are prone to overthrow.

In addition to the conundrum faced when previous theories and fact are overthrown, scientist face yet an additional problem. Since the time of the early scientists, science has presumed mathematics can be used to establish empirical truth. Both positivists and realists share that assumption. Yet, as shown in the scientific discoveries of the twentieth century, this match is often filled with "noise," and even chaos. Despite this, some authors, such as Lakatos (1978) and Chalmers (1990), argue scientific theories maintain value when general principles lead to active and productive research. Falsifications are merely aberrations to be ignored until a preponderance of evidence exists to overthrow the theory. Consequently, science still has room to work. Yet, others hold noise and the historical overthrow of scientific theories characterizes the limited utility of science.

At stake is whether twentieth century science outlaws the ability of science to provide an accurate picture of reality. In this regard, quantum mechanics inflicts the most serious damage. Where science traditionally employs realism, and views micro and macro physical phenomena as integrally related, quantum mechanics denies this relationship. While quantum theory does not preclude macro phenomena, nor macro stability, it nullifies a cohesive relationship between micro and macro phenomena. Thus, quantum mechanics undermines the validity of general scientific theories claiming a relationship between the two levels (Cushing and McMullin, 1989).

Two principle reactions to quantum mechanics and chaos exist in science. The first is from those authors who accept Bell's theorem (1964), which states determinate projections are incompatible with quantum mechanics. The second and more accepted notion, promulgated by authors of the Copenhagen school (e.g. Born, 1926), suggests micro phenomena is indeed unpredictable and cannot be used in direct predictions of macro. Nonetheless, studying macro phenomena remains a more definite process. Thus, the Copenhagen school suggests not all levels of reality may be equally understood. The best to be accomplished at the micro level is a sense of the probabilities involved (Cushing and McMullin, 1989 p. 2-6).

Inspired by the work of Bohm, later authors such as Humphreys, Railton, and Salmon have stretched science even further to escape from this dilemma (Salmon, 1989). Their work remains inductive (and ascendant) and asserts the proper scientific approach is to uncover hidden variables that can explain the micro level. One prime example of this approach is the wave/particle thesis, a widely accepted idea that at the sub-atomic level, phenomena is not made up of either a wave or particle, but is a duality of both. While this duality was hidden from earlier scientists, it remains theoretical with all of the problems inherent in the distinction between theory and observation. These problems are made even more difficult since particle/waves are both unobservable and unpredictable. In short, as Davidson (1976) argues, scientists are left with less than what their historical predecessors hoped for.

Others (e.g. Hempel, 1966) have taken a deductive (and descendent) position, asserting macro reality may be reduced for micro phenomena. This allows for a possible, if not perfect, description of micro reality. If terms can be made equivalent in both levels, micro phenomena can be reduced from their macro equivalents. It would be impossible of course to move from the micro to the macro because the quantum dilemma would halt any connection. To date, there is no scientific empirical proof to give credence to this proposal.

Thus, while the purpose of science is to initiate general theories with universal application, it has not reached that goal. Each major theory in science has been superseded or overthrown entirely, and quantum mechanics has sent philosophers of science back to old inductive and deductive paths. Finally, authors such as Kitcher (1989) argue for a modified unification theory, where less-than-perfect knowledge progresses by reducing the number of independent assumptions about reality. In this view, the explanatory power of generalized principles are maintained, despite the absence of a perfect picture of reality. Explanation, then, is transformed into a means only of classification and categorization of reality.

Describing the limits and dilemmas of philosophies of science is not meant to imply older or more recent theories have no value, or that empirical proofs be ignored. Even if Kuhn is right, paradigms, even if based on false ideas, can produce beneficial scientific findings, and it is still possible to account for good vs. bad scientific practices and methods.

However, it is equally true that twentieth century science requires foregoing the aim for universal truth, and recognizing that unifying micro and macro physical reality has become impossible. Even if science consents to a reality that is not perfectly attainable, probability is a dagger aimed squarely at the heart of unification. Whether one accepts the "frequency of an event" thesis, where repetition increases the probability of occurrence, or, as Popper has suggested, the "propensity theory", where repeated experiments or observations lead to statistical stability, the obstacle of probability, especially probability founded on observations, remains. Moreover, relegation to isolating probable relationships between one class of events and another class of events leaves scientists unsure, particularly at the micro level, that yet other classes of events do not influence the two being studied. In short, scientists and philosophers of science are looking squarely in the eyes of autonomy and contingency.

Time, Space, and Social Theory

What implications for social theory emerge from the scientific discoveries of the twentieth century? Before answering this question, it is legitimate to ask whether any implications should be drawn at all. While some theorists, such as Weber, insist a divide exists between scientific and social scientific research and issues, the first three chapters of this work reveal an overwhelming scientific influence on social theorists. Almost all have postulated theories in concert with, or as a reaction to, fundamental scientific discoveries of their time. Social science, itself, is inconceivable outside the parameters of Enlightenment science. Early social science debates revolved around controversies of empiricism, and quantifiable and value-free methods. While social science entered these discussions in the nineteenth and twentieth centuries, and were, therefore, late arrivals for scientific debates, the influence of science is irrefutable. And while direct relationships between science and social theory may, and indeed should, be questioned, the foundations of social science are plainly built from scientific discoveries. It is legitimate to ask, therefore, what twentieth century science means for social theory.

While social science came late to the classical scientific party, it has remained long after the party favors have been distributed. Science has, itself, moved far from the classical notions. The Newtonian views of gravity, time, and space have all been transcended, and the mechanical universe no longer exists. In its place, and founded on cumulative twentieth century scientific discoveries in areas of biology, geology, quantum mechanics, and astro-physics, is an expanding endorsement of contingency. At the micro level, a degree of unpredictability also must be included.

The philosophical and scientific legacy inherited by sociology maintained an inherent debate between rationalism and realism. Where the indictment theories have forcefully questioned rational universals, twentieth century science has undermined realism. Maintaining the realist notion that subject and object are mutually constituted is no longer tenable. Even at the physical level, quantum mechanics proves that micro and macro phenomena are autonomous. Philosophers of science are recognizing the implications of autonomy, and so too should social theorists.

One example of the potential influence of twentieth century science on social theory is in considerations of time and space, an area receiving growing attention from social theorists. Unfortunately, contemporary social theorists ignore contemporary science. What follows is a discussion of what a social theory of time and space might include if it seriously considered recent scientific discoveries.

From the review in this chapter, it should now be obvious that classical ideas of time and space have been undermined by scientific discoveries in the twentieth century. Notions of universal and absolute time, as well as the separation of time and space were abandoned after Einstein introduced the theory of relativity. In contrast to classical absolute time and space, relative time and space indicates observers moving in space carry their own sense of time, and although each observer comes to different conclusions, both are correct. This, of course, is the famous concept of curved space-time, but inherent in this revolutionary idea are daunting questions. Are time and space totally subjective and imaginary, and if they are, can time move forwards and backwards equally?

The classical scientific answer to these questions is no, and the traditional reason given for why time and motion are not imaginary rests in the second law of thermodynamics. The second law states that disorder, or entropy increases with time. This explains why mechanical devices break down, rather than fix themselves. If time were arbitrary and reversible, cars abandoned on the highway would run again rather than get towed away. The second law requires, then, that any ordered state will become more disordered in the future, and moreover, the more ordered a state, the more intense the rate of disorder. This disorder is absolutely essential for individuals. If time were reversible and totally imaginary, practical life as we know it would be unbearable. Thus, ironically, entropic disorder allows both for a practical grasp of reality, and the ability to take social action.

But a more contemporary view of space and time suggests that thermodynamics also must be seen in relation to dynamics. Dynamics is that branch of mechanics which addressing systemic motion, especially motion originated by forces outside the system under consideration. In dynamics, the aim is not to explain growing disorder, but to explain how systems move. Moreover, the theory of dynamics implies time is reversible and subjective, because absolute motion differs according to the frame of reference of the observer. This takes Newton's laws of motion, and Einstein's relativity into account, and the question arises: what is the relationship between entropic disorder and systems moving through space?

The answer is that entropic disorder brings causality to dynamics; motion no longer becomes totally relative because the second law requires systems move from order to disorder, the most probable state. However, causality is not the same as predictability. As discussed earlier in this chapter, biurfication of steady states is common in the physical world. That is, fluctuations at far-from-equilibrium states are both necessary for equilibrium, and can cause their change. While natural equilibrium exists and can be studied, some processes reach equilibrium and some do not; in either case, both predictable and nonpredictable factors help shape the formation. Moreover, while systems may become increasingly disordered, the form of disorder cannot be predetermined. In short, the second law of thermodynamic disorder allows the concept of contingent time and space to be applied to motion of systems. Obviously, large scale systems are created, exhibit motion, and are able to obtain a state of relative stability. However, their eventual movement is toward unpredictable disorder, often caused by fluctuations existing far from the system. All these factors may combine into a new relatively stable system.

Consequently, the notion of time has changed dramatically from Newton's absolute time. Instead, time now must be seen as containing relativity (time depends on where you are), contingency (it is impossible to predict the path or speed of disorder) and biurfication (even large scale systems may be created and/or changed by distant events). This combination of thermodynamic and dynamic time will be combined here and referred to as dynamic time. But the physics of time is only part of the equation.

A second form of time is human time. Human time is the subjective sense of passing through life, and includes not only an individual's sense of his/her own passage, but also includes both spatial and temporal relationships between individuals and others, as well as relationships between individuals and the course of external society. Human time, then, allows for a sense of history, but like dynamic time, cannot provide an inevitable direction for the future. Since human time is impossible with out the direction of entropy, human time and dynamic time are closely related. Moreover, since it remains impossible to predict how entropy and dynamic systems will interact, it is just as impossible to predict precisely when (time) and where (space) human beings and social systems will interact.

A third form of time is cosmological time. Whether or not the cosmos is expanding or contracting is at the root of cosmological time, and directly influences both dynamic and human time. Scientists postulate the universe began a period of rapid expansion after the "big bang", followed by a more stable period where expansion slowed. This slower expansion allowed for the creation of galaxies and solar systems. Nevertheless, while almost all physicists believe the slower universal expansion enabled life as we know it, the expansion has continued unabated. Continued expansion raises a troubling dilemma. Either the universe will continuously slow down due the force of gravity, or it will continue to expand at a rate allowing it to escape the force of gravity. Either choice yields calamity. If gravity is strong enough to end the expansion, then the universe will begin to contract, slowly at first, but eventually at unimaginable speeds. The inverse scenario is no less a predicament; if the universe escapes gravity and continually expands, the physical laws as we know them come to an end. Either way, life on earth eventually is doomed.

If one wishes not to contemplate that physical enigma, another, only slightly more imaginable, theory is available: why did the universe develop in the precise manner necessary for life in this galaxy and solar system? Despite the cataclysmic start, and unpredictable future, the universe created a relatively orderly and smooth formation allowing for the eventual creation of human beings. Of course religious beliefs come to the fore here, but my aim is far more mundane. Put simply, cosmologists now conclude humans live in a universe which accidentally developed in a manner temporarily capable of engendering life. Inherent to cosmological time, then, is substantial uncertainty and contingency, both in its past and for the future.

Several conclusions may be drawn form this discussion of time. First, dynamic time and human time are closely related; that is, the very development of disorder is what gives individuals a sense of time. Second, entropy cannot predict the relationship between the general tendency of disorder and dynamic systems (entropy cannot determine what the evolutionary form of disorder will be). Third, the form of time disorder is unpredictable not only because entropy itself is unpredictable, but also because human and dynamic time are not necessarily related to cosmological time. Cosmological time has its own form of time and is autonomous from dynamic and human time. The autonomy between human and dynamic time and cosmological time remains, even if the universe ends its expansion and begins to contract. In that case, the arrow of time will not simply reverse itself and repeat previous events. Instead, the cosmos will contract in new and different ways. Thus dynamic, human, and cosmological time will all remain pointed in the same direction (Hawking, 1988 p. 149-50). Nevertheless, dynamic and human time remain distinct from cosmological time. Separately and together the notion of contingency endures as a defining principle.

Once again, social theorists have ignored these ideas from science. As discussed earlier, it is legitimate to ask whether these findings of science should be incorporated in a discussion of social theory. But if it is reasonable to raise such an objection, it is also legitimate to reveal that social theorists already use science for assumptions about time. Unfortunately, these assumptions are grounded in an old science, now long out of date. While new explorations of time have recently appeared within social theory, the boundaries of discussion are closer to Newton's classical formulations than they are to the science of the twentieth century. In brief, the mistake repeatedly made by contemporary social theorists is three-fold. First, only human time is examined, with little or no discussion of dynamic or cosmological time (e.g. Kern, 1983). The second, and related mistake, is that human time is assumed equivalent to cosmological time. This is believed for the same reasons explored in previous chapters: first, social theorists retain their emphasis on social integration and thus cannot conceive of time as dynamic and contingent; and second, social theorists search for universal explanations and thus cannot conceive of human time as different from any other form of time including that of the cosmos. This results in social theory failing to see the various time paths that exist between micro and macro processes. Instead, social theorists view time and space as coincidental.

One social theorist who has consistently raised issues of time and space is Giddens (e.g. 1990). Giddens constructs a concept of time-space distanciation which describing general conditions in which time and space become humanly organized. He intentionally limits this concept to explain only the relation between what is present and absent. Like many of the concepts devised by Giddens (see Chapter Two), the concept of time-space distanciation is not meant as a path for universal knowledge, but rather is limited to a practical understanding of time and space by individuals, both in their everyday lives and in their relations with institutions.

Giddens argues that in premodern societies, time and space were directly connected, but with the advent of clocks, time and space became separated. Clocks require thinking about what can and cannot be done, or has or has not been accomplished. The social organization of time in modern societies furthers the separation between time and space. For example, premodern societies perceived place and space as equivalent. In modern societies however, distance is not only incorporated into subjective understanding of space, but individuals are additionally influenced by places far distant from their locale. The logic of technological social organizations, then, places distant events directly within the sphere of spatial relationships of individuals.

Modern forms of time-space distanciation also affect social relationships. Relationships are no longer purely local, and are structured along indefinite lines of time and space. To remain rational and socially integrated requires a high degree of trust in both social organizations and on more mundane levels, such as expecting electric lights to turn on at night. Since individuals are often far removed from events affecting them, and cannot absorb all the information necessary for both individual and societal well-being, trust is an essential ingredient for the continuation of society.

Giddens does suggest the outcome of trust is not predetermined. Contingency plays a role in trust, as what is expected is always at some risk. Contingency is also present because practical individuals continually evaluate levels of risk and may act to reform any practices they choose.

Giddens, then, disputes the postmodern view that anything beyond the locale is beyond comprehension. Rather, Giddens argues modern forms of time space distanciation change modernist definitions of time and space, but still may be conceived outside subjective location. This is accomplished by grasping the mutual creation of time space/relationships between micro and macro phenomena. His approach is, of course, an implosion, where individuals create time and space through interaction with particular institutions. Thus, repeating principles outlined throughout his theory (see Chapter 2), Giddens views time and space as not entirely beyond objective analysis, but maintains general definitions are impossible to perceive. Consequently, the relativism of postmodernism is replaced by a modified realism, where not all elements influencing time and space may be understood, but enough critical components are clarified through the implosion of subject and institutions.

The shortcoming of Giddens' analysis is its exclusive concentration on human time. When compared to dynamic and cosmological time, human time becomes a mere blink. In this light, humans have existed for a minuscule period of time. Moreover, while the analysis of modern time/space distanciation may be true, this is so only for human time and space (and the same may be said of the postmodern view of time and space). In contrast, cosmological time proceeds at a different rate than human time. At the time of the "big bang", events developed at unimaginable speeds, while the current formation of the cosmos, with its incremental expansion, proceeds at a painstakingly slow pace. Consequently, human time must not be conceived as the only form of time.

Giddens' work also ignores the notion of dynamic time. Since he believes practical individuals are capable of coming to an understanding of time, albeit based on trust and containing a certain level of uncertainty, he nevertheless argues a comprehendible connection exists between individuals and larger macro institutions. This is his implosion bias, a bias resulting in contemporaneous micro and macro time. Dynamic time implies, in contrast, that divisions and biurfications exist in time. While a subjectively coherent and practical apparatus for time may exist, this is not inevitable. It is also possible the postmodern description of disjointed junctures in time may be an accurate generalization for society. Leaving open the possibility that either approach may be right seems an appropriate idea. Implosion, however, leaves no openings.

Similar comments can be made about space. Human space may be viewed as changed in the modern era, but when viewed as part of cosmological space, changes in human space have trifling significance. Thus human time and space are not the only forms available. If other forms exist and develop independently of human forms, and if those forms have a potential influence on human forms, than the relationship between them requires investigation.

David Harvey (1990) also considers time and space, and views these concepts as basic human categories. Time is perceived alternately as providing a sense of security (e.g. birthdays and holidays), or conflict (e.g. use of resources for the short or long term), and may even trick the individual (e.g. time passes quickly when having fun). Despite the variety of time perceptions, social actors always see time as moving inexorably in one direction. Harvey asserts people believe the natural direction of time is linear.

For Harvey, however, time and space cannot be understood either by providing primacy to subjective concepts, or to its conditional development. Harvey suggests modern time and space relations are characterized by the rising importance of being, as opposed to the more long-term concern for becoming. To explain this idea he discusses time and space distanciation, the appropriation of space (different forms of

housing, land use etc.), the level of domination of space by the powerful, and a description of how new ideas of time and space are generated
(1990 p. 219-22). But even these conditional concepts are not enough,
for they must be placed in a broader situational context, and for Harvey, this means distinguishing the social relations of society. Social
relations do not determine time and space, but cannot be understood
without them. Following Gurvitch, Harvey suggests the relationship
between time and space and social relations can be understood through
an analysis of power (Harvey, 1990 p. 223-225).

Like postmodernists, Harvey is convinced the modern era has
made time and space subjectively confusing and disruptive, but insists
a logical explanation of disruption exists: the development of capitalism. He formulates the concept of time-space compression to describe
this process, where time and space are objectively and subjectively
compressed, life moves more quickly and spatial barriers are torn
down. Unlike pre-industrial societies, where distinct and isolated time
and space were possible, and unlike even the early stages of capitalism,
where it was still possible to place oneself in a particular time and
space, contemporary capitalism is characterized by international
spaces, a global reality, and the knowledge that speed and timing is all
important. Computer information and the management technique of
"just in time delivery" are but two of the examples cited. Long-term
planning is made difficult in this situation. Simultaneously, while the
world is shrinking in many ways, an ironic resurgence in the importance of locale emerges. With a global system of production and marketing, where businesses can locate wherever they choose, and in some
cases are required to locate production near consumption, the location
of capital becomes a series of local battles within each nation, with
region and locale in competition with each other.

The political ramifications of compressed time and space are immense. Local organizations may establish themselves in their locale,
but not over distances. Local groups and organizations may not, given
the general increase of the speed of life, even fully grasp distant developments. Yet what happens at a distance may well influence their locale. Within the context of time space compression, levels of political
access is a serious issue. At most, politics is viewed as a national event.
Yet, even assuming locales are thoroughly engaged in national politics,
which is almost never the case, national space is, itself, divorced from
global events influencing the nation. Establishing a United States of
Europe is a prime example. The intent of unifying Europe is to more
effectively compete economically and politically with Japan and the
United States of America. To support such an effort requires an under-

standing of economics and politics at the global scale. This is not an easy proposition at the local, regional and even national levels. To accomplish the unification will be a long and arduous process, where time space compression will have to be overcome continually.

Harvey, then, includes a clear autonomy between subjective and objective perceptions of time and space. At the subjective level, perceptions of time and space are confusing and compressed. At the macro level, the situational context of compression is the development of capitalism. Harvey, however, does not imply macro developments determine subjective perceptions. Instead, they are autonomous, and while they develop in relation to one another, no micro or macro determinism is present in his analysis. Instead, Harvey's analysis implies that space and time, as experienced by the individual, are different than space and time of large-scale structures. Although not specifically stated in his work, a contingent notion of human space and time is applied.

A third social theorist who develops a theory of time is Norbert Elias (1991). One of Elias' important ideas was that human beings accumulate knowledge through the generations. For Elias, time is a human conception. Without the ability to synthesize information, which is uniquely human, no need or utility for the notion of time exists. But time should not be conceived as an object. Rather time is a process, where humans, especially those living in modern societies, establish a frame of reference between two points to measure change. In order to measure time, humans created symbols (clocks, calendars etc.) so accurate they are granted an objective status (Mennell, 1989).

The objective status granted to human symbols of time is, for Elias, a serious mistake, one that has been repeatedly made by western philosophy. He argues that from Descartes to Kant to Heiddeger, time is seen as a universal form of consciousness, which individuals may use to order events (Mennell, 1989 p. 213). Elias asserts, by contrast, that time is neither universal or objective. Rather, time is a subjective process established by groups to evaluate past, present and future. Thus, time is a collective idea necessary for social integration, but must not be given objective status. Evident in these ideas is the notion of contingency. Each group collectively formulates its own conception of time. While Elias rejects subjective relativism, contingency remains.

The three theorists discussed all add important content in the social understanding of time and space. Giddens' time space distanciation, Harvey's time-space compression, and Elias' emphasis on the collective synthesis of time conceptions are important features in any discussion of the topic. Moreover, when taken together, their views fit

nicely as preliminary investigations into the concepts of autonomy and
contingency. Harvey is correct to point out that material structures have
an influence on the subjective notion of time and space. Elias is correct
to point out that the normative process integrating the collective formation of conceptual time must not be overlooked. And Giddens is
correct that the relationship between subjective and institutional space
and time must be analyzed.

However, the common error in these approaches is only an
analysis of human time is developed. On what basis do we believe any
of the theories postulated? Giddens' theory is implosion, where subjective time and space are mutually constituted with institutional forms of
time and space. An interesting idea, but why believe it? Harvey argues,
similar to descendent approaches, the development of capitalism influences, but does not determine, subjective time and space. An interesting theory but why believe it? And Elias argues, similar to ascendant
theories, all humans synthesize concepts of time in order to be integrated within a group. Here too, is an interesting theory, but why believe it? Moreover, all have allowed for different levels of autonomy
and contingency within their ideas. On what basis should we believe
the level chosen is the correct one? When limited to an analysis of human time and space, (either in the form of combinations of personal
time and space, collectively perceived times and space, or temporal and
spatial relationships between individuals, collective and societies) the
dual biases of rationalism and social cohesion are too often the result.

Like many contemporary theorists, Giddens, Harvey, and Elias
allow for some flexibility in their conceptions of time and space. However, failure to comprehend autonomy and contingency in other forms
beyond human time and space vastly diminishes the scope of the theories presented. This repeats the mistakes of their predecessors. For example, Marx, Weber, and Adam Smith gave preference to time over
space. Their concept of space remains relatively fixed and stable, a
product of human creation and changed by human actions. Foucault
(1972) observes space as a point where socialization and punishment
are inflicted, and to escape, individuals carve out spatial freedom. De
Certeau (1984) believes space is open to micro processes and is created
through social action. Bourdieu (1977) suggests space sets the context
for both groups and spatial structures, which, in turn, are created by,
and influence, the group.

These alternate explanations of spatial relations roughly follow
descendent, ascendant and implosion theories. Either space is conceived as an objective category and remains stable and fixed unless
changed by human endeavors (descendent); space is conceived as

nothing beyond the social creativity and actions of individuals (ascendant), or space is mutually constituted through micro and macro process (implosion). What is common to each explanation is that space is both rationally logical, and while it may change, is contemporaneously and humanly constructed at micro and macro levels. Positioning humans as dominant over space, and accepting space as a rational and humanly created phenomena neglects both the importance of space as it exists outside of human control, as well as its development external to human action. Once again, these biases lead to an ignorance of contingency.

What is missing form these analyses is a recognition of contingency based not only in the difficulty of making universal assumptions, but in recognizing that time and space are variable, not only in human relations, but as they exist external to human beings. Without the physical laws of thermodynamics, human time is inconceivable. A human life, itself, follows this law. Humans are born in relatively orderly states and begin the process of physical disorder that eventually brings death. Moreover, without the second law of thermodynamics, time becomes irrelevant and human thoughts about space and time are mute. Finally, without the development of cosmological time, human life, itself, would be impossible. As ecological theory instructs, this is human arrogance at its height. Human time and space must be viewed in relation to physical properties and to the ecosystem. And when that is done, subjective and collective time and space are no longer linear, but curved and independently observed. To explain temporal and spatial relations, then, requires consideration of all three forms of time and space. They must be seen as both autonomous and contingently related. Discussions concentrated only on the human aspects of time and space will always be based on philosophical assumptions and, as such, will be found lacking.

The evidence for contingency and autonomy, then, is not found solely within the realm of human perception and constructions. Rather, contingency and autonomy is also found outside the realm of purely human endeavor. In short, the paths of human, dynamic, and cosmological space and time are distinct. They may, or may not be, in harmony, may or may not be conflictual, and may or may not influence social formations, natural ecosystems, or the general development of the cosmos.

Accepting autonomy and contingency as general principles does not repeat the mistakes of so many contemporary social theories. Instead of accepting a set of assumptions, the aim of contingency theory is to allow for all possibilities. To that end, the most reasonable application of the current discussion is to perceive human time and space, like dynamic and cosmological time space, internally and externally autonomous and contingent. That is, individuals and groups absorb and create time and space differently, and so too do institutions, regions, social formations, and global formations. Moreover, the various combinations are further related to dynamic and cosmological time and space.

The particular social time and space paths generated, then, are neither inevitably cohesive or deconstructed. Rather, they are contingent and based on the specific characteristics of the micro and macro processes that generate them, and to the development of nature. Finally, it reasonably follows contingency theory accepts as a fundamental principle that micro and macro social processes move along autonomous and contingent time and space paths.

This is not to deny the compelling analyses by theorists of human time and space. Each highlights important aspects of human time and space, subjective time and space, collective time and space, and societal time and space. Moreover, each of these elements may be thought of as autonomous. However, subjective perceptions of time and space are simply not the same as collective perceptions, and neither are equivalent to societal time and space. Each develops along different time and space paths. Taking cues from the theorists discussed above, material, normative, and subjective time and space must be seen in relation to each other, but not as if they consume identical time and spaces. No other avenue is present to arrive at the dynamic between them, and it is the autonomously derived dynamic that allows for each, and all combined, to be revealed.

Conclusions

How, then, should these findings be related to social analysis in general? To begin with, like all scientific discoveries, twentieth-century science is only descriptive of physical regularities, empirical findings, and technological effects. Moreover, science has been more productive at the micro level than the macro, where general theories are continuously overthrown and transcended. Despite prodigious time, money, and practical results, scientific discoveries cannot sufficiently explain how people perceive or are affected by nature, nor explain the social aspects of human society. As such, it is justifiable to contend social science is at least as relevant and essential to humankind. If science not only undergoes change, but is related to both macro political and economic developments, and in any case is variably perceived by people, then no reason exists to grant science its current lofty intellectual position. Understanding the development of society, and vital social issues such as war and poverty, may well be equally useful to humankind, for example, as developments in health sciences.

Nevertheless, twentieth-century scientific notions of contingency, autonomy of micro and macro physical phenomena, curved time and space, and the contradiction between rationalist and realist viewpoints and physical realities, all must be synthesized with the other findings of this work. What is clear is that the issues of autonomy and contingency have replaced the older universal principles founded in classical science. In the words of Nobel-prize winning biologist Jacques Monod (1972), "We would like to think ourselves necessary, inevitable, ordained for all eternity. All religions, nearly all philosophies, and even parts of science testify to the unwearying, heroic effort of mankind desperately denying its own contingency."

While the transcendence of old scientific assumptions proves nothing about social reality, it raises questions about social theories fundamentally influenced by classical scientific ideas. In short, new science shakes the foundations of every classical social theory and ascendant, descendant and implosion versions of micro/macro syntheses. Classical scientific notions of realism, where micro and macro phenomena are inherently related and cohesive, have been undermined, and scientific universals are now mute. Autonomy and contingency are the new watchwords. Even chance has emerged in a variety of arts and sciences, including sociology (Manis and Meltzer, 1994). As a result, the scientific and philosophical ideas that were borne from early science, and in turn, begot social theory's fixation with ideas of social integration and universal assumptions, are gone. It is time these theoretical boundaries be eclipsed. Authors that come closest to doing so are discussed in the next chapter.

Chapter Five

Contingent Clues in Non-Traditional Social Theory

Four central lessons can be gleaned from the previous discussions. First, one primary emphasis in social thought must be dropped: the obsession with social cohesion between micro and macro levels. The enlightenment legacy of explaining the social world in rational and universal ways has historically monopolized micro and macro social analysis. At the micro level, phenomenology suggests people make sense out of the social world, exchange theory argues people rationally engage in economic and psychological cost/benefit choices, symbolic interaction asserts individuals rationally interpret social interaction, and rational choice theory is, by definition, a rational process.

For their part, macro theories also conduct a rational, logical, explanation of social reality and development. In their effort to construct rational, universal explanations of reality, macro theories construct a societal vision that is either knowable in its realism (e.g. Marx) or reduce the importance of the individual actor (e.g. structural functionalism, and the orthodox version of Marxism). In either case, society is viewed as a comprehendible, logical social apparatus that at its core is a coherent social order.

These rationalist and realist positions no longer prove adequate in social analysis. Rather than social order and integration, the ordinary state of social affairs between micro and macro processes is contingent. This message has been correctly criticized by the indictment theories of postmodernism, feminist theory and ecological theory, and through the scientific discoveries of twentieth century. The indictment theories and contemporary science highlight how much social and physical reality has been excluded by maintaining the enlightenment paradigm. At the social level, much of the analysis is irrelevant for pressing social issues. Applying social theory has become an exercise in abstraction, or mere description with little regard for theory at all. If social integration between micro and macro is eliminated as the theoretical exemplar, social theorists would find themselves in the thick of society, with much to investigate and much to offer.

Second, the rationalist and realist interpretations of social order and integration have led to a misunderstanding of time and space. Many social theorists still operate on the classical scientific assumption of universal time and space. While new ideas discussed in this chapter suggest time and space are altered in the postmodern era, most theorists ignore what contemporary science has shown: time and space is curved, variable, and contingent. This error grounds the mistakes made by contemporary micro/macro integrationists: ascendant theorists argue rational individuals can contemporaneously construct macro structures; descendent theorists maintain that rationally organized structures contemporaneously influence individuals; and implosion theorists assert a modified realism which states micro and macro are mutually instantiated in time. In place of these errors, social analysis must transcend enlightenment universals and grasp the notion of various time and space paths. If accepted, variable time and space will allow theorists to view micro and macro phenomena autonomously, and generate forms of social analysis extending far beyond traditional efforts.

Moreover, accepting notions of autonomous and contingent time and space requires neither micro or macro theorists give up what they hold most dear: a belief their area of inquiry is a legitimate and fruitful exploration of reality. No inherent contradiction exists between micro and macro theorists, nor the inductive and deductive methods springing from their suppositions. Predilections aimed at explaining everything are the only concessions needed. Imperialist attacks on opposing theories give the impression that social thought is hopelessly variable, wrought with ideology, and the softest of the sciences.

Third, the enlightenment conception of human relationships to nature also must be transcended. While social theorists construct various accounts of natural processes, social analysis has absorbed the enlightenment impulse to assume human domination over nature, if nature is considered at all. This is a serious mistake, and has led to a confusion over the very definition of the concept of structure. It is a common truism that structure means whatever theorists want it to mean. Structures are variably defined as a group, an aggregate pattern, a social institution, a political and/or economic process, or as a world system. Part of this confusion stems from the belief that macro structures are integrally human, and natural processes are dominated through these structures. Nothing could be further from the truth. Natural processes, such as global warming, the ozone layer, and pollution, etc., suggest humans interrelate with ecological processes in an intimate way, and nature provides the necessary elements allowing people to be social.

The enlightenment, then, granted supernatural characteristics to social structures, and this allowed social scientists to redefine the origin and implications of structures. With structures celebrated in this way, it becomes impossible to see the autonomy and contingency of micro and macro processes. If, however, structures are viewed as humanly created, but as mediating and contingent elements between people and nature, structures become explicable. They can be evaluated not only in relation to micro processes, but in relation to nature. This elementary lesson from ecological theory must be embraced by social theorists.

And fourth, the lack of understanding of contingency has led social theory to ignore and misinterpret pressing social concerns. One example is social inequality. Explanations of inequality have many faces in social theory. Macro theorists variously claim inequality is due to individual talents and activities as actors function relative to social structures (e.g. structural functionalism), as a result of political economic developments (e.g. Marxism), and as a result of social position (e.g. network theory). Contemporary descendent theorists repeat this explanation, although giving some flexibility to micro processes (e.g. neofunctionalists). Micro theorists present inequality as a result of individual processes, either as a set of subjective rational choices, or exchanges, or aggregate actions, often accompanied by differential access to available resources. Ascendant theories repeat the formula, commonly attributing macro patterns to aggregated social actions. Implosion theorists see inequality as a consequence of structural and individual processes that fold into one another. Here individuals both are responsible for inequality patterns the potential to change them, at least in an aggregated way.

However, if autonomous and contingent micro and macro phenomena are viewed over variable time and space paths, a far different explanation of inequality becomes possible. Inequality remains the consequence of both micro and macro phenomena, but unlike ascendant, descendent and implosion notions, both macro and micro sources of inequality are analyzed separately. Once again, neither micro or macro need abandon their perspectives. The micro processes influencing inequality, including rational decisions, social constructions of reality, and symbolic interpretations, will maintain their inherent theoretical and concrete explanatory power. Simultaneously, macro analyses of inequality, both as a function of the system, and as a result of political and economic developments, may also be included. All that is eliminated is the effort to differentiate micro from macro assumptions, and macro from micro assumptions.

The concepts of autonomy and contingency, then, will have potential practical and political applicability. Currently, no contemporary explanation fully explains autonomous micro and macro sources for growing inequality in societies like the United Sates. Nor are their explanations for why sociology, which by definition should shepherd any discussion of these matters, has yielded such an avalanche of description, but dearth of explanation.

However, the immediate task at hand is not merely to reiterate the need for autonomy and contingency in social theory, but to begin the search for pivotal elements which illustrate how contingent and autonomous micro processes relate to contingent and autonomous macro processes. The discussion that follows investigates social theories which consider this relationship, even if only in limited ways.

Systems Theory

Partly as a consequence of postmodernism, a number of theorists are accommodating contingent autonomy within their frameworks. While some theorists already discussed (e.g. Alexander and Habermas from the descendent approach, and Coleman from the ascendant approach) provide some autonomy for various aspects of micro and/or macro phenomena, or for general societal development (e.g. Giddens), the theorists discussed below straightforwardly include autonomy in their work. It will become obvious, however, that autonomy between micro and macro phenomena is not equivalent to contingency. Autonomy implies separation between and within levels of analysis, and the authors discussed below open the possibility that sectors do contain independent development. However, they uniformly do not concede contingency. Contingency implies not only that autonomy exists between and within levels, but no universal or integrated explanation can scientifically predict social outcomes. By not accepting, or ignoring the notion of contingency, these theorists have eliminated the power of indictment theories, and the scientific findings and philosophical discussions of the twentieth century. Nevertheless, as autonomy is a central feature of their theories, these social theorists uncover and explore important areas missed by descendent, ascendant, and implosion theorists.

Of all current social theories, autonomy is most seriously addressed in systems theory. As such, and given the continued assent of enlightenment principles within sociology, it is not surprising that systems theory was exported into social theory after developing as a hybrid of natural and other social sciences. The foundational disciplines of systems theory include cybernetics, information theory, and economics (Ritzer, 1992 p. 517). Systems theory is opposed to any division of micro and macro phenomena, but unlike the ascendant, descendent, and implosion integration theories, system theory searches for the relational development between levels of reality. Nonetheless, systems theory maintains the rationality and coherence of dynamically changing social systems (Buckley, 1967; Ball, 1978).

How, then, can a theory simultaneously assert autonomy between micro and macro processes, and claim system cohesiveness? To begin with, systems theorists conceive social systems as increasingly complex elements and processes, all related to the physical world (e.g. Buckley, 1967). This leads some systems theorists, such as Luhmann (1987), to assert a functional primacy of collective phenomena over micro processes, especially since macro structures are judged more resistant to change, and individuals react to system needs. Despite the domination of collective, almost biological, system needs for preservation, the future of collective structures is not wholly predictable (Schwab, 1989). Moreover, patterned after cybernetics, system theorists allow for feedback between and within systems, where each may have an influence on the other. This combination of feedback, coupled with an overall system logic, allows for autonomy and social integration.

Systems theory, then, begins where fractured theories end. Where fractured theories divided micro from macro and had difficulty in explaining both levels, systems theories emphatically oppose that division and grant some measure of autonomy to micro and macro. Perhaps the best example of an autonomous systems is found in the work of Margaret Archer. In her book, *Culture and Agency: the Place of Culture in Social Theory,* Archer devises a clear autonomy between micro and macro level processes. She believes autonomy is warranted because micro and macro processes do not co-exist in time. For example, within the system of culture, the main focus of her book, cultural structures are perceived as predating agency, and thus the cultural system predates any actions that develop within it. Moreover, culture, itself, must be seen as autonomous from other structures, and viewed in this light, analysts may examine what is often left in the dark: the interplay between the two main levels (Archer, 1988 p. ix-xxv).

To analyze the interplay between macro and micro processes of culture, Archer makes a distinction between the cultural system (macro) and socio-cultural processes (micro). The interplay is uncovered first by analyzing each of the two levels, and then examining the contradictory or complimentary relations between them. Contradictory or complimentary relations provide social actors situational contexts from which to act, or do nothing. Thus while Archer's theory allows for autonomy between levels, and some flexibility for actors, a systemic structural logic exists. When an attempt is made to alter the macro cultural logic, a process of change is enacted, especially when the shift is also contradictory to the micro socio-cultural process, (Archer, 1988 p. 103-105).

Archer, then, opposes the traditional aim of explaining social cohesion between micro and macro levels. In her view, the mistake of granting primacy to social integration requires theorists to interpret culture as a manifestation of either the cultural system, or social action. This ignores the possibility for inconsistencies and contradiction within and between the two levels, and this means social change is never made clear.

To reveal autonomous relations of levels, Archer offers several proposals about cultural development. 1. The macro cultural system exhibits "logical" relations between its components. 2. The cultural system also generates "causal" influences on the micro socio-cultural level. 3. Causal relationships also exist between groups and individuals at the socio-cultural level. 4. Socio-cultural activity modifies the logical relationships existing within the cultural system, and therefore, generates reforms or changes at the system level. (Archer, 1988 p. 106).

Central to the analysis, Archer delineates logical cultural systems, and the micro causal relationships they create. As a systems theorist, Archer sees cultural systems not only as autonomous from micro processes, but as part of a systemic logic discrete from micro influence. She concludes from this both that objective relations may exist without people's knowledge, and that invariant logical analysis may be used to uncover the dynamic of system components. The cultural system, then, while humanly originated, develops an objective existence that can influence social actors. There is, she argues, no other explanation for the fact micro processes contain a higher degree of variability than macro processes (Archer, 1988 p. 108).

This is Archer's relief from the philosophical choices of rationalism, relativism, and realism, choices at the root of most contemporary social theory. She wants to allow for autonomy, contradiction and inconsistency, especially at the micro level, so rationalism must be eliminated. Simultaneously, she wants to avoid relativism, so she pronounces an analytic coherence of the logical cultural system. Moreover, since micro and macro are autonomous, realism provides no help. In sum, the cultural system is logical and the sociocultural level is causal. This allows Archer to have both autonomous creativity and a logical system to analyze.

Both advantages and disadvantages of systems theory are evident in Archer's analysis. The main advantage is autonomy allows systems theorists to analytically separate levels. The disadvantage is that by viewing overall systems as objective entities, the micro capacity to generate independent social action, and the multitude of processes that combine at the micro level, are diminished. Despite the autonomy, and allowance for contradictions and inconsistencies in Archer's framework, the situational context is nonetheless omnipresent. Consequently, micro responses to objective conditions are conceded in Archer's work, but internal micro processes are given short shrift. The underplay of micro processes is a common problem among system theorists. In Archer's work, for example, the objective system, as well as situational responses to it, are analyzed in useful detail, but since social actors may have variable responses to situational contexts that are not determined by systemic conditions, micro responses become inexplicable. But on what basis should we assume the macro system sets logical parameters for micro responses, or that a higher degree of variability exists at the micro level? A quick perusal of the Sunday papers show many of the structures of the social world in upheaval.

Archer further asserts power resides in the micro socio-cultural level, where ideas are imposed and challenged. Groups play meaningful roles and mediate between the socio-cultural and cultural realms, and yet are shaped by both. While this is a complex process, systemic objective conditions designate micro ideas consistent or inconsistent with the cultural logic. Powerful interests attempt to influence the process, but cannot be guaranteed of their success. One advantage available to powerful groups is that logical structures are often hidden from social actors. This often enables the powerful to manipulate the sociocultural realm in effective ways. Archer also acknowledges that segments of the elite may also embrace ideas contradictory to cultural structures, and this can ignite a cultural debate among the powerful (Archer, 1988 p. 187-217). Thus, possibilities for cultural change reside in the socio-cultural level, where old and new ideas are defended and attacked by both the elite and other groups in society.

In Archer's view, then, ideological struggles, whether complimentary with or contradictory to the logic of the cultural system, contain both a micro causal element and a logical structural element. The two levels of struggle are not identical, however. The macro can profoundly influence micro cultural processes, but micro processes have limited influence on the structural logic: when micro struggles are complimentary or contradictory to the cultural structures, new ideologies are developed within the socio-cultural level, but always either compliment or never engage the cultural system. In either case, the unfolding dynamic, according to Archer, cannot be analytically deduced because it is causal, not logical. The result of micro socio-cultural processes, therefore, is contingent, but never seriously threatens a rational, logical understanding of the overall system.

Archer also recognizes that while culture is her focus, it is insufficient to portray culture in isolation. Culture, itself, is penetrated by other material structures. Moreover, social action is relative to both material resources, interests and power, and to cultural ideas and beliefs. Material social groups which initiate ideas find themselves in the cultural milieu described above, and are forced to account for that situational logic. A social give-and-take evolves, where material and/or cultural groups may be in opposition, agreement, or outmoded. Archer sees these micro material and cultural processes, once again, as contingent, with neither pre-determined as dominant. When in concert, the two can provide the basis for long-tern societal stability. When the relationship is unstable and even contradictory, material social groups will explore the logical cultural system for major weaknesses, if any exist, and attempt to exploit them. Thus, cultural development has its own importance in the process, autonomous from material structural development. Even when change emerges, the old cultural system plays a role in what is accepted and rejected for change (Archer, 1988 p. 282-300).

When either cultural or material systems undergo change, and the other remains stagnant, the unchanged system acts to brake, but not eliminate, change in the other. Moreover, cultural and material system change involves social actors who may have status in both sectors. Consequently, change in one sector influences the structures of the other. At the micro level, then, social groups crisscross looking for allies and affiliations, sometimes temporarily creating odd alliances. This endless maze of socio-cultural and micro material interaction ends when some dominant group gains control over the situation, and the process starts anew.

Taken as a whole, several notions developed by Archer seem problematic. The source of these problems rest in the assumptions of systems theory. First, on what grounds is macro to be considered logically objective and micro causally contingent? Systems theorists seem to want to accept indictment theories, and the new scientific notion that much of the world is contingent, but are unable to escape the rational legacy of the past. They simply refuse to yield the idea that general societies are beyond rational universals. The systems theory solution is to give up what is least important to them: micro processes. These are tossed off as contingent and inexplicable, and they are left with what they always wanted, to talk about rational, logical systems.

By designating micro processes as causal and contingent, systems theorists assign the messy, human concept of power to the micro level, where it receives little attention. By contrast, structures are viewed more objectively. People may act on, or react to, structures, but these are evidently logical, not social, structures. However, no empirical evidence exists for assuming the logical nature of structures. Moreover, if ecological theory is accepted, these social structures are not as macro as systems theorists believe. Social structures, instead, should be viewed as mediating structures that mediate differences between humans and natural processes. In this light, mediating social structures lose much of their logical allure. It may be worthwhile for systems theorists to consider natural processes as logical, and micro and macro human processes as causal, but even this would both deny the scientific findings of the twentieth century and force systems theorists to move away from the logical scientific method they have inherited from the enlightenment legacy.

If social structures include human beings as full, active participants, then the objective, logical structures envisioned by systems theory is eliminated. Social actors and groups must not be relegated to only micro activity. While it is true not all actors may equally participate in structural activity (and Archer explains this is mistake of many micro and implosion theorists), it is also true that structural change is both autonomous and contingent, and creates unintended consequences. As such, it becomes unnecessary to claim, as Archer does, the capacity to transform structures is logically independent of the power of agents (1989, Chapter). The systems theory view of structures, as part of a larger, independent logic, is both theoretically and empirically indefensible. The ability to manipulate structures is the very definition of power correctly supplied by many macro theorists, and is at the core of their productive empirical work.

Nevertheless, system theories at least entertain a modified notion of autonomy and contingency, something beyond most social theories. Moreover, Archer's work is a fascinating, perhaps groundbreaking, analysis of the complimentary and contradictory systems of culture. Systems theorists are right to grant autonomy to structures, but are wrong when they give structures philosophical and methodological primacy.

Neo-Marxist Autonomy and Contingency

One area Archer cited as significant, but left unexplored, is the dynamic between material micro and macro processes. This has traditionally been the domain of Marxists, and some Neo-Marxists have seriously taken autonomy into account. Marx's own work (see Chapter One) included a level autonomy between macro productive forces and micro relations. However, for Marx, the developing forces of production provide a causal link to the relations of production, and set parameters for social activity. Neo-Marxists have revised some aspects of Marx's historical materialism, and allot various levels of autonomy.

Claus Offe (1972, 1976) adopted a systems theory approach to Marxist questions. He sees the macro level as divided into three main compartments: the economic system, the political-administrative system, and the normative/legitimating system. In modern late capitalism, the political-administrative system increasingly dominates society. Offe asserts the traditional Marxist concern for class struggle is misplaced in the modern nation-state. Instead, the politics of inequality and power is amplified, regardless of economic forces and relations between people. The state, not the economy, sets the parameters for social struggle, for the state can reach into areas of social life beyond economic relations.

Offe suggests the political-administrative rise to dominance explains why many modern social struggles focus on issues of democracy, not purely economic interests. The interest groups leading these political movements are inconceivable outside the democratic, capitalist state. The concept of class remains compelling, but modern economic classes may be revealed in relation to political structures, and non-economic interest groups also must be considered. Moreover, inequality is explained in political, not economic terms. For Offe, those suffering from inequality are not simply exploited economically, but lack ability to influence political events.

Like other system theorists, Offe allows for crises to emerge within the overall system, and crises heighten awareness at lower level subsystems. Crises are endemic because in late capitalism maintenance of the general system is evermore dependent on the political and normative systems. The elite need these systems to exercise power, but also need to ensure subsystems do not become autonomous. Subsystem autonomy has the potential to generate a general crisis. Thus the state must play two roles simultaneously: it provides its own political and normative justification to gain popular support, all the while protecting elite interests. When economic structures misfire and the state must act directly in favor of the elite, popular support becomes increasingly difficult to maintain.

Two mistakes of systems theory are repeated within the work of Offe. First, while elements of the general system are given some autonomy, they also are seen as conditional and objective. As such, a rational and logical explanation for the general system is provided, in this case, by granting primacy to the political apparatus. Second, once a logical and objective description of the system is authorized, little choice exists but to diminish the importance of micro level activity. Social action, then, is not emphasized and made dependent on the overall development of the system.

A similar problem emerges in the work of G. A. Cohen (1982). Again, as a Neo-Marxist, he is concerned with the link between forces and relations of production, but like Offe, diverges from classical and orthodox Marxism. In Cohen's view, the primacy of the forces of production, at the heart of classical Marxism, must be abandoned. Instead, Cohen speculates that humans are at least somewhat rational, try to improve their reality, and operate in a framework of scarcity. This setting gives rise to relatively autonomous social actions and creates structures of social production. The material question for Cohen, as was the cultural question for Archer, is to uncover the consistency or inconsistency between the forces and relations of production. Cohen claims, moreover, this methodology can uncover both material and nonmaterial developments. Nonetheless, as in Archer's work, social action is relegated to the micro level, and while, for Cohen, macro forces of production are not granted primacy, they are still supplied an objective status.

Ernesto LaClau (1985, 1990) develops the Neo-Marxist argument toward similar conclusions. Relationships between forces and relations of production is one worthy problem area, he argues, but the struggle between social groups and classes is not identical to an objectified process. While contradictions may emerge between objective micro and macro elements, Marxists are wrong to assume class struggle inevitably emerges. LaClau argues social actions are not determined by ab-

stract definitions of social forces or relations. Instead, and again similar to Archer's non-Marxist approach, LaClau calls struggle between
social groups antagonisms, and is careful to point out antagonisms do
not fit neatly into predetermined logical contradictions. Moreover, antagonisms may or may not be between social classes, and may occur
outside the framework of the relations of production (Laclau 1990 p. 6-
16).

Social activity, then, only can be complimentary or antagonistic,
and once antagonisms are established, objectivity necessarily comes to
a halt. Objectivity ends because antagonisms transcend logical conclusions derived from contradictions between objectified relations and
forces of production. Consequently, while forces and relations of production are theoretically objective, antagonisms are concretely contingent (Laclau, 1990 p. 17-18). Social actors, therefore, are autonomous
from social structures, yet act within the situational context structures
provide. Actors influence structures, but only to the extent that actions
are complimentary or contradictory to structural development.

As in Archer, then, Laclau relegates social activity to the more
micro field of antagonisms. And like Archer, power is initiated as a
micro process. Moreover, Laclau suggests power develops within the
non-material sphere of social life. Groups vie for power to objectify
their positions in the non-material sphere, but since this can never be
completely realized, weaknesses are displayed and antagonisms are
sparked. This process is not void of objective or even material conditions; the more contradictory the objective conditions, the more antagonisms likely will develop. However, objective contradictions
remain separate from, and do not determine, the form of non-material
micro antagonisms. Autonomous micro, non-material, antagonisms are
contingent (Laclau, 1985 p. 122-45).

Another Neo-Marxist attempt to include a notion of autonomy
can be found in the work of E.P. Thompson. Like other Neo-Marxists,
Thompson pays deference to the concept of class, but extends his
analysis beyond this single element. Here again, class is seen as an objective relation, but has no direct connection to class consciousness or
social action. Thus, consciousness and social activity follow no universal prescription. Although class-oriented activity should not be ignored,
neither should subjective responses to both economic and non-
economic factors. Concrete experiences, then, become a critical element in Thompson's analysis (Eley, 1990).

Thompson does not totally ignore or deny the facts of political
economic development. Political-economic development has an obvious influence on other macro phenomena and on subjective individu-

als. The influence, however, is not deterministic. Other macro phenomena, as well as social actions, are autonomous from political and economic developments, and in turn, must be included in any analysis of economic systems. In this context, culture and ideology have an autonomous logic and development, and the economic sectors of society are, in some ways, irreducibly social. Thus, it is conceivable that subordinates may become stronger proponents of capitalism than elites (Wood, 1990).

A final example of Neo-Marxist autonomy is contained in the concept of "dominant ideologies" suggested by Abercrombie, Hill and Turner (1990). Like other Neo-Marxists, these theorists suggest that economics, while playing a significant role in the development of ideology, must not be granted determinist qualities. The role of culture is elevated and equated with ideology, and autonomous from the economic structures. Rejecting the notion of false consciousness, and that social actors ideologically are led astray by a dominant class, these theorists see the role of ideology as critical for the dominant, but not the subordinate, class. A primary reason for limiting the role of ideology to the dominant class is the existence of autonomy and contingency: the connections between economics, culture, and social action are contingent and beyond universal application. No single set of ideas, then, are applicable to all sectors of society, and moreover, no ideology is necessarily aligned to particular economic and social systems. Capitalism, the authors argue, is compatible with various forms of ideology, ranging from liberalism to state regulation of economies. As this is the case, cultural autonomy is necessary to establish specific belief systems to correspond to contingent social formations (Turner, 1990 p. 229-40).

Autonomous structures, culture, and ideology, then, may have various forms at various times. Individualism, for example, was traditionally aligned with the development of capitalism, but in the era of late capitalism the two have drifted apart. And while social order is of concern to Abercrombie, et. al., a common culture is seen not as a requirement for social order, only as a possibility. Even a coherent dominant class culture is not required. All that is indispensable for social order is the continuation of a materialist reality compelling individuals to work to maintain their existence, and which "binds them to the social order." This is not a purely negative relationship, as most workers in capitalist countries view their society as superior to those of other countries and social systems. Social actors, therefore, have the capacity to gain a practical knowledge of their surroundings (Turner, 1990 p. 240-252).

Once again the notion of contingency suggested by Abercrombie, et. al. is in a limited form. By maintaining the notion of social cohesion as a key feature of social analysis, the exploration of contradictions and inconsistencies existing within structures, and between structures and social actors, is qualified.

In summary, Neo-Marxists certainly propel the issue of autonomy to the forefront of theory. All see the need to do so because of the particular history of Marxism. Marx and the classical era of Marxism did not fully articulate the connection between political-economic contradictions and social action. Each of the neo-Marxists cited were responding as much to the development of Stalinist orthodox interpretations of Marxist economics and to poststructuralist Marxism (see Chapter 2) as to Marx himself (see Chapter 1). All want to release various aspects of social life from economic determination. Offe divides macro phenomena into three elements and places the political-administration of society above economics; Cohen divides economic from non-economic aspects and asserts that the economic factors have no primacy; Laclau and Thompson separate social action from objective conditions; and Abercrombie et. al. suggest culture and ideology are autonomous sectors of society. Each theorist also pointedly reduces the importance of class struggle, because such struggles are viewed within Marxist orthodoxy as predominantly economic activities.

Another common feature among Neo-Marxists, except for Thompson, is macro level objectivity. This is ironic since much of the intent of neo-Marxism is to eliminate determinism. Offe, Cohen, Laclau and Abercrombie et. al., while providing more flexibility to micro phenomena than found in Marxist orthodoxy or poststructuralism, nevertheless maintain an objective status for structures. Offe simply selects politics instead of economics as the dominant macro element, and while granting autonomy and thus more opportunity for micro social action, his systems theory approach requires a conditional status for the general system. Cohen, while granting social action more importance in the development of the forces and relations of production, nevertheless searches for consistency and inconsistencies between micro activity and what already exists at the macro level. While Cohen denies economics a deterministic primacy, it remains conditional nevertheless. In both Offe and Cohen, micro activity is restrained by these conditional propositions.

Laclau's theory contains similar themes. Once again economics loses its conditional primacy over social activity, but Laclau asserts social activity may not be viewed logically since it is beyond objectivity. Similar to Archer, Laclau argues social action is simply complimentary or antagonistic to objective conditions. The process of social action, itself, is beyond such logical determinations. Thus macro phenomena may not be purely economic in Laclau's view, but the situational context of objective conditions remain. For Laclau, macro is objective, but not deterministic, and social action is micro and beyond the pale. And while Abercrombie, et. al. release culture and ideology from any economic base, social cohesion is maintained as a condition of society. While other sectors of society may be autonomous, Abercrombie, et. al. are analytically forced to find a common denominator for social integration. Their answer is economics, albeit promoted by the social actors themselves.

Thompson's approach is different than the others. Like Laclau, Thompson sees the forces and relations of production as objective categories, but unlike Laclau, Thompson does not relegate social actions to purely micro phenomena responding to the situational context. For Thompson, social action can maintain, reform, or create the situational context. In order to allow for this, Thompson must draw distinctions between material and nonmaterial society, allow for micro activity to influence nonmaterial structures, and allow for nonmaterial structures to influence material structures. Each has a logic of its own and defies universal explanations. While logical categories of objective material life may be uncovered, it is impossible to predict subjective material and nonmaterial experiences. And since micro responses to these experiences may influence macro phenomena, neither micro nor macro is subject to any universal laws of history. What is evident in Thompson is not only autonomy, which characterizes many of the theorists in this chapter, but also an element of general contingency, where more than micro social action is contingent. Instead, the entire relationship between autonomous micro and macro processes proceeds towards contingent results.

Of all the theorists discussed in this chapter, Thompson's work most directly incorporates the concepts of autonomy and contingency. Thompson, of course, is an historian, not a sociologist. Leaving aside any discussion of that coincidence, another field outside the realm of sociology deserves attention. That field is philosophical hermeneutics.

Hermeneutic Autonomy and Contingency

Another field of inquiry grappling with issues of autonomy is hermeneutics. According to Gadamer (e.g. 1984), who is primarily responsible for its contemporary revival, hermeneutics tries to grasp the

meaning of the present and past, as well as meanings subjectively difficult to understand. Subjective comprehension is made difficult either
because of false understandings or ideology. The goal of hermeneutics,
then, is to investigate genuine interpretive processes.

Hermenuetic theory contends not only that the past is genuinely
knowable, but that presumptions about the past can be avoided.
Moreover, the genuine past can be uncovered through an intellectual
process of the present. To believe otherwise makes the connection between the past and present logically impossible, and renders history a
waste of time (Jameson, 1988 p. 150-51). An individual interpreting
meanings of the present and past, however, immediately faces mi-
cro/macro issues: Does the individual interpret micro or macro phenomena, or both?

Each of the hermeneutic authors reviewed below deal with these
issues in one form or another. Gadamer's primary concern is to establish the hermeneutic experience of individuals. To do so, he provides
both a macro and micro level description of individual experience. At
the macro level, experience is derived from cultural meanings influencing the individual. Cultural meanings are continually in flux and represent a mass of enormous proportions. Particular meanings may be
grounded within one stable segment of the fluctuating mass, but no
universal direction or generalized logic exists. History, then, is constituted in the various meanings derived from, and affected by, various
cultural meanings. Thus a rational interpretation of history and society
is feasible, but is construed from unique meanings which are, themselves, derived from a contingent fluctuating mass. Gadamer's contingent macro process requires a dismissal of both universal explanations
of history, and descendent explanations where cultural meanings are
objectively self-evident to individuals (Schwab, 1989; Shapiro and
Sica, 1984 p. 4-7).

At the micro level, individuals respond to the meanings presented.
This is partly an internal, subjective process, but also a hermeneutic
process, where individuals respond to historically specific meanings,
mediated by the process of hermeneutics. This hermeneutic understanding is a rational process, but is far more limited than ascendant versions
of micro rational activity. In hermeneutic understanding, a rational
process takes place, but individuals are incapable of creating historical
and fluctuating macro meanings that set parameters for interpretation.
Only limited command is available to individuals. Although hermeneutic processes can yield a historical consciousness and lead to a rational socio-political unity, such unity is not predetermined. Consequently, macro normative properties of meanings may or may not

exist, and individuals may or may not come to understand them. If objective normative properties do emerge, Gadamer believes individuals will make the effort to interpret their meanings, because this is what all rational individuals strive for. (Schwab, 1989 p. xxvii-xviii).

In Gadamer, then, the hermeneutic process moves full circle. Objective meanings are contingent, but individuals are able to rationally strive for subjective meanings, and this in turn, leads to both objective understanding and the possibility of micro influences on macro meanings. What holds the entire process together is the inherent rationality of subjective individuals.

Another hermeneutic effort is proposed by Ricoeur (e.g. 1981), whose ideas differ greatly from Gadamer. Ricoeur discounts all objective reality, even if hermeneutically created. Instead, the emphasis is placed solely on subjective meanings found in everyday existence. But these subjective meanings are derived from more than purely internal processes; interpreting cultural symbols is also used in micro perception. Thus, cultural symbols represent both micro and structural elements. The apparent contradiction between denying objective reality but allowing for structural elements causes no problem for Ricouer, because his interest is restricted to how symbols are used by individuals, not their source.

For Ricoeur, locating the source of cultural meanings is wasteful because they remain hidden from individuals (Frank, 1989 p. xxix-xxxi). Instead, cultural symbols are subjectively encountered as mediating elements between individuals and larger situational contexts; symbols reflect some part of the cultural milieu, but are also constituted by the individual. Consequently, while meanings are admittedly established through a combination of macro and micro forces, they are useful only at the micro level, where individuals gain a sense of self and generate social activity. Social action, then, is neither left to subjective whim, nor objectively determined (Frank, 1989). In sum, rational individuals hermeneutically gain knowledge of rationally created symbols (Schwab, 1989).

A third example of hermeneutics is the work of Manfred Frank (1989). Unlike Ricouer, Frank asserts signs and symbols are initiated by structures. However, the structural constitution of symbols requires meaning to become subjectively known. Consequently, micro and macro processes of interpretation are inherently related; without micro interpretation of symbols, no reason exists for their structural creation. Nevertheless, while subjective interpretation springs from external sources, the subjective process is a threat to the order exhibited in structures.

Taken as a whole, autonomy and contingency are central features in hermeneutic efforts. The discussion of these concepts, however, is limited by the theoretical frameworks created. Gadamer wishes to avoid the pitfalls of descendent theories which eliminate the hermeneutic project. Thus he allows for some level of contingency by denying a universal logic within cultural meanings. Instead, culture is considered a fluctuating mass. But if culture independently fluctuates, this crimps micro social activity, in this case by limiting the hermeneutic influence on macro processes. Individuals, no matter how rational, cannot influence that which has no logic.

Ricouer and Frank represent two different versions of implosion theories, although the element of contingency does peak from under Frank's theoretical constructs. First, Ricouer denies objective reality and replaces it with an implosion between culture and individuals, where meanings act as a mediating force. While this allows for an analysis of social activity, it, like many implosion theories, requires the macro structures to be beyond subjective reach. Frank's work also exhibits implosion, although structures are accounted for. Individuals are knowledgeable about structures and culture because of the structural and cultural meanings that they fasten. Thus, Frank's hermeneutic process requires that micro and macro phenomena be mutually instantiated. Contingency has a limited role, as meanings help shape both micro and macro, but are not determined by either.

Nevertheless, the concepts of autonomy and contingency are not fully explored by the hermeneutic effort. Instead, hermeneutics' main purpose is to highlight symbolic understanding, a substantial and often-ignored aspect of individual and social life. Symbolic understanding does require rational individuals, but why should this aspect of subjective perception be given primacy? If symbolic understanding was accepted as one of many areas worthy of exploration, a different hermeneutic agenda could be visualized. If it was unnecessary to defend symbolic understanding from structural attacks, hermeneutic inquires might allow structures to maintain an inherent quality worthy of investigation. To do so, once again, requires that micro and macro been viewed autonomously, and if neither has primacy, their interrelationship must be contingent.

One theorist who combines elements of hermeneutics, postmodernism, and Marxism, and articulates a theory of autonomy is Jameson (e.g., 1988). He includes the hermeneutic emphasis on cultural meanings and interpretation, the postmodern notion of deconstructed reality, and combines both with a reformed Marxist concept of the mode of production. Following the hermeneutic and postmodern efforts,

Jameson concludes that contemporary capitalism has dissolved into varied cultural forms. However, a logic exists within this development, one construed and financed by the dominant class (Jameson, 1984). Thus, for Jameson, the postmodern reality is beyond neither analysis, nor rational social action. While not all members of society may engage in rational social action, or rationally comprehend contemporary cultural forms, the dominant class does both.

Jameson's framework is a unique effort at synthesizing three theoretical programs, but how, then, are the issues of micro and macro phenomena, as well as autonomy and contingency resolved? Jameson's solution is to hearken back to Marx, who showed the mode of production contains not only elements of the present, but both the past and future possibilities. Granting individuals the capacity for symbolic interpretations of the past and present stages of history challenges the traditional dichotomy between individuals and social structures; temporal interpretations of the mode of production depict the past, present, and future in confrontational and dynamic ways. The past, present, and future, then, become available to individuals, and moreover, individuals realize social actions taken or not taken are vital to the future complexion of the mode of production (Jameson, 1988 172-77).

Of all the approaches discussed in this chapter, Jameson most clearly points out both autonomous relationships between micro and macro phenomena, and the contingent nature of social development. Moreover, he explores ways in which the two levels dynamically relate. Jameson's main concern nevertheless rests primarily with subjective interpretation, and this leads him to make assumptions about the rational ability of individuals to interpret historical development. While he concurs postmodern deconstruction is due to elite aims and efforts, he simultaneously believes rational individuals will come to interpret and gain a meaningful understanding of this process on their own (Jameson, 1988 p. 208). There seems to be no imperative to believe individuals will do so.

Jameson accepts autonomy, but it is in a rationally comprehendible form. Macro phenomena is historically and presently separate from individuals, but through rational understanding, individuals can make sense of, and act on, structures. Jameson also accepts contingency, but again it is rational. The interrelationship between micro and macro does lead to alternate results, but historical diversity is confined to rational elites creating rational structures, to which potentially rational individuals either act, or do not. Within this context, history is not truly contingent; it is controlled at the structural level, and mistake-prone at the micro level.

Conclusions

Either overtly or unconsciously, issues of autonomy and contingency have crept into much of contemporary social analysis. Systems
theory, neo-Marxism and hermeneutics all have wrestled with these
issues, albeit for distinct reasons. What is clear, however, is that each
approach considers autonomy, and occasionally contingency, as secondary, not primary concerns. Consequently, each proposal maintains
either a micro or macro form of rationalism. As such, all three approaches skirt the fundamental transcendence required of social theory.
In response to universal theorems that suppress their special areas of
interest, these authors entertain autonomy between levels. But clinging
to rationalism, they are reluctant to take the additional step of recognizing contingency. In sum, these approaches have not seized upon, or
have ignored, both indictment theories and developments in twentieth
century science. Instead of unpredictable contingency, these authors
continually posit either micro or macro phenomena as objective, and/or
logical, and/or causal, all within a rational process. Depending on the
chosen point of interest, other levels, or sectors within levels, are ignored or made vague.

Nevertheless, potent lessons for autonomy and contingency can
be inferred from these varied theories. First is the notion that micro and
macro processes, and sectors within each, may be complimentary or
antagonistic. This is a fundamental step forward from fractured micro
and macro theories, and improves ascendant, descendent and implosion
theories of integration. The mistake in the latter, is the continual search
for social cohesion. In ascendant theories, aggregate social actions create social cohesion. In descendent theories, social structures create the
situational context for social integration. And in implosion theories,
social integration is mutually constituted through codeterminous micro
and macro processes. The recognition that micro and macro processes
may generate either social cohesion, or antagonisms, is a necessary step
for a contingency theory.

A second valuable guideline offered by several theorists is to
separate material from non-material processes, and to see both sectors
containing micro and macro processes. Often, however, even among
many theorists who include some degree of autonomy, either micro or
macro, or material, or nonmaterial processes are given primacy and/or
objective status. The chosen area is then crowned more valuable for
analysis. This is nonsensical, unless a theorist wishes to establish what
he/she has already predetermined. Contingency, however, implies that
neither material or non-material realms, nor micro or macro processes

within them, may be accurately forecast. Instead, internal and external complimentaries or antagonisms must be investigated without a priori conclusions.

A third important point illustrated in this chapter is the concern for the issue of power. Power becomes a necessary element when complimentarities and antagonisms are accepted concepts. It is simply impossible to establish the contingent level of social integration without revealing the empirical level of power in society. Power itself must be viewed as contingent. It may exist in any or all of the micro and macro, material, and non-material levels. This contingent notion of power has been uniformly ignored or misunderstood in social theory. Power has been objectified through structural and descendent analysis, seen only as a micro process in micro and ascendant theories, or viewed as a result of both in implosion theories. This is wrong. Power is contingent and may exist in any of these or other forms, but will never be uncovered as long as universal and rational assumptions replace an exploration of the complimentarity and antagonisms of power.

This raises a fourth important notion: the fundamental role of empirical investigations. Any theory which directs what will be found in empirical applications nullifies the research effort. While theory inevitably relates to research, battles over accurate descriptions of reality belong as much, if not more, within bodies of research, as theoretical articulations. Instead, contemporary theoreticians engage in endless confrontations with other theoreticians, where the ammunition is faithful assumptions. Sociology is left with the spectacle of theorists dueling other theorists on the basis of theory. Unless a pious stance toward theoretical assumptions is adopted, along with shutting out indictment theories and twentieth century science, it becomes obvious that theory can never foretell empirical reality. Unfortunately, this practice is so common that researchers either divorce themselves from theory entirely, or fill libraries and bookstore shelves with research governed by theoretical assumptions. Contingency demands, however, that theory be constructed as a useful tool for uncovering contingent relationships, not a decree for empirical reality.

This does not mean that social inquiry must revert back to empiricism. Empiricism asserts the concatenation of empirical events is open to rational, universal explanations. This, as has been discussed, is impossible. What is possible is to develop theoretical models which aid in uncovering contingent empirical reality. No ultimate closure to these revelations exist, not only because micro and macro interrelationships are so complex, but also because they change over time. It is hopeless, then, for any rational, universal theory to prove its assumptions in reality. It simply cannot be done.

At the very best, a provincial relationship between universal assumptions and empirical reality may be uncovered, but such relationships are not equivalent to all social reality. Since it is misguided, social theory should end its internal search for one true theory of social action and/or structure. The solution to the social action and structure dilemma within sociology will be found in empirical studies modeled after a theory that is useful for asking the right questions, but is unassuming about what the answers are. The prospect of limiting theory to a model applicable to contingent relationships will require theorists to limit both the scope and import of their theories. This may well cause a noticeable level of dissonance in the social psychology of social theorists. Some will see the contingent approach as lacking and argue that the problem with autonomy is the infinite number of factors that may be included in both micro and macro analysis, and an infinite number of theories corresponding to the selection of factors. But this is precisely what it means to abandon universal objectivity and rationalism. Moreover, this does not mean social theory is limited to relativism. Rather, advancements in knowledge of reality can take place by building theoretical models which are ever-more precise guides to empirical investigations, and in turn, allowing empirical investigations to influence theoretical models. In this way, theory and research can build a body of knowledge that is both explanatory of social reality, and continually open to question and debate.

Contingency does not hamper social theory; it places it squarely where it belongs: enmeshed in the social reality of the day. This places sociological practice, as well as methodology, not only on an equal footing with social theory, but necessarily integrated into its development. If this proposal were adopted, sociology could expect heated disputes over the legitimacy of theoretical models as proper tools for empirical analysis, and over the relative accuracy and significance of specific empirical findings. In short, sociologists would begin to behave like social scientists.

Taken as a whole, a contingent theory must include a nondeterministic exploration of complimentary and antagonistic elements existing within and between micro and macro processes of material and nonmaterial sectors. In this exploration, power must be accounted for. The general aim of contingency theory is to provide a non-determining model for empirical analysis that will allow its own development to be shaped by what is found within empirical findings. If this is done, social theorists and researchers, I believe, will inevitably find themselves participating in the most fundamental and critical issues of the day. If, however, sociological theories continue the rationalism and universal effort that is the legacy of the past, the discipline may well be in jeopardy.

But this is merely a sketch of what such a model must include. These issues must be more formally analyzed and presented. Before some conclusions may be drawn, however, one additional area concerned with issues of autonomy and contingency, this time directed purely at the level of the individual, must be explored. A discussion of psychological and social psychological principles as they relate to autonomy and contingency follows.

Chapter Six

Contingent Clues in Psychology and Social Psychology

As in other aspects of social relations, the desire to uncover laws of social cohesion has led micro theorists to misconstrue the relationship between individuals and groups. The goal of social cohesion, coupled with the U.S. emphasis on individuals, often have led micro theorists to view collectives as little more than grouped individuals. Routinely, social theorists simply apply theoretical assumptions to the activities of people and groups, all within the context of searching for keys to social order. However, if social integration is screened as an overriding principle, and findings are sifted through that screen, valuable findings and data appear. From this process, a picture of autonomy and contingency emerges at the individual and group level (Greenwood, 1991).

Any investigation into micro level contingency must begin by acknowledging that individuals and collectives are two distinct entities and processes; individual processes are not the same as collective processes. The two disciplines that separately impart autonomy to individuals and collectives, and must be accounted for in the formation of a contingent social theory, are psychology and social psychology. The association between these disciplines and social theory has a long, but often distorted, history in social thought. Most social theories have simply usurped some principles of psychology and/or social psychology to further accepted ideas. For some contemporary examples, Giddens uses concepts of trust and security, Collins selects emotional motivation, and Alexander's choice is borrowed from exchange theory's use of behavioral psychology. However, there seems no rhyme nor reason for these selections, except that they fit nicely into a particular set of assumptions. Psychology and social psychology must be viewed differently. Each must be given credit and investigated on its own merits.

The first task is to differentiate between the two disciplines. Psychology is the study of human behavior and the forces influencing that behavior. The primary focus is on the subjective individual. Psychology includes the study of physical and social processes of memory, sense perception, language, emotions and drives, motivations, conflicts, personality development, and environmental conditioning of behavior. Social psychology, by contrast, focuses on subjective behavior and how it is influenced by the behavior of others. Social psychology focuses on the social perception of others, and attitudes including prejudice and discrimination, conformity, aggression, cooperation, and group behavior. Obviously, it is beyond the scope of this work to analyze the entire breadth of these disciplines. Instead, the focus will be on areas adding to the body of knowledge necessary for a contingent social theory.

Psychology

Nothing inherent within psychology dictates the separation of subject and object, yet, like in philosophy, the separation exists. Biological, behavioral, and cognitive schools of psychology all study individuals removed, for the most part, from general objective conditions. This is not so much a matter of granting intentional autonomy to the individual, as it is a lack of interest in macro processes. While psychological theories have come under increasing criticism for purely individualistic explanations (e.g. Senn, 1989), and have reformulated contemporary theories to include both individual and environmental factors (e.g. Werner et al. 1988; Stokols, 1988), the subjective individual remains entrenched as the main focus.

Psychology traces its roots to the first laboratory experiment conducted by William Wundt in the late 19th century. Swayed by the scientific method and physiology, Wundt developed rudimentary physical experiments to test for conscious reactions by his subjects. Conducting tests and using the subject's own analysis was called introspection, and was further developed by William James (1890), whose psychology was based on his interpretation of the stream of consciousness. James argued, however, introspection could not lead to universal discoveries because one stream of consciousness is different from all others. From its beginnings, then, psychology accepted some degree of autonomy for individuals.

Psychology came to accept subjective autonomy partly because of the influence of early biology and the belief that human development was akin to evolutionary adaptation. This meant human introspection and consciousness must be distinct from the environment to enable humans to adapt to their environmental surroundings. And as John Dewey (1922, p.313) argued, this gives humans a degree of freedom and dominance over their surroundings. However, subjective autonomy did not mean early psychologists argued for contingency. Instead, they argued universal principles of psychological development were discoverable, and could provide clues for constructive adaptation. Their aim was to reduce social disorder.

Sigmund Freud (1963) altered previous psychological assumptions, by rejecting both behavioral recall through introspection, and streams of consciousness based on previous experiences. Instead, Freud argued the cause of behavior, especially mental disorders, was the dynamic unconscious. Unconsciousness is repressed and cannot be recalled by normal processes, he claimed. These assumptions led Freud to hypothesize about human drives and personality, and while later psychoanalysts, such as Adler (1931) and Jung (1972) disagreed with particulars of Freud's ideas, they accepted the general methodology. What is common in psychoanalysis is an interest in the unconscious, which not only is methodologically separated from the study of macro conditions, but is separated as well from the very consciousness of the individual. Once again, the goal was to bring conscious recognition to unconscious disorders, thereby enabling individuals to choose socially constructive goals.

Autonomy, then, is an inherent component of psychoanalysis. The concept of the unconscious requires that autonomy be granted. However, once again, autonomy is not accompanied by contingency. Freud and later psychoanalysts have continually searched for universal principles to uncover the physical and evolutionary laws of human development.

Thus, in these early applications of psychology, a rigid concept of the subjective individual is present. Whether the individual is considered capable of analyzing subjective feelings as little more than pragmatic instruments in the pursuit of constructive societal adaptation, or as unable even to recognize their own emotional disorders, the study of individuals apart from macro processes in which emotions and pragmatic decisions are made became an inveterate psychological principle. However, autonomy is also entrenched. By consistently pointing to the uniqueness of psychological processes, and individuals as worthy of investigation, early psychologists infused individuals with autonomy.

The separation of micro and macro phenomena also was evident in the behaviorist school. Founded by Watson (1930) and carried on by Skinner (1974), behaviorists suggest psychology should examine behavior, not consciousness. Modeled after natural sciences, behaviorists study individual behavior as it responds to varied stimuli, and attempt to explain, and even predict, natural human behavior. Skinner believed individuals search for, conceptualize, and categorize objects only to give an appropriate response to stimuli. While Skinner does not totally rule out mental activity, he rejects the "mysterious" realm called the mind. Instead, behaviorism asserts only a selection of various positively and negatively reinforced environments are available to individuals. The root of subjective feelings, then, is not found within subjective mental activity, but rather in the environments where individuals exist.

Part of the explanation for the behavioral emphasis on the environment also should be seen within the context of the nature vs. nurture debate. Those stressing nature believed evolution meant human beings were influenced by genetic heredity. Those proclaiming nurture asserted individuals were influenced by their environment. The nurture perspective allows for two possibilities. Either humans have the ability to adapt to, and even control their environment, or environments determine individuals. Behaviorism chose the later. Thus where the early psychologists and psychoanalysts grant autonomy to individuals, behaviorists grant autonomy to environments surrounding the individual.

This debate over the source of individual behavior is similar to micro/macro issues within sociology. On the one hand, early psychological research was geared toward understanding individual feelings, and used autonomous self-description as the basis for findings. By contrast, behaviorists argue varied immediate environments set parameters for behavior. However, neither approach considers contingency. For example, including a variety of environmental factors does not deter behaviorists from the belief that adequate control of the environment can lead to the control of human behavior. Behaviorists hope to uncover laws that will allow for the control of conditions, not grant them contingency.

In opposition to behaviorism, an early effort to study psychological phenomena as a continuing process emerged. The Gestalt school (e.g. Kohler, 1947) allowed for introspection and consciousness, but argued these elements are merely internal influences. External influences also exist, and when the two are combined the entire context of the whole individual is made clear. Gestalt psychology rejects behaviorism on the grounds that general, not local, patterns of stimuli are central to understanding behavior. These patterns are based on facts, both experiential facts gained from inner life, and external facts perceived outside the self. That is, individuals first perceive the external world as a whole, and then form categories in order to make sense out of the external reality. Gestalt psychology, then, rejects the behaviorist method of isolating independent stimuli because it underplays both the general influence of environments, and the individual process necessary for categorization. In short, Gestalt psychology allows for a dialectic between individuals and their environments; people can emit stimuli which give rise to perceptual facts, and stimuli from outside sources have the potential to influence subjective perception.

The most prevalent psychological school in the modern era, the Cognitive school (e.g. Criak, 1952, Latsky, 1980), also stresses categorizing environmental stimuli. This school attempts to combine both the stimulus-response method of behaviorists with the Gestalt emphasis on holistic entities. Cognitive psychologists assert humans actively process information and seek diverse forms of knowledge. For the Cognitive school, emotions are conscious experiences, and may result from an interrelated series of biological and environmental factors synthesized within the mental process. The synthesis occurs as a result of the ability of senses to perceive the environment, and the physiological capability to send sense impulses to the brain for interpretation. The result is behavior.

Once again the autonomy of individuals is reaffirmed in Cognitive psychology. In this case, processing information is seen as separate from, and not determined by, the environment. However, as in other psychological perspectives, the aim is not to understand the contingent nature of these processes, but to unlock universal explanations common to all humans. Contingency is not considered as a possibility.

The purpose of this discussion is not to select one method of psychology over all others. Indeed, by limiting their explorations to the level of the individual, all psychological perspectives may be criticized. However, it is worth noting that all schools of psychological thought overtly or covertly contain elements of autonomy. For that reason alone, psychological discoveries are worth discussing, but that is not the only reason. If micro and macro levels are to be seen as autonomous, disciplines concentrated on the individual are as critical for the formation of a theory of contingency as any other area. Although psychology may be flawed by ignoring macro influences on individuals, these theories are more than worthy of exploration.

One area of psychological study ignored by most social theorists is the influence of physiology on behavior. While sociobiologists (e.g. Wilson, 1975) have attempted to analyze the consequence of genetic makeup and evolutionary "inclusive fitness" to explain human behavior, most psychologists have targeted their analysis on the functioning of the brain (e.g. Kagan et. al., 1984) The brain is seen as the main storage and distribution center for various physical components and processes affecting behavior. Humans have brains larger than other species, containing ten billion interconnected nerve cells called neurons. The brain acts as the control center for a host of physical needs and processes. However, the brain, specifically the cerebral cortex, is responsible not only for physiological needs, but for the processes of memory, and thinking and planning, often referred to as consciousness.

All sense perception is transmitted to the cortex for analysis, interpretation, and possible action. To accomplish this task, neurons flash back and forth through untold billions of pathways available in the brain. Neurons contain both a sending and receiving mechanism. When ignited, an electrical impulse carries a message that travels from the neuron sender through its length to its receiver end. Between neurons lie synapses, which are intermediaries between neurons. Sometimes synapses are activated by the electrical impulse of the neuron, but more often by the chemical release of neurotransmitters, which are released by the neuron and flow across the synapse to the next neuron. The chemicals contain messages which instruct the next neuron to either fire or refrain from activity. Even more amazing, any given synapse is in close proximity to as many as several thousand neurons, all sending and receiving messages. Thus whether or not a neuron fires depends not on a single message but on a pattern of messages.

The patterns developing within the brain are not universal. While common physical processes exist within human brains for memory, communication, etc., no two people develop patterns of neuron firings in exactly the same way. One of the best examples of this process rests in the often-cited "two sides of the brain" theory. The brain is divided into two hemispheres; the left side of the brain controls the right side of the body, and the right side of the brain controls the left side of the body. Moreover, each side displays important and distinct functions. The left side of the brain specializes in individual items of information, reasoning, and logic. The right side specializes in analyzing things as a whole and is more adept for spatial, musical and intuitive functions. But people do not utilize either side in isolation. The two sides are connected by the corpus callosum, which allows messages to pass back and forth in individualized patterns.

Contingency evidently is involved in the brain process. Individuals do not transmit message patterns flowing through the brain in precisely the same way, or have equivalent levels of cooperation between the left and right sides of the brain, nor even which side they favor. All of this is contingent and no universal principles can establish this process for all human beings. The same is true for memory. Memory is the process of storing, sorting and retrieving of messages. If a synapse is activated continuously, it is thought to become more efficient, and thus the pathway becomes easier to activate. Moreover, new synapses may emerge between neurons forming new connections. Why and how this actually takes place remains undiscovered, but the process is unique to each individual. Individuals associate long strands of items in association with one another, but what is remembered is not an exact copy of what was happening at the time. Instead, only the process of memory is remembered. The same is true for loss of memory. Various theories exist about memory loss: the pathway falls out of use, a failure in the retrieval process, interference from other information stored, and the notion that old information gets in the way of the new. What is common is that memory and memory loss differs from individual to individual.

Contingency also plays a role in language. While the ability to learn languages appears universal in human beings, the brain processes have a direct influence over language (Chomsky, 1972). Speaking and writing requires recalling stored memories. Without this ability language is impossible. The same is true of concepts, which are rough approximations of similar or different objects or ideas. These concepts make it possible to develop categories at various layers, and this both greatly simplifies the process of language, and makes it more flexible (Smith and Medin, 1981). Language, concepts, and categories allow for the possibility of problem solving. Again, individual differences are abundant.

A similar contingency exists in emotions. Cognitive psychologists suggest that emotions have both an environmental and internal origin. Individuals collect information about the environment through messages sent to the brain from the senses. The brain interprets this information through its memory. Patterns of nervous brain energy affect the general nervous system and create bodily changes, which in turn send messages to the brain. Thus emotions are created through a combination of environmental and physical factors. It should not be surprising, then, that different levels of emotional activity will be generated, even when the environmental factors are exactly the same. The sensitivity of the nervous system and the size and activity of the endocrine glands cause individual differences in all people (Izard, 1977). A similar combination of environmental and physical factors influence the human drives. For example, hunger is a combination of brain activity, messages sent from other parts of the body including the liver, but also the influence of the sight and smell of food, eating habits, and cultural mores.

Finally, personality development is seen by psychologists as a total pattern of thought, feelings and behavior that constitutes an individual's relationship to the environment (Hall and Lindzey, 1978). Whether based on Freudian theory, humanistic theories, or social learning theories, all perspectives believe a common core personality exists among human beings, but through individualized development each person develops a distinct personality. While a variety of explanations are available as to why some individuals are not only distinct, but develop personality problems, such as anxiety and stress, individual differences remain.

The essential message from psychology, then, is that a great deal of difference exists between each person. This is true both at the physiological level, and at the level of consciousness. However, these findings have not led psychologists to concentrate on, or even include, contingent analysis. By contrast, psychologists have sought universal explanations for behavior. Like social theory, psychology has been highly influenced by pre-twentieth-century science, and has searched for universal laws of human behavior. Their hope has been to use such laws to generate social integration and social order. Thus, despite the abundance of contingent evidence accumulated through the study of the brain, language, emotions, and the personality, psychology remains plagued by old ideas and beliefs. This sets the stage for the continual overthrow of new universal assumptions. Promoting human behavior and psychological problems as logical and comprehendible may have a practical payoff for practitioners, but advances neither an understanding of general behavior nor social theory.

While psychological commonalities do exist among human beings, the process of individual development results from a variety of factors and possibilities. Psychological research, itself, tells us this must be so. Put in the vernacular of social theory, the micro level of individual behavior is both an autonomous and contingent process. This is an important fact that must be realized in social theory, but the micro level is not enough. Social theorists have long argued, correctly I believe, that it is impossible to theorize about the individual in isolation. For the purposes of this chapter it is necessary to investigate the relationship between individuals and groups. That is the intellectual domain of social psychology.

Social Psychology

Social psychology also spent the early part of its history trying to develop universal laws to explain social behavior (Allport, 1968). Patterned after scientific studies, social psychologists in the beginning of the twentieth century employed the scientific method in search of lawlike statements. By the 1930s, however, some social psychologists concluded social behavior is influenced by a variety of factors (e.g. Sherif, 1935; Lewin, 1939). While this did not eliminate generalized theories, new concepts and theories began to hint at contingency. For example, social psychologists have studied the varied influences of external conditions, such as heat, noise and crowding, and their diverse influence on behavior. Nonetheless, the traditional view of social psychology has been to examine individuals as they interact within groups, and to search, primarily, for reasons and causes of social integration. Again, a theory of contingency and autonomy between micro and macro processes cannot accept this traditional approach. Nevertheless, social psychology contains important elements relating to the topic at hand.

One of the areas discussed within social psychology is attitudes (e.g. Bem, 1970; Bandura, 1976). When individuals generate a cluster of beliefs around a person, group, object or idea, and it is relatively long-lasting, an attitude is created. The emphasis on social integration has led social psychologists to discuss such items as conditioning as causes of attitude development, but they also entertain concepts of attitude-discrepant behavior and cognitive dissonance (e.g. Wicklund and Brehm, 1976). Cognitive dissonance suggests that human beings dislike inconsistency both between various beliefs held, and between beliefs and behavior. Often, individuals will either alter beliefs and attitudes to be consistent with their behavior, or reevaluate their beliefs as more appealing and denigrate the alternative not taken. Moreover, when individuals are required to change attitudes to be consistent with some behavior, they take the path of least resistance. That is, individuals will change attitudes which are cognitively least resistant to change. Even in the face of dissonance, then, attitudes and beliefs are not easily changed.

Other powerful influences exist that discourage people from changing attitudes. First, if individuals place a high value on personal freedom, any person or group trying to change an attitude may be viewed as a threat to that freedom. Second, if individuals have advanced knowledge of a particular subject and already have formulated an attitude toward that subject, individuals are less likely to change their minds. In part, this is true because counterarguments have already been categorized. And finally, if counterarguments to an established attitude are presented weakly, then later counterarguments, even if more powerfully presented, have less influence over attitudinal change.

The social psychological explanation of attitudes and dissonance can add important elements to a theory of contingency. Above all, the process of attitude development is seen as both an individual and a group process. Because they are autonomous, the dynamic between the two may be uncovered by investigating each process and by allowing for a variety of results. Moreover, autonomous individual and group processes may then be distinguished from, and analyzed in relation to, macro processes. A contingent social psychology would add vital insights to current micro and macro searches for universal laws. For example, the systems theory of culture as suggested by Archer (Chapter Five), could be made all the more powerful if these principles were included. Archer's insistence on including consistency or inconsistency when describing the relationship between the cultural system (macro) and the socio-cultural process (micro) would no longer be based on assumptions, but would have a micro and empirical basis. Unfortunately, Archer's systems theory claims the micro process is causally created from the macro, and is, therefore, inexplicable. By contrast, a contingent theory must accept the autonomous existence of both micro and macro to search for their dynamic relationship. This requires, moreover, that either inconsistency or social integration may exist in micro and macro levels.

Another important area discussed by social psychologists is conformity and obedience (e.g. Wheeler et al, 1978). Conformity appears when individuals alter behavior to be consistent with generally accepted ideas and beliefs. Individuals tend to conform when a group is subjectively seen as influential, when the group is relatively small, when more than one influential group holds similar beliefs, and when individuals have no allies in support of alternative positions. Individuals may also comply with requests of others when flattered, when requests start small and gradually build, and when large requests are removed and replaced by smaller ones. Perhaps most interestingly, compliance also is enhanced when individuals are first asked to comply with a small request, and after having done so, are asked for a larger request, even where the logic of the request is changed. For its part, obedience is related to following orders. When responsibility for following orders can be transferred to someone outside the individual, obedience is more likely.

While commonalities exist between people as they conform or comply, not all people react to conformity and compliance in the same way. Moreover, commonalities discovered by social psychologists are based on the theoretical constructs they employ. Since social integration is used as the base assumption in most research, topics such as conformity become biased toward the acceptance of the norms. That is, the question for research becomes "how and why will people conform to already established norms and values?" Despite this bias, the tendencies leading to obedience and conformity are highly valuable for a theory of contingency. It helps explain the stability that may be present in groups and even larger structures. Since stability is a contingent possibility, these areas must be understood. However, it is not enough. Assumptions of social integration eliminate the possibility of other contingent results, and as such, explanations of change and inconsistency within groups are removed. Hogg and Abrams (1988) suggest social psychologists turn their investigations on their head and ask: what are the mechanisms that lead to individual and group uncertainty, disagreement, and dissensus? Issues of obedience and conformity are undeniably important, but contingency must still play a role.

The most interesting topic for this work conducted by social psychologists is their analysis of groups and group behavior (e.g. Condor and Brown, 1986). People become members of a group either through ascription, which is relatively non-voluntary (families) or through acquisition, where individuals join others. Groups have a forceful influence on individuals. At the purely individual level, being part of a group is subjectively arousing, and this encourages group behavior and acceptance. For example, individuals will perform tasks within groups they would not perform alone, often throwing off constraints that inhibit individual action. Group decisions also tend to be more radical in nature as individuals shift their ideas within the group context. While the shift in subjective ideas does not include a complete overthrow of established beliefs, the beliefs are made more extreme.

But what of conflicts emerging within groups? There are two basic approaches that establish conflicts within groups. The first emphasizes the individual. One topic within this framework has revolved around the development of authoritarian personalities. Adorno et al. (1950) attempted to explicate why individuals were willing to participate in Nazi war atrocities and the mass extinction of Jews. Modeled after Freud's psychodynamic model, these authors conclude individuals who were more authoritarian were also more ethnocentric, and the source of these personality traits was child rearing practices. Others (e.g. Bierly, 1985) suggest it is not personality, but perceptions of in-groups and out-groups that determine the level of prejudice. [Still others (e.g. Hogg and Abrams, 1988) suggest that more macro forces, and not just personality, must be considered.]

Another explanation of intergroup conflict is presented within the frustration-aggression hypotheses (Dollard et. al., 1939). It suggests that frustration always leads to aggression. A related theory is relative deprivation theory (Davis, 1959). It suggests that when one feels subjectively deprived relative to other groups, frustration sets in and can lead to aggression, protest, and violence. One form of deprivation stems from studies of individuals (egoistic deprivation), but another stems from the study of dissimilar individuals, particularly between groups (fraternal deprivation). Understanding the difference between the two is a matter of understanding how much importance is placed on the situational context. Sherif (1962) asserts that groups and individuals are two different entities, and moreover, that it is impossible to arrive at an understanding of group dynamics through the search of subjective social psychology. Nevertheless, subjective feelings cannot be ignored. Even when separate groups are neither competitive or cooperative, in-group feelings toward the out-group are formulated, and this is due to subjective attitudes (Brown and Abrams, 1986).

Yet another theory of group conflict is presented by Deschamps, (1984) who suggests the very act of cognitive categorization leads to conflict between groups. In part, this is so because any mental categorization leads to further categorization by groups. That is, one category becomes related to other already established categories, and differences between groups become subjectively more pronounced. But as Hogg and Abrams (1988) point out, this explains only part of the process. In the real world there are not only psychological differences between groups, but differences of status, power, prestige, legitimacy, stability, size, geographic location etc., and these factors are outside the realm of individual psychology.

Taken as a whole, the social psychology of group conflict has limitations for a contingency theory. Despite some signs of macro inclusion within the social psychology of conflict, the main focus is misplaced for two reasons. First, almost all conflict becomes a description of individuals within groups. This downplays the autonomy of individuals, but equally important, it ignores the dynamics of intergroup conflict. Nevertheless, analysis of the psychological propensity for conflict and authoritarianism, and for frustration-aggression and deprivation, are important findings worthy of inclusion in any social theory. However, these autonomous and contingent psychological and social psychological processes do not develop in isolation. The autonomous and contingent macro factors must also be included, albeit that individuals within the group engage in the development of perceptions that influence how macro factors will be perceived.

One school of thought that entertains not only external objects in its social psychology but also the potential for conflict, and combines both toward an understanding of social change is the social identity theory (e.g. Hogg and Abrams, 1988). This theory encompasses the mental process of categorization, which provides an order to the information absorbed by individuals. But the information is not about the individual only. It also operates on external objects and on other people. Thus the social identity theory suggests subjective categorization places the individual in relationship to other people and the external world. Moreover the process of categorization, combined with a motivation to view the self positively, requires that individuals make judgments about the information categorized and groups joined, and this is what leads to intra and intergroup conflicts, collective action and social change (Hogg and Abrams, 1988 p. 209).

How, then, can these various social psychological ideas of subjective and group processes, and external objects, be included within social identity theory to explain social change? That is, how does social identity theory explain not only how individuals and groups entertain ideas of conflict and inconsistency, but contingent change? One psychological element is that individuals perceive groups as having a status. If the objective status is subjectively perceived as subordinate, negative implications emerge for group membership. Since group status is perceived as objective, individuals and groups cannot escape this conclusion through simple redefinition. Three strategies are available to such groups and the individuals within them. The group may find new criteria in which to judge themselves, and if accepted as legitimate by dominant groups, this may change the objective perception. The group may also redefine values attributed to various attributes of the group. Clothing, cars, fashions, etc. may be granted more importance. But a third and particularly effective strategy, according to social identity theory, is to select new out-groups, so that the group defines itself less in comparison to superior groups, and more in comparison to similar or less status groups. This process may be encouraged by superior groups in order to maintain their domination. A final possibility emerges when comparisons between subordinate and dominant groups are perceived as legitimate, and a change of status between groups be-comes the subordinate group's goal.

The goal of group redefinition is more likely when it becomes legitimate for the subordinate group to perceive change. However, the subordinate perception of legitimate change may or may not be ac-cepted by other groups in society. During change, perceptions may also be altered by dominant groups who wish to either maintain or unravel the legitimacy of the subordinate group (Hogg and Abrams, 1988 p. 92-115).

While the social identity theory outlines important, often ignored, issues of social psychology, and escapes the traditional mistake of viewing only the individual within the group, it ignores the question of autonomy and contingency. Psychological and social psychological processes must not merely be attached to macro processes, or as the new trend in interactional psychology suggests, view the situational influence on personality (e.g. Elder and Caspi, 1988; Magnusson, 1988; Caspi, 1989). Instead, the dynamic relationship between the two must be uncovered. Although external objects may be taken into ac-count, doing so solely from the individual and group perspective can-not uncover the autonomous and related dynamic between the two levels. Intergroup relations are often conflictual and hostile, and to be understood, analysts must first combine both individual and group as-pects of psychology and social psychology, and also must relate these to macro processes. Moreover, the three processes must be seen as in-ternally and combinationally contingent.

Finally, a group of social psychologists have begun to extend their analysis beyond even social identity, and to concern themselves with societal influences on individuals (e.g. Himmelweit and Gaskell, 1990). Called societal psychology, this school argues sociocultural contexts motivate subjective attitudes and beliefs. For example, U.S. culture encourages individuals to be "self-contained" while Japanese culture encourages individuals to be "embedded" in obligations and social harmony (Sampson, 1988). Linkages between individuals and society must be fleshed out, as well as social change where individuals and various societal elements interact. In short, societal psychologists assert social psychology requires a systems approach where the indi-vidual life cycle and wider society are seen in mutual relation (Himmelweit, 1990).

While including macro conditions is a step forward by societal psychologists, a systems approach to understanding individual and group behavior undermines the autonomy of micro processes (Chapter Four). Instead of micro autonomy and contingency, societal psychologist seem to suggest that while individuals and groups may have some effect on macro conditions, macro conditions are seen as objective, and micro processes become their causal effect (Himmelweit 1990 p. 22-27).

Neo-Marxist Psychology

The two authors who come closest to a contingent analysis of psychology are Erich Fromm and Frantz Fanon. Both develop their psychological principles within a neo-Marxist context. This creates a bias in their work, but nonetheless, contingency emerges. Fromm (1965) attempts to integrate psychological, economic and ideological factors. In doing so, he rejects both psychoanalysis and behaviorism. Fromm rejects the Freudian interest in instinctual drives, and argues the key question between subject and object is not satisfaction or frustration, but rather the interrelationship between individuals and the external world. External objects are granted primacy in their relationship to individuals, but this is not equivalent to the behaviorist belief that subjective individuals have no part to play in the process. Fromm plainly believes individuals have an important role to play.

Fromm also asserts specific elements of human nature are unchangeable, including the need for satisfaction, physiological drives, and the need to avoid isolation. Within these confines, individuals are accorded enough flexibility to dynamically adapt to external situations, and in doing so, create new drives and anxieties. In combination, then, humans are more than their drives, and are not totally conditioned by external environments. Nevertheless, the primacy, but not determining nature, of the external conditions remains. Fromm also argues that modern freedoms establish isolation as a common subjective reality. This presents humans with a modern choice between freedom and security; either individuals give up security by seeking to unite with others in an open and spontaneous way, or individuals can give up freedom for the security of authoritarianism.

The relationship between internal needs and external conditions is not, for Fromm, direct. A lag may exist between the developed character structure and external, primarily economic, conditions. These inconsistencies can cause subjective difficulty as individuals pursue economic interests. Since internal drives need to be satisfied, as does the need to avoid isolation, periods of lag and inconsistency may give rise to authoritarian tendencies.

Some elements of Fromm's theories fit well with a theory of contingency. The idea of autonomy between character structures and external conditions allow for contingent relations between the two. Fromm also allows for inconsistencies to develop, and this too must be included in a contingent theory. However, two of Fromm's ideas must be rejected. First, he grants universality to the internal drives of satisfaction and the need to avoid isolation, and sees these elements as unchangeable. In contrast, aside from the physical need for survival, a contingent theory of human nature carries with it no universal explanation of drives or motives. Contingency implies not that anxieties and psychological motives are non-existent, but that they develop in the autonomous and dynamic relationship between micro and macro processes.

Second, Fromm is wrong to assert the primacy of economic elements. While this is a possibility, whether or not economics should hold primacy over other structural elements, for example culture, is a contingent question, not a predetermined answer. Related to this is the relatively small amount of flexibility granted to individuals to adapt to economic developments. Inconsistencies between character structure and economic development may or may not give rise to authoritarianism. Again, the process is contingent, and empirically verifiable, not predetermined.

Like Fromm, Frantz Fanon (1963) considers external conditions, specifically their influence on the process of psychological development in Africa. Fanon concentrates on the influence of colonialism on individual personality and distinct groups. He argues that psychoanalytic responses vary, given different historical periods. During colonialism, when natives are dominated and suppressed, a loss of self-identity occurs, defensive attitudes reach their limit, and neurosis is the outcome. This process is due, in large part, to the violence characterizing colonialism; natives may be struck, violated and killed. Structured violence leads to internal violence against other natives and external violence (in feeling if not always in action) toward the colonial power. The only other escape is into mysticism and the belief that evil spirits are the cause of any dilemma.

During periods of liberation, violence also acts as a cleansing force for feelings of inferiority, and for previous inactivity of natives. Ultimately, liberation movements diminish violence as the enemy is made clear, and freedom becomes feasible. But not all groups react to either economic or psychological processes in the same way. Peasants maintain the most potential for violence, in part, because nationalist movements promise only indirect connections and relief for this group.

Rural people distrust urbanized collectives because of their ability to act like colonialists. Fanon argues peasants find sophisticated political programs irrelevant. The peasant view of the future is direct and concrete: foreigners must be driven off the land. Peasant revolts are, therefore, often spontaneous, but largely unsuccessful. Ironically, this makes them susceptible to colonial compromises that ease, but do not eliminate, their burden.

Fanon asserts colonial powers, along with members of the indigenous bourgeoisie, coalesce not only to carry out violence, but to destroy native cultures. By eliminating the significance of the past, colonial powers are able to justify their own superiority. Fanon suggests nationalist intellectuals defy colonialism by preserving the past at every opportunity. At times this comes in the form of purely tribal or national cultural revivals, and at times in pan-African movements.

Above all, Fanon suggests the working class has the best opportunity to create liberation movements. The working class, unlike peasants, has endured relatively less violence, and unlike intellectuals, is rooted in the present and sees the current situation of society. The working class, therefore, suffers from fewer psychological maladies.

Fanon's combination of elements of psychology, culture and political economy is suggestive of a theory of contingency. First, he sees all three elements as related, but autonomous. Second, the developments in international political economy are related to the autonomous development of culture. Third, both political-economic and cultural developments are related to the micro processes of the individual. This process is not seen as identical for all groups, nor is the response to these developments pre-determined. Finally, Fanon allows for micro processes to influence more macro developments. Although Fanon's political desire to end colonialism affects his theories, his approach allows for more autonomy and contingency than any other theorist concerned with psychological and social psychological processes.

Rethinking Individuals and Groups

Despite the advantages of Fanon's, and to some extent Fromm's, insights, they have had little influence on social theory. By contrast, traditional psychology and social psychology have stimulated many social theorists. One theory whose roots rest squarely within the traditional framework is symbolic interaction. Symbolic interaction contends societal influence on individuals is mediated by a process of self-conception, where self-conception is derived through the interaction between individuals and others. Social psychological principles are evidently important here.

Psychology also played an important role in the formulation of functionalism. In search of a mechanism which could grant motivation for social action within structural constraints, Parson chose Freud's personality theories. For its part, exchange theory unabashedly accepts principles of psychology in developing ideas of cost-benefit analyses. Here, individuals become more likely to engage in exchanges when a perceived economic or psychological interest exists. Finally, the phenomonological social construction of reality is at least partly indebted to cognitive theories of psychology. Yet, despite these variations, little help is provided for a theory of contingency. While autonomy is evident through the sheer elimination of macro phenomena, contingency between the two levels is obviously excluded. This abridges the very process that could illuminate critical findings in psychology and social psychology.

Nonetheless, psychology's autonomous view of individuals and groups does provide significant ideas. From psychology, we learn that micro psychological processes are autonomous. Whether one accepts the unconscious, immediate environments as conditioning elements, patterns of internal and external stimuli, or mental processes as a mediating force between internal and external environments, all major schools of psychology include elements of autonomy within their frameworks. Moreover, the mental process of memory, language, emotions and personality result from the autonomous interplay of internal and external factors. While psychologists stress social integration and universal findings, the psychological lesson for a contingency theory is that psychological development cannot be determined by macro processes.

From social psychology we learn groups and their dynamics also are autonomous from both individual psychological and macro processes. Moreover, principles establishing how individuals relate to groups, and how groups influence individuals, are essential elements in uncovering the autonomous micro level. Compelling findings of individual relationships to groups include: individuals strive for consistency in behavior and attitudes; individuals reevaluate attitudes to make their choices of behavior more appealing; individuals dislike changing categorized attitudes; and if individual attitudes change, a path of least resistance is followed, where new attitudes are incorporated with the old as much as possible.

Important findings of how groups influence individuals include: the desire by individuals to fit into influential groups, especially when the group is small, and no allies for non-conformity are present; that group feelings are enhanced when a strong comparative out-group is established; and that intergroup conflict depends, in part, on whether groups are perceived as having high status, power, prestige, and/or legitimacy.

And finally, neo-Marxist psychology suggests character structures develop from autonomous relationships between individuals and external processes, that these character structures may be inconsistent with macro developments, that different groups or social classes within society respond differently to changing macro phenomena, that culture has an influence on the individual process, and that micro developments may influence macro changes. How then can these disparate elements be combined into a more coherent approach that is useful for the creation of a contingency theory?

One important finding of psychology and social psychology is that individuals do not experience the entirety of social structures, but only that which is perceived. Moreover, the perception is highly influenced by group processes and objective environments. It is an error, therefore, to either elevate or deny subjective psychology. The brain process of categorization, and its influence on the ability to communicate and form attitudes, is an individual and unique process. So too are emotions and the motivations they generate. Nevertheless, individual psyches do not develop in a vacuum. Groups aid in filtering information absorbed by the brain, and affect the development of beliefs and attitudes. But where does the information come from? It cannot be from individuals, nor solely from the group. The information must come from external objects and processes. Within this scenario, groups are mediating structures between individuals and social structures. This does not mean structures determine group or individual processes. Rather, external conditions are refracted within each individual as subjective responses help shape both objective conditions, and the parameters for which conditions will become subject. If this is so, social structures are an autonomous and missing element from psychological and social psychological discussions.

Moreover, the dynamic process between the three elements is contingent. That is, no universal law can predict precisely what the relationship will be. This is so not only because of the contingent relationship between the three elements, but because each process contains its own internal contingency. No sweeping principle can explain or predict how individuals will psychologically develop. No universal wisdom can explain how group dynamics will proceed. And no general law can predict how structures will develop. All three elements are autonomous and related, but that relationship is contingent.

How does this contingent relationship express itself at the individual level? While individuals autonomously and contingently process information to form beliefs and attitudes, it is legitimate to ask, what information? Even when limiting knowledge according to the Kantian notion that individuals do not rationally understand external objects "in themselves," the rationalist presumption that individuals can understand all that is necessary must be rejected. This may or may not be the case.

A more grounded approach would suggest the foundation of individual comprehension is the natural and social environment necessary for survival. This is different from Marx's conception, who argued that subject and object are materially related. They are not; each is contingent. This means that while survival is a basic fact of human nature, and while macro processes surely influence the survival process, each individual develops a contingent and autonomous process toward survival needs.

Within this process, social structures and groups act as autonomous and contingent mediating forces. Consequently, a fourth element must be added to autonomous and contingent elements of individuals, groups, and social structures. That fourth element is nature. Natural objects, then, are both necessary for survival and socially manipulated. Thus no direct links exist between these natural objects and human perception. Instead, natural and social objects of survival are filtered through structures and groups, and individuals perceive these filtered natural and social objects contingently.

The dynamic process existing between these four elements means individuals may or may not clearly perceive their subjective situation, and are influenced in various ways and to varying degrees by groups, social structures, and nature. And since individuals autonomously and contingently create concepts and attitudes, groups must not be conceived as simple aggregates of individual conceptions. To do so underplays both the uniqueness of the individual process and the autonomy of the group process. Groups are more than cumulated individual wishes and desires. The group process can, itself, actuate the individual. This is especially true since multiple groups may variably influence individuals. Thus, what occurs at the group level must be autonomous from the individual, and because it is autonomous and not equivalent to aggregate individual processes, the group process, itself, must be contingent.

One example of this dynamic interrelationship can be considered through the concept of work. Work may be considered an individual concept, a group dynamic, and a social structure. Moreover, when an individual works, a survival relationship exists between the individual and the natural environment. The clearest example of this is in hunting and gathering societies where members either hunt or gather. In modern societies, the relationship may be more complicated, but remains nevertheless. One example is when a production worker manipulates raw materials and fashions a social object. But the process is no less true of someone who provides a service. This process may involve the circulation or distribution of the social object, or provide technical expertise to allow for more efficiency in the creation of the social object, or training of individuals who create the social object, or aiding in the reproduction of social life to make it easier for individuals to create social objects. In any of these cases, the fundamental relationship between individuals and nature remains primary, albeit indirect. This is the limit in which one may speak of human nature. Beyond the needs and drives to survive (and even this is variable among humans), there are no psychological drives or motivations which can be claimed as universal.

This means, in our example, the only commonality between people as they work is a shared concept developed within the subjective process of relating to the natural environment for survival. Thus the information processed and conceptualized by the brain to create attitudes about work has an external source, yet is uniquely individual. Moreover, in modern societies the individual process is necessarily more abstract. Because of the rise of social structures and modern groups, the direct relationship between individuals and nature, as expressed by their work, is more oblique than in hunting and gathering societies. Individual processes become correspondingly abstract. The result, as Durkheim correctly pointed out, is more room for individual differences, not only in the kinds of work performed, but in individual attitudes and beliefs about work.

Each individual, then, conceptualizes and forms attitudes and beliefs about work, whether or not they are related to unconscious or cognitive motivations and emotions, or conditioning. And while it is true that the mediating forces of structures and groups make the individual process more abstract in contemporary society, it also is true that without abstract thought no mediating structures may be created. Thus some individuals develop a condescending attitude toward workers who do not directly produce a product, while others view white collar work, even when paid less than factory workers, as an increase in status. Some believe hard work pays dividends in the long run, while others only work to make fast money. And some would rather die than not work, while others would like to retire tomorrow, or never have to work at all. Individual responses to work are just that: individual. The emotional response to work also differs in modern society because of the creation of mediating structures and groups. While it is true that modern responses may be more confused and more variable than in hunting and gathering societies, (because relationships are more abstract) the traditional sociological analysis of the modern condition as alienating or creating anomie does not necessarily follow. Alienation or anomie may or may not develop, depending on the autonomous and contingent relationships between individuals, groups, social structures and nature.

The functional and neofunctional notion of a personality system, therefore, must also be rejected. Structures cannot determine personality, for personality is an autonomous individual process. While it is possible that macro and group processes may highly influence individuals acting within groups and institutions, such influences on behavior cannot be pre-determined. Any suggestion that structures generate common personalities is created from an assumption of social integration.

Simultaneously, however, individual responses to work do not develop in seclusion. Collectivities and structures play an substantial part in the process. Indeed, contemporary emotions and attitudes are not conceivable without mediating collectivities and structures. Nonetheless, while groups and structures maintain an influence on individuals, they have differed widely over time, and from place to place. The reason for such differences is that groups and structures are, themselves, autonomous and contingent. The result of each of these processes, and the relationship that forms between them, is unpredictable. Regrettably, the social-integration bias, historically expressed by psychologists and social psychologists, has encouraged a fruitless search for universal explanations of the human psyche.

To correct this bias, emotional and conceptual individual processes must be seen not only as part and parcel of the development of groups and social structures, but as a process of autonomy and contingency. It is true that abstract emotions and concepts are due to relationships formed with social groups and structures. But it is also true that groups and structures mediate between individuals and nature. This means individuals need not necessarily develop in tandem with the group and structural developments. The result may be a postmodern confusion and fragmentation, as individuals become more distant from groups and social structures, or a period of stability and cohesion between the elements. Only empirical investigations can provide the answer. And finally, the reality that individual processes are autonomous from groups and social structures means individuals are not only a derivative of external developments, but that what proceeds at the level of the individual may, in turn, contingently influence groups and structures.

The concepts of contingency and autonomy are evident not only in individual processes, but also within collective processes. Individuals either are ascribed to or may choose to enter groups which are variable and change continually. These variations and changes cannot be deduced from a purely individual perspective. The variety and types of groups also are combinations of individual, group, structural, and natural developments. For example, the number of groups to which a contemporary individual may join are more numerous than were available for a hunter and gatherer. Moreover, group forms also are influenced by macro developments. Time and space distanciation and compression have directly influenced both the form of contemporary groups and their dynamic. Changes in technology, forms of communication, and social relationships to nature have both widened the space and shortened the time for group dynamics. What results from these dynamic relationships is contingent. Either contemporary processes will lead to a decrease in importance of groups for individuals, or more significance will be placed on groups as individuals emotionally and conceptually feel isolated and in need of group communication.

This means groups are influenced both by macro processes and individual processes, as each proceeds in relation to nature. Groups, therefore, should not be seen as mere cumulations of individual and/or structural influences. The formation and development of group dynamics, including levels of dissonance, conformity, frustration and group status, all contribute to the autonomous role of collectivities. Moreover, the combination of influences generated from internal group processes can neither be determined from universal principles applied to all groups, nor from individual or structural theories. In short, group dynamics are not only autonomous, but the relationship formed with other levels is contingent.

This can be illustrated through continuing the example of work. Almost all individuals engage groups through work. Production workers may be part of the general workforce, members of a particular department, and may be part of smaller cells of workers. Office workers engage groups in similar ways, as do service workers. While the size of the group may differ in each example, the existence of groups is almost always present, and thus, group dynamics must exist also. Individuals at work must relate to varying levels of conformity required of them. There is no universal level asked, however. At some workplaces, levels of conformity are extremely high, perhaps including dress codes, and behavioral expectations at and outside of work. At other places of work, innovation, creativity, or even eccentricity may be prominent. Obviously, this may be viewed as another form of conformity, but the point is levels and forms of conformity vary greatly.

Since conformity varies, so too will levels of frustration and aggression. An individual who is relatively non-conformist may chafe at the prospect of a formal dress code and expected behavior. Dress codes are often traditional in large corporations, and the lack of options may raise the frustration level of an individual who views such dress as demeaning to human creativity. Conversely, within a business that does not stress conformity (perhaps in a computer software company) individuals who feel comfortable wearing conservative clothing may find themselves ridiculed. Again the frustration may rise. Varied expectations of behavior has the same effect. Companies promoting value and stability, and a belief that family commitment leads to higher worker productivity will generate frustration and aggression from unmarried workers, or those who are unhappily married.

The group dynamic at work can cause other forms of individual reactions. Dissonance is a prime example. For individuals who have processed a set of beliefs and attitudes, working within a group may present inconsistencies. For example, assume an individual has processed a set of beliefs and attitudes which includes some level of environmental awareness. Such an individual may seek to work for a company that sells solar hot water panels. These panels are placed on the roofs of homes, and on sunny days will heat water, lessening the need for energy-wasting hot water systems. However, if the company selling the solar panels is located in an area that does not receive much sun, if the company uses a tax break scam and false facts to convince customers to buy the panels, and if the type of panel used destroys the roofs of homes, dissonance will likely rise within the individual.

The rise of dissonance caused by this situation is grounded in all four elements previously discussed: the individual process, the group dynamic, macro social processes and nature. First, the group dynamic. While under normal circumstances the individual may choose not to sell solar panels under these conditions, individuals are more likely to perform a task within a group than they are when alone. Moreover, if the buyers have been established as a strong out-group, that is, the company has been effective in categorizing buyers as obstacles to overcome for personal success, this will affect the individual and the response to dissonance. Finally, if the group is subjectively perceived to have high objective status by the salesperson, this too will influence the individual and any action taken.

However, the group dynamic alone cannot determine the individual response to dissonance, nor the level of dissonance created. Individuals bring their own autonomous process to the group, and while each has an influence over the other, neither can be determining. Moreover, individual and group processes are additionally related to macro processes. For example, whether a group is perceived as objectively dominant or subordinate is another social psychological finding that makes an important difference in the relationship between individual and group processes. But the relative level of dominance and subordination can only be investigated with the inclusion of macro factors.

At work, various levels of dominance and subordination emerge. Often, clear hierarchical levels are established. Whether or not individuals and groups perceive these differences as legitimate depends in part how individuals perceive power and subordination in society. This means individuals not only are related to group dynamics, but view those dynamics in relation to macro processes. This is not to say that macro processes determine individuals or their views of group dynamics. Each is surely related, but the levels are distinct and autonomous. The macro processes, however, must be included in the analysis. In relation to work, such topics as the relative position of the society compared to other societies may make a difference both in individual conceptions of work, and in group dynamics. A perception of a society as relatively wealthy or poor may influence the individual process, but in ways that are impossible to predict. Relative wealth may encourage an attitude of shared entitlement (relative deprivation), but conversely, an individual might reject spending one's creative talents simply in the search of money, and will view the society as overly materialistic. Either case, and many other factors, will have an obvious impact on group dynamics, including conformity, feelings of frustration-aggression, levels of dissonance etc. In turn, both the individual and group processes may have an influence on macro processes. The intermixing of the three are interrelated, but unpredictable, autonomous, and contingent.

In a relatively poor society, individual, group, and macro processes again are related, yet autonomous. While contingent international and political economic developments have a definite influence on individual and group processes, micro processes remain self contained. A peasant who forcibly has been removed from his/her historic position on the land and enters a high-poverty urban area obviously has been affected by international political-economic developments. However, emerging individual and group processes cannot be universally pre-determined from these macro events. Individuals and groups may or may not conform, be obedient, develop authoritarian personalities, be-come violent, perceive relative deprivation, or choose to change their situation. The outcome is contingent, and depends on the dynamic that unfolds between the autonomous levels.

Individuals, groups, macro structures and nature, then, are con-tinuously influenced by existing subordinate and dominant relations. As individuals develop their mental processes, including emotions and personality, power plays a role. Dominant and subordinate relations exist within families, at school, at work, and even in leisure activities. In every point of the life cycle, human beings face and/or exert some level of power. Groups also are inconceivable without domi-nant/subordinate relations. Whether it is the group attempting to use its power to influence individuals, or to influence other groups, power is evident. Within social structures, powerful individuals, and more often groups, have the potential to generate fundamental macro changes. Finally, the exercise of power also may influence nature (see Chapter Three).

Power, then, must be included in any theory of contingency. Power may or may not lead to conflict, but it must be assessed. If groups and macro structures are conceived as mediating forces between individuals and their natural and social environments, then those who have variable control over these mediating forces may be seen as hav-ing varying levels of power. But power should not be seen as omni-present and determining. The autonomy of individual and group processes ensures a perfect match between micro and macro processes, no matter how thoroughly controlled, will never be absolute. That is, individual processes may produce attitudes, emotions, and personalities inconsistent with macro phenomena, and group dynamics may produce variable levels of dissonance and deprivation that are inconsistent both with individual and macro processes and with other groups.

Finally, it is also evident that individual, group and structural processes are carried out in relation to nature. The examples of work and relative wealth are both enabled and constrained by the autono-mous and contingent natural environment. Many individuals and so-cieties have bumped against natural parameters. Storms and floods have destroyed homes and places of work, and many societies through-out modern history have been limited by endless consumption of en-ergy and fuel. The examples are endless, but the common need for nature to carry out work, and the natural parameters influencing that process, means nature must be considered another autonomous and contingent part of the process.

Taken as a whole, psychology and social psychology have provided valuable insights for autonomous micro level activity. However, like other areas discussed in Part II, much of what is done right is for the wrong reasons. The inability to escape the boundaries of previous theories has encouraged psychological theorists to seek universal laws and social cohesion. This leaves autonomy divorced from contingency. Doing so underplays the unique power of autonomous micro activity, and fails to uncover both the relationship between individuals and groups, and micro from macro.

Part III begins the process of considering the implications for social theory when both autonomy and contingency are taken into serious account. That discussion follows.

PART III

CONCEIVING A NEW MODEL

Chapter Seven

Contingent Social Perception

This chapter outlines the autonomous and contingent relationship between individuals and groups. While micro relationships to structures will be referred to, the formal treatment of macro processes is developed in the next chapter, and the interrelationship between the two is explored in Chapter Nine.

Principles of psychology and social psychology previously demonstrated the unique and unpredictable quality of both individual and group processes. The valuable findings of inquiries into individual and group processes were seen as most productive when the bias toward social integration is eliminated, and replaced with the concepts of autonomy and contingency. When viewed contingently, micro processes create either consistency or conflict.

What was not discussed in the last chapter is how autonomy and contingency between individuals and groups relates to philosophical debates covered in Chapter One. Philosophy, like psychology, and especially social psychology, has gradually accepted external influences on individuals. Beginning with Hume, who used social interaction as a unifying force between individuals and society, philosophy has struggled to escape universal, scientific explanations for individual behavior. Although Kant held individuals universally interpret and categorize data from external sources, in a major break from the past, he nonetheless placed individuals independent from external objects. In more recent times, analytic, structuralist, and postmodern philosophies all emphasize language as a micro connection to the social world. However, where Kant believed individual thought formed a universal social tie, each of these modern perspectives argue relativism is the social result.

In its popular form, relativism has been the source for believing all perspectives are equally significant. For example, debates over multi-culturalist viewpoints has raged in U.S. higher education for some years. Relativism also has been a catalyst for epistemological arguments within anthropology, where no culture may be seen as superior to others; in feminist theory, where no particular vantage point may be granted preeminence; and finally, in postmodernism, where no one statement may be more truthful than another.

As relativism makes a critical point and leaps to faithful conclusions, it begs the most important question. It is true that individuals cannot have accurate accounts of all social reality and, therefore, universal explanations of social reality are spurious. The end of universal reality, however, does not mean the end of all social reality. The essential question begged by relativism is: What are the elements of a social situation, even if granted a relative status?

The beginning elements of micro social situations are provided for in psychology. Psychology has slowly come to the cognitive conclusion that divisions between physical and mental aspects of individuals must be abandoned, and while physiological factors and the senses are vital, the mental process, perception, learning, and consciousness all have social content. For social psychologists, these social elements have their source outside the individual, and depend on who and what individuals interact with (Hormuth, 1990). Many sociologists agree.

Mead (1962) maintained a clear separation between individuals and their social surroundings. He then granted social elements primacy over the individual, even when discussing such topics as the mind. Mead believed individuals select actions on the basis of subjective, internal conversations and categories, and from the ability to select from a variety of stimuli. But consciousness, mental images, and meaning are social, not subjective. This is so because of the use of symbols, such as language, which provide the framework for both internal conversations and meanings. Moreover, for Mead, the only source available for symbols used in internal conversations is social interaction between people.

Mead asserts the social "self" also develops through interaction, first with "particular" and then "generalized" others, where the self learns social roles. This is required if individuals are to participate in group and organized activities. Both individuals and society benefit; individuals become members of the larger society, and the society becomes better coordinated. The result, however, is not pure coordination and conformity. While many selves participate in a coordinated society, each self remains autonomous. Moreover, social coordination leads neither to invariant societies, or uniform individuals. Instead, Mead suggests social variety leads to multiples selves, and to people having the ability to change society through the capacity to think of new generalized roles and behaviors.

Changing society through new conceptualizations of roles and behaviors is made possible by a relationship between the "I" and the "me." The I is an immediate, unpredictable response of individuals to others. Even the individual is unable to predict what response the I will have in various situations. Autonomously, but simultaneously, the "me" represents attitudes of others which have been absorbed into the self. While Mead sees the me as a more social, logical, and recognizable property, it is the combination of both the unpredictable I and the social me which Mead believes most accurately reflects the micro process.

Mead, then, represents one example where predictability and universal explanations are rejected, yet pure subjective relativism is avoided. Instead, Mead recognizes multiple possibilities for actions and reactions between individuals and others, yet still maintains that social interaction is discoverable. As discussed previously in this work, the unifying potential of social relationships has been recognized since Hume, but too often ignored. While social relationships may not make reality perfectly clear, individuals do think, learn, and act in relation to others, and therefore, these relationships become both understandable and necessary to include in any social theory. Thus external objects are not directly apparent to individuals, nor does awareness come about because of purely subjective, rational processes. Rather, external material and social objects, as well as the relationships formed between and among them, is interpreted by individuals through their interaction with others.

Many macro and micro theories have ignored interaction, or redefined it, because it would require eliminating long-held assumptions. At the micro level, phenomenology and most perspectives within psychology, for example, cannot accept interaction, because individuals would no longer be the primary catalyst for all that is social. For micro theorists, interaction conceived as truly social is an expressway to macro considerations better left untraveled. For their part, structural theorists also ignore social interaction, because they continue to maintain the objective nature of structures, and ignore the autonomy of individual and group processes.

Curiously enough, many micro and macro theorists believe their assumptions result in liberating individuals. Micro theorists seek to liberate individuals from constraining structures, and Marxists, for example, argue a macro concern for humankind will aid people in attaining their full potential. By contrast, this chapter will suggest it is social interaction that increases the human potential. By replacing macro and micro assumptions with a recognition of contingent social interaction, a humanly created world of knowledge becomes both open to individuals, and a collective responsibility. That is, when people interact, it becomes possible for individuals to interpret more than if left in isolation, and simultaneously, macro structures become collective creations and responsibilities, not objective processes separated from individuals.

The autonomy and contingency of social interaction does not eliminate the need for micro and macro theories. It simply means any assumption which logically denies either process must be discarded. Micro and macro assumptions are retained in mainstream theory, however, because of the obsession with social order and integration, and the assumed relationship between social order and social action. This has continually led theorists astray, as macro theorists have concentrated on social order and then secondarily on action. Micro theorists, in contrast, have concentrated on social action and secondarily on order. Instead, contingency theory accepts the possibility that social interaction may or may not lead to social order, and that social action may or may not be consistent with macro conditions. Moreover, contingent social interaction does not necessarily imply an open, free, democratic form of interaction. Not all people interact with all other people. While it is true that macro phenomena cannot be created apart from human intervention and interaction, it is also true macro conditions are not influenced equally by all individuals. This is one reason why power also must be discussed in this chapter and related to social interaction.

The significance of social interaction, then, blends well with the concepts of autonomy and contingency. The autonomy and contingency between micro and macro, and between individual and group within the micro level, means relativists have, at least partially, won their point. Autonomy and contingency concedes both an external reality not entirely knowable to human beings, and that no universal explanation of reality exists. But autonomy and contingency do not accept these principles as all-or-nothing propositions. What remains is both real and discoverable. At the micro level, what remains is the social creation of individuals and collectivities, where both inform and influence each other. An exploration of the autonomy and contingency as it exists within and between individuals and groups follows.

Individual and Group Social Perception

Autonomy and contingency implies that individuals may or may not accurately perceive external groups, and are variably influenced by them. While the breadth and scope of individual processes may vary widely, the unknown remains unknown. That is, a hunter or gatherer, with no contact with the contemporary world, has no desire or interest to question subjective and group categorizations of attitudes and beliefs. The inability to subjectively know everything means no universal pattern can be assumed between individuals and groups. While the relationships that develop are contingent on a myriad of factors, what is common among individuals and groups is social interaction. Social interaction remains the unifying force among and within micro and macro levels. But the result of interaction is unpredictable. To accept contingency, then, requires a rejection of simple realism. In its place, one can accept what might be called clustered realism. That is, the dynamic within and between individuals and groups can never be extrapolated for all times and in all places, but the social process of interpretation and interaction can be established within clustered matrices of reality.

For example, in contemporary industrialized societies, interaction between individuals and numerous groups is far more prevalent than in hunting and gathering societies. Moreover, contemporary interaction may be considered more abstract; that is, time and space is distanciated and compressed through technology and the media where individuals may interact with other people and groups in ways removed from personal contact. This undoubtedly is one modern influence on subjective perception. Contemporary groups are not eliminated, but the form of social interpretation and interaction is certainly different from hunting and gathering societies. Since subjective perceptions and group perception systems vary from place to place and over time, their relationship requires examination.

While individuals interpret interactions to develop a subjective social perception, groups develop what may be termed a social perception system. The difference between them is that individual social perception is formed as a result of individual processes as they relate to group dynamics, while a social perception system develops as a result of group dynamics. Since groups and their dynamics are autonomous from individual physical and psychological processes, group social perception systems remain distinct and separate. This autonomy is one source of group influence on the individual, but while the social perception system and the dynamics of the group can influence individual social perception, they cannot determine it. Moreover, since groups are made up of autonomous individuals, it follows that an individual's social perception and social actions potentially influence, but cannot determine, some groups.

But what is the source of individual interest to perceive or interact with groups? Why, at the individual level, are some perceptions and groups accepted or rejected? One traditional answer to this question within psychology, and a growing answer within sociology, is that emotions are a central feature for individual interest and action. How, then, are emotions defined, and what is the relationship between emotions and social perception and interaction?.

The traditional sociological view is that emotions are inconceivable except as a response to social contexts (e.g. Goffman, 1974), but as de Sousa (1991) outlines, emotions also may be placed solely within the realm of autonomous individuals. The source of purely subjective emotions is variously described in the literature as amorphous "feelings", as cognitive information (Solomon, 1976), as psychological responses to brain patterns (e.g. Panksepp, 1982), as intentional or collective strategies to change the world (e.g. Sartre, 1948; Barbalet, 1992), and as determined by social developments (e.g. Scheman, 1983). Finally, Elliott (1992, p. 9-11) suggests that the unconscious is a necessary window to the social world, where social symbols are received and acted on within a particular set of social relations and psychological desires, and Lazarus (1991) develops the concept of "core relational themes", where individuals evaluate the relevance and consistency of goals in relation to ego.

These various explanations place emotions as a purely subjective phenomena. The view of emotions suggested by de Sousa, however, closely parallels a contingent view of micro processes. He proposes emotions are social in that they are based on social interaction with others, but the autonomy of the individual remains protected. While de Sousa concedes that emotions provide information for cognitive perceptions of the external world, emotions also have a subjective origin. The two levels interrelate as innate emotions (e.g. an infant's ability to smile) are mixed with reactions received from social interaction. This creates an "emotional paradigm" from which individuals build a repertoire of emotional responses. Neither the social context nor innate ability to experience emotions is determining. Each can influence the other as the individual matures (de Sousa, 1991 p. 171-186). Or in terms useful for this work, intrinsic emotional capability, coupled with social interaction, creates an emotional perception system within individuals.

These emotional paradigms act as filters for new perceptions constructed over a lifetime as individuals interact with others and groups.

Adding emotions to the equation, even when connected to social settings, does not expedite a clear vision of micro processes. Are there no alternatives to relativist conclusions? How is it possible to sort out the complexities involved with individual and group perception, and interaction? Since autonomous and contingent individuals relate to other autonomous individuals and groups, yet cannot have an accurate account of all reality, is anything other than a relativist account of the social world possible? Despite the complexities of micro processes, autonomy and contingency imply individual and group perceptions and acts are not beyond comprehension. While never universal, individual and group perceptions and acts are nevertheless categorized, both emotionally and cognitively, by individuals and groups. This allows the process to be understood.

However, since neither individuals or groups carry out this process in total isolation (for without interaction between the two, neither may be said to even socially exist) or in total coordination, individual and group processes maintain autonomy. This sets the foundation for future relationships between the two levels. Subjective emotional paradigms and categorization -- social perception -- interrelates with perceptions and categorizations at the group level -- social perception systems --, and the dynamic that occurs between the two can change either or both.

For example, a situation may arise where one family member considers breaking a long-standing tradition of attending family gatherings during a particular holiday. The subjective decision whether or not to take such an action is based on the perceptions of the individual and the perceptual system of the family group. No matter the individual decision, there are only two possible outcomes in this case: the perception of holidays may remain the same or may be changed subjectively and/or by the group. But the decision has not been an arbitrary one. It is made through the emotional paradigm and cognitive process of categorization by both the individual and group, where the whole history of family perceptions and relations are taken into account. That is, the potential action is perceived and categorized by both. Thus the autonomy between the individual and group, and the contingent nature of the decision, does not mean the process is beyond comprehension. A first step toward understanding individual and group social perception, then, is to uncover the emotional paradigms and categorizations that have developed within and between the two levels.

For their part, individuals do not merely look inward when evaluating their thoughts or actions. People generally come to self-conclusions in relation to others. This is an important part of the subjective emotional and cognitive categorization processes. Without emotional paradigms and categorization, individuals would be overwhelmed by the amount of information and decisions necessary to generate thoughts and interactions. If it were not for the ability to select and categorize sensual, emotional and intellectual data, humans would be in a constant state of informational overload. Every sense and every thought would send the brain into a dizzying compilation of uninterpreted feelings and data. Instead, the uniquely human quality of selection and categorization of sense data, thoughts, and feelings allows people to learn of their physical and social surroundings, and to store data for almost instantaneous recognition. This process is the basis for the social perception of individuals, and social perception is one necessary element for social interaction.

Subjective emotional paradigms and categorization, however, are inconceivable apart from the social context. Language, attitudes, and emotions must be related to persons outside the subject. But while categorization opens the potential for understanding the complex external world, something is lost in the process: a complete and accurate picture of social reality. There is no guarantee that what is subjectively perceived is accurate or complete. Any theory of individuals claiming otherwise must be based on universal assumptions, and misunderstands the autonomy and contingency of individuals. Subjective autonomy and contingency means people individually develop social perception, and that they do so in relation to others. The form of interrelations with others may differ, e.g. hunters and gatherers relate to others differently than computer networkers, but the net result is a social perception system that may or may not reflect real situations, and may or may not be consistent with other individuals, groups, and macro phenomena.

The contingent nature of individual and group social perception is made most obvious when inconsistencies develop within or between the two levels. Once again the process is not purely relative. As one limited example, assume an individual develops the right side of brain and becomes oriented toward spatial and intuitive processes. The individual may be adept at comprehending large complex issues, and develops creative and intuitive attitudes and beliefs which correspond to an emotional paradigm developed over a period of years. However, as the individual interacts with particular groups within the context of family, schools, and other social groups, more emphasis may be placed on practical skills and talents. These are granted a high value by these particular groups because of their own perceptual processes. Since the group has developed attitudes and beliefs corresponding to their assumptions, the group encourages conformity and obedience within the individual.

However, the physical and psychological development of the individual is inconsistent with these group dynamics. This causes dissonance and conflict. The relationship between subjective social perception and the group perception system, then, will be a consequence of the dynamic relationship between individual and group processes. While neither process can determine the other, and the result must be considered contingent, clearly distinguishable patterns can be detected. Detection is made possible through the analysis of the process of subjective and group social perception, and the consistency or inconsistencies that develop. In this case, examination of both individual and group processes and the extent to which perceptions are held, is necessary in order to make reasonable projections about the outcome of future interaction.

Although contingency is present, then, the process of social perception is not haphazard. Psychologists have long held the identity of objects and features in the environment supplies individuals with a feeling of stability and security (e.g. Vernon, 1971). Our recognition of objects allows us the potential to proceed from understanding. If the selection and categorization of objects were humanly impossible, then it would be just as impossible to obtain a social perception, or engage in social interaction.

As we perceive the world around us as children, and master the categories of shapes, sizes, language, and symbols, we become prepared to classify similar objects into familiar patterns. Moreover, individuals come to expect objects to correspond to learned categories, and incorporate newly identified objects on the basis of these categories to broaden their understanding. To do otherwise would force individuals to analyze each and every object, and this would make life impossibly difficult, placing individuals in the world of child-like bewilderment.

Moreover, when new objects or thoughts are beyond the boundaries of developed categories, or are too difficult to categorize, individuals will either simplify the object or thought to fit what is already known, or will abandon the object or thought entirely. Social perception presumes the social reality existing when you fall asleep will remain when you awake the next morning. If you were to wake each day in a new part of the world, with new norms, language, and means for material well-being, you would not know how to socially interact and survival would be unlikely.

This leads to another important element for individual social perception. A common feature among almost all human beings is that social perceptions are partly created in relation to base survival needs. Making sense of the external world is not an abstract process at this base level. Without the ability to construct social perceptions, humans would become unable to interact and obtain minimal material existence. This does not imply that social perceptions need be wholly accurate, or in concert with all other individuals, but it must contain enough social consistency for the individual to survive.

The need for survival, then, is not some base drive hidden in the consciousness, or even unconsciousness, of the individual. Rather, contemporary material survival is obtained through the interaction of individual and group processes and the creation of categorizations at both levels. In brief, survival is a social process. Thus individuals and groups are not free to perceive at will. Nor is there any necessity that developed social perceptions are merely rational choices played out in a zero sum game. In contrast, it is entirely possible individual and group social perceptions may be irrational or even non-rational. The need for material survival may be a common feature within many people's development of social perception and interaction, but it is not imperative that subjective and group perceptions be rationally chosen, or even an accurate reflection of reality. Different social clusters contingently give rise to different individual and group perceptions of material survival.

As individuals categorize perceptions they obviously include far more than what is purely necessary for material survival. A similar process develops within non-material perceptions including religious ideas, cultural norms and values, a philosophy of life, family and friends, etc. Here again, non-material perceptions require individuals to interact with others, and as such, group dynamics again become relevant. Moreover, material survival perceptions cannot determine other non-material perceptions because they are not developed solely in relation to the need to survive. Non-material perceptions are autonomous and influence not only material survival perceptions, but also the formation of subjective social perception and group perceptual systems.

Music provides a good example of the process of non-material perception. Traditional Chinese music is alien to the western version of harmony, and vice/versa. For individuals accustomed to harmony, oriental music is atonal and disrupts learned patterns of harmony. That is, within the learned categories of harmony, Chinese music does not fit into the perceptual understanding of music. "Western" listeners will tend to rebuff oriental music [and not listen to it.] Moreover, non-material factors also influence group dynamics. Music is a common cultural component of groups. In part, music helps groups identify themselves as in-groups, and distinguish themselves from out-groups. Music may be learned from childhood and, through interaction with others, is placed within a group context. The emergent group perception of music can have important meaning for the development of a general perceptual system. Zorba's Greek folk dance, a tribal dance for rain, or the U.S. baby boomers' experience with the Twist, all fit into important group categories and dynamics. Dissonance, deprivation, and intergroup conflict all can be related to the perceptual understanding and use of music.

Finally, it follows that a relationship may exist between non-material individual social perception and group non-material perceptual systems. Moreover, as previously discussed, subjective perceptions cannot be seen apart from emotional paradigms. But to elevate any of these factors as the integrative force between individuals and groups requires the faithful acceptance of some previously accepted theoretical assumption. Individuals and groups are concretely connected only through contingent social interaction as it provides the one common denominator in the formation of subjective perceptions and group perceptual systems.

Individual social perception and interaction, then, is not void of logical characteristics. Although micro processes are not causal aftershocks of macro developments, and contain their own autonomous and contingent process, neither are they totally arbitrary. The fact that individuals must socially relate to and interact with groups acts as a powerful force on subjective perceptions. The individual is not wholly isolated, and this is so not because of some assumption about innate psychological needs, but because of the necessity of individual/group interplay. This interrelationship, then, is at the root of conformity. Even the most rebellious individual spends the vast majority of time conforming. The use of language, no matter how unusual, wearing unconventional clothes no matter how out of the ordinary, following road signs no matter how often rules of the road are bent etc., are for the most part inescapable. To completely rebel, an individual would need to create a totally alien pattern of life. This is why compromise between the autonomous individuals and groups takes place, and this is what forms the basis for the social perception system and interaction.

To continue a previous example, the right-brained individuals and students must learn to come to grips with dissonance and conflict between their own individualized thoughts and actions and that of groups. This is done both within material and non-material perceptions. Materially, perhaps, individuals are able to divide time between work and their own interests, or find a job that allows for intuitive and creative expression. Whatever the case, the dynamic existing within and between individuals and groups creates social perception systems. In the contemporary era, individuals must form some relationship to work and money in order to gain what is necessary for survival. This means that no matter how individual the micro process, people must still form a relation with others, and this requires individuals to come into contact with groups and their dynamics. But this also means that the relationship between the two must be contingent, since neither the individual nor groups can pre-determine the relationship formed.

In summary, then, emotional paradigms and the process of categorization develop within and between both individuals and groups to form social perceptions. Although the process develops autonomously in each, and the result of their interplay is contingent, contemporary individuals and groups are required to form interrelationships. It is logically possible, therefore, to discover the development of subjective social perception and group perceptual systems, and to uncover if individual and group perceptions are internally and externally consistent or inconsistent.

It is on this basis that relatively common social perception systems may establish themselves among generalized groups in society. These groups are constituted of individuals who share relatively common social perceptions, and may be formal or informal, small or large, and even beyond personal interaction. Such diverse groups as families, religious organizations, and social classes may share social perceptions. Not all group members necessarily share precisely the same emotional paradigm, or external world view, and dissension can exist. However, when individuals establish similar social perceptions, and are part of groups that establish social perception systems, it becomes possible to understand generalized interaction within and between those groups.

While a need exists for social connection within and between individuals and groups, contingency remains evident in all realms. This is true within the group itself as it creates the group social perception system. No imperative exists for the social perception system to develop in any particular manner. The only boundary is that social perception systems are created within the context of social interaction. Moreover, as individuals interact with groups, emotional paradigms and categorization come to play not only in the subjective evaluation of the group, and in the social perception system of the group itself, but in establishing positive or negative social interactions with other groups. Social psychologists have forcefully pointed out that groups do not stand in isolation, and since groups interact with other groups, the perception of others also comes into play. Thus autonomy and contingency within and between groups' perception systems can influence not only subjective social perception, but intergroup dynamics. That is, as groups perceive and categorize out-groups, the interrelationship between groups becomes contingent. Moreover, this fundamental process remains whether or not group perceptions reflect reality. Thus, intergroup perception systems may or may not place groups in concert or conflict with each other.

Once again, contingent intergroup dynamics does not lead to a relativist position. Just as contemporary society requires individuals to interact with groups, it also requires interaction between groups. The complexities of the contemporary era means that groups, no matter how large, find themselves existing within a maze of other groups, and necessarily interacting with them. Indeed, an endemic part of the group dynamics is to define out-groups, and this obviously requires at least a perception that other groups exist. This feature seems common to all groups in all societies, no matter their racial, ethnic, religious, or social class characteristics.

Regrettably, the continual emphasis on social integration has led psychologists, social psychologists and sociologists alike to a misplaced explanation of these processes. Traditional explanations are dominated by universal assumptions of psychological or structural developments which view out-group development as dysfunctional. But the existence of outgroups cannot be explained within the context of social integration, nor by universal principles predicting interaction between groups. Rather the process is contingently constructed, where the interaction of groups remains necessary for categorization of perceived reality, but its outcome is dependent on whether social perception systems develop in consistent or inconsistent, and cohesive or conflictual, ways. Thus the process may not be universal, but it is comprehendible.

A contingent approach to out-groups helps explain the discrimination, prejudice and ethnocentrism so prevalent in the contemporary world. Rather than viewing the cause of out-group beliefs and attitudes as a result of psychological deficiencies, (e.g. authoritarian personalities, or feelings of deprivation) a contingent approach would begin with autonomous individuals. At this individual level, people select and categorize feelings and information about other groups in the same way they select and categorize all feelings and information. That is, feelings and information about racial, ethnic, social class or gender groups are sorted according to developed social perceptions. But once again this is not a totally individual process. Instead, the process is shared with members of identified groups, where beliefs about in-groups are given favorable status, in part, because this benefits the self-conception of group members. Moreover, since levels of discrimination, prejudice and ethnocentrism rise and fall over time, this process is not only based on the relationship between individuals and groups, and the processes between groups, but between both of these and macro phenomena.

While these micro and macro processes combine contingently, the common feature between them is the social nature of their interrelation. The socially necessary process of group interaction, then, provides a common denominator from which intergroup relations may be analyzed. Autonomy and contingency only imply universal explanations must be rejected, not that analysis is impossible. Without preconditions, and using categorization of group social perception systems as they relate to material and non-material ideas and objects as a starting point, it is possible to uncover social interaction as it unfolds between groups, and even to uncover contingent possibilities. This is the limit of social inquiry.

The dynamic development of a social perception system, then, is not a process of implosion. Individuals and groups are not mutually constitutive. This is so both because individuals and groups are two autonomous levels, and because they develop along two different time and space paths. The physical and psychological process of subjective maturation is both related to social objects and relations, and reflects the subjective social perception of the external world. Individuals, then, cultivate their social perception based on their entire personal history, including their interaction with others. This ultimately forms the backdrop from which individuals perceive their interrelation with groups.

But the group dynamic autonomously plays its part as well, and exists within a time and space frame separate from individuals. Put simply, the history of the group is distinct from the history of the individual. Thus, the formation of individual social perception cannot be purely a subjective biological or psychological process, nor are group social perceptions formed purely from social or objective processes. Instead, both are sophisticated, uniquely human expressions, where the autonomous individual and group processes mesh.

In sum, social perception is the totality of biological and psychological processes of memory, perception, attitudes, emotions, and personality combined with conformity, deprivation, conflict, and dissonance. This combination allows individuals and groups to be related, yet develop along distinct time and space paths. It also allows both individuals and groups to mutually influence each other to perceive thoughts, feelings and actions, and choose alternatives. For example, new and unfamiliar thoughts, feelings, and actions present little difficulty when they correspond to established social perceptions. Whenever possible, choices are made amenable to individual and group perceptions. However, inconsistent interpretation and actions also arise. Since social perception and social interaction are mutual requirements for either to exist, inconsistent thoughts or actions are received as potentially destructive. Consequently, whether consistent or inconsistent, all actions are judged by individuals and groups through developed social perception systems.

This process can be seen as individuals make everyday decisions. Individuals at a group gathering must make a judgment about when to leave. Part of the decision is based on subjective social perception. Attitudes, emotions and personality will help shape the decision. Whether it is a good idea to stay will be based, in part, on perceptions of what good is, and whether it will be better to leave. This single subjective decision relies on a complex web of perceptions categorized since childhood. However, the decision is not totally subjective. Group dynamics, including conformity, conflict, and the group perception system comes into play. If the gathering typically lasts for hours, but the individual wants to leave ten minutes after arrival, the group perception will have a dynamic relationship to the subjective decision and action. The contingent decision will vary from individual to individual, and from group to group. Even how the question is subjectively phrased or perceived by the group makes a difference. The subjective phrasing of "should I go home?" requires complicated perceptions of home. If the phrase was, "should I leave here?" other places to go must be perceived. At the group level, the perceptual system may relax conformity standards depending on the perceived reason for leaving. If someone at home is ill, or if work needs to be done, the individual may more readily be excused. If the group perceives the individual simply does not want to be there, the group may act to encourage conformity. Despite these contingencies, the process remains comprehendible.

Once social perception systems are developed, dramatic calls for change are problematic both for individuals and groups. Moreover, the reality of the need for change is not the deciding factor. People do not enjoy dissonance, and develop a variety of social psychological mechanisms to avoid it. These include altering beliefs and attitudes, often within the path of least resistance, and the perception that dissonance is an attack on personal knowledge and freedom. Group dynamics also are adept at redefining in-groups and out-groups as dominant or subordinate, selecting new criteria to evaluate groups, or finding new groups to reshuffle group rankings. The resistance to change is sensible because social perception systems are fostered over long periods and include complex categorizations, feelings, attitudes and behaviors. No individual or group will easily accept inconsistent ideas or attitudes into their social perception systems. This is a primary catalyst for stability and conformity within society. Change threatens the difficult and uniquely human process of constructing a social perception system.

Resistance to change does not eliminate transformation of social perception systems, but it does mean perceived inconsistencies must be strongly evident. Biology, emotional paradigms, cognition, behavioral effects, and group dynamics create a continuing process aimed at consistency, with developed categories ingrained in the social perception system. This is a life-long process for the individual, and spans the entire history of the group. When individual and group social perceptions are consistent, social perception systems are difficult to challenge. Such systems have great capacities to defend against and outlaw minor inconsistencies and conflict, and when needed, are flexible enough to select alternatives that fit most neatly into the pre-existing system.

It is a mistake, however, to see social perception systems as cast in stone. These systems can and do change, and the source of change can be from either individual or group processes. While neither source of change develops in isolation from the other, their autonomy allows them to be distinguishable. At the individual level, the need for social interaction is a powerful influence on both the already-established social perception system and the potential for its change. Social interaction can act to encourage attitudes and emotions consistent with established social perception systems, but interaction may also cause individuals to question what was previously believed. For example, someone who is unemployed for an extended period of time may question long-held social perceptions that have historically been consistent with ascribed or achieved groups to which he or she belongs. Similarly, a college student may begin to question the utility of gaining a college degree if it becomes unlikely graduation can be transferred into a good job. No matter how carefully constructed, if new situations are not easily absorbed into established categories, change becomes possible.

A variety of biological, cognitive, and emotional changes may alter subjective social perceptions, and a variety of group processes may alter group perception systems, but it is only in extraordinary situations that these processes will fundamentally change social interaction. Individuals, for example, may change their attitude toward personal health and this may lead to an effort to eat better foods, exercise

and reduce stress. This will have importance for individual social perception, but does not require a fundamental change. The individual and
group dynamic will be altered, and some groups previously a part of
the individual's interactions may be refashioned, but psychological
mechanisms are available to incorporate these changes into accepted
social perceptions. At the group level, a regular informal gathering of
friends may collectively decide to read poems, or engage in a charitable
effort, but once again this may be accomplished without fundamentally
changing group perception and interaction. Undermining subjective
social perceptions is a painful and difficult process, and occurs only
when profound inconsistencies and/or conflicts develop between individuals, or between individuals and groups. The inconsistencies must
be severe, because fundamental changes are selected as a last resort,
attempted only when the variety of alternatives have been thoroughly
exhausted.

   At the group level, change involving inconsistencies is not simply
a process of developing in and out-groups, as suggested by many social
psychologists. Group social perception and interaction are more complex than group dynamics as defined in social psychology. While the
selection and categorization of group perceptions by definition is resistant to change, out-groups are not merely the result of psychological
needs. Rather group perception develops, as well, from concrete inconsistencies that emerge between groups, and are based, in part, on
inconsistencies between groups and macro developments. For example,
social conflict over abortion in the U.S. is illustrative. Neither pro-
choice or pro-life groups may be said to be in conflict solely due to in-
and out-group processes. Macro phenomena must enter into the analysis, and at a minimum must include such factors as the historic, social,
economic, and political position of women, along with elements of
religion, families, and children, to mention just a few. An understanding of the conflict and a call to action in any direction, will be incorporated and analyzed within group social perception systems, but also
will be perceived through macro processes that interrelate with groups.
Consequently, change of existing social perception systems do not develop solely due to either macro or micro factors, but are a combination
of the interplay between the two. This means, at a limit, that even fundamental change will always be colored by the existing social perception system.

   A final area of inquiry needing exploration is the potential for
large scale, or national social perception. Here I would accept elements
of both Collins' and Giddens' work (see Chapter Two). Collins argues
an interactional chain develops into large-scale networks. Social per-

ception systems may develop in a similar manner beyond any single group, no matter how large. Autonomy and contingency expressed within a national social perception system makes it possible to generalize differences. For example, agrarian societies will have a distinctive social perception system, separate from one formed within a highly industrial society. Differences also will exist between a society with an unmixed population vs. one that has a high percentage of various ethnic immigrants, and between a small entirely mountainous society from a transcontinental one.

Moreover, this more macro social perception system filters messages received by groups and individuals. An agrarian society, with corresponding perceptions of land and family roles will generally categorize children's rights differently than a mostly industrialized, urban society. New ideas, thoughts or national actions are selected, categorized and acted upon or ignored through existing social perception systems. This is so whether or not the new ideas, thoughts, and contemplated actions accurately reflect the social situation. Thus despite the autonomy and contingency of national social perception, it is still possible to make some generalized statements. But, as Giddens argues, these statements must be only of the most general nature. Since not all people develop social perception in relation to all social groups, limits exist for generalizations.

However, limitations on examining national social perception systems become less severe when macro phenomena is taken into account. As suggested in the beginning of this chapter, an effort has been made to isolate individual and group processes from that of macro phenomena. It is obvious that this is an analytic, and not a real, or even practical idea. Macro processes affect both autonomous individual and autonomous group processes at every step, and vice versa. Before turning to an explanation of the macro processes, however, one further micro element must be explored. That is the element of power.

Power and Social Perception

Traditional theories of micro power revolve around empiricist and behavioral definitions. Empiricists believed humans emulate natural law, and this encouraged theorists such as Hobbes to articulate power as analogous to physical mechanics. If A exerts a force onto B, a change will occur. Power becomes the behavioral ability for A to exact change in B. As the behavioral model unfolded, theorists expanded definitions to recognize that power may exist whether or not force is directly used, that 'interest' is necessary for power to be effectual, and that power is sometimes used to gain willing compliance, even when compliance is not in the interest of the powerless (Ball, 1992).

Three contemporary forms of power analysis attempt to transcend behavioral explanations. However, each is inadequate for a contingency theory. The first contemporary perspective, the communicative model, has already received some attention in this work (see Chapter Two). The communicative perspective defines power as the ability to communicate a powerful message. Weber used this idea to claim power is the force of one's own will on others, where an individual or group purposively realizes their aim through action and obtains compliance. In contrast, Hannah Arendt defines power as the communal ability to communicate ideas and convictions, where agreement is the goal (Ball, 1992, p. 20-25). As discussed earlier in this work, Habermas also seizes on the idea of communicative action. His work is combination of Weber and Arendt. From Weber, Habermas accepts the notion of strategic power, rationally institutionalized, but from Arendt, Habermas accepts the idea that power is generated, ideally, through communal communication. Habermas combines the two by placing communicative action as a goal, and denounces institutionalized forms of power that inhibit its development.

Even this short description points out the reasons why communicatively defined power is inadequate for a contingency theory. Its failure rests in the lack of autonomy provided at both macro and micro levels. Autonomy implies that power is more than a mechanism that ties micro and macro together. Instead, power must first be analyzed in each level. Weber's analysis of power stems, in the first instance, from a macro analysis of how power is transferred and maintained at the micro level. Arendt begins at the more micro level, and investigates how power is ascended. And Habermas' approach accepts Weber's macro assumptions, but holds hope for ascendancy. While insights from communicative power should be incorporated within a contingent approach, power must first be analyzed as it develops within autonomous micro and macro levels before any unifying mechanism can be established. By doing so, both micro and macro assumptions can be avoided.

The second contemporary perspective of power is realist. Realism rejects causal models of power, and defines power as the consequence of varying social roles. That is, power simply is generated through positions of power. Here, individuals are not viewed as intrinsically powerful, but social roles are. In addition, realists define power as: necessary for the coordination of society; containing no guarantee that powerful social roles will be used successfully; not power 'over' some-one, but rather power to do something; and not used in opposition to the interests of the powerless. In sum, power may be used in a variety of ways, and since power is always relative to social roles, it is possible for the powerless to become powerful (Ball, 1992, p. 25-27).

The realist perspective on power also is inadequate for a contin-gency theory. With power embedded in social roles as a main focal point, realists confine the autonomous influence on power relations created by individual and macro processes. For example, what part does biology play in aggression and power; and what of cultural differ-ences encouraging different values; and what of tangible material or normative power differentials between people (Argyle, 1992)? The social aspects of power as discussed by realists remain significant, but from a contingent point of view, this form of power is merely one among many contingent possibilities.

The third contemporary perspective on power is postmodernism. Once again, the traditional model of power, defined as the ability to force some action, is rejected. Foucault adds the concept of specializa-tion, where experts gain power over knowledge, including administra-tion and surveillance. However, knowledge power is not centrally maintained, rather it is locally dispersed in a multitude of situations and in a multitude of forms (Ball, 1992, p. 27-30). But as discussed earlier (see Chapter Three), postmodernism, in general, and Foucault's theory of power in particular, are again inadequate for a contingency theory of power.

Contingency theory cannot ignore the autonomous level of macro phenomena where power also evidently exists. Once again, this is not to deny the insight of postmodernism which suggests that power cannot be universally described solely from a macro analysis. Nonetheless, the autonomous macro process must be included. Wartenberg (1992) makes a similar point by developing a theory of situated social power. Power is seen as situated because no individual may exercise power without the cooperation of 'social others.' Power is impotent unless the powerful, and others, generate an interest in the disempowered to comply. If interest is not situated, compliance will not develop. Thus consent is not a process of free will, but rather a response to situated power. Moreover, power is not exercised in the absence of alternatives for the powerless, but in the presence of power situated beyond the dyad of the powerful and disempowered, where the disempowered have an interest in something that the powerful have (Wartenberg, 1992, p. 79-90).

In ways similar to Bourdieu, Wartenberg's analysis of power makes use of a concept of field. Situated power is more than institutions, or fixed patterns of interaction. Rather, power may be situated in a variety of ways and for various periods of time. Moreover, individuals may or may not be aware of situated power. For example, Wartenberg uses the example of sexism to show that even males who believe themselves to be non-sexist cannot escape the fact of situated power where women are culturally and economically discriminated against. In such a scenario, no relationship can be non-sexist.

While Wartenberg correctly sees power as more than the dyad of two individuals, one powerful and one not, and correctly suggests that more macro phenomena must be included in any analysis of power, his theory also remains inadequate. He sees power as external to the individual, and moreover once a field of power is created, the individual and/or group only has the ability to adapt to, not change, it. In short, Wartenberg's analysis of power denies the autonomy of the micro process. For example, Brown (1988) has shown that low-status groups show increased in-group bias only when the power differential is seen as illegitimate; Argyle (1992) suggests that positive shared goals work well on a small scale, but aggressive goals are needed at the national level; Ross and Nisbett (1991) point to the cognitive strategies individuals use to make judgments, stressing personal meanings of situations and power. Thus while insights from Wartenberg's theory should be included, it cannot be the sole basis of a contingent theory of power.

What part, then, should power play in a contingency theory, and how does it relate to the development of social perception? The discussions of social perception and power share some common components. These include the social nature of their development, that both micro and macro phenomena are highlighted, that social perception and power may not be understood by all social actors, that social perception and power are complex and beyond universal explanations, that social perception and power at the micro level requires a different analysis than macro social perception systems and power, that social perception and power may or may not develop in consistent ways, and that the possibility exists that social perception and power relations may be changed. A contingent theory can additionally include two vital elements to these considerations. First, all of these features have room for examination because no micro or macro assumptions are adopted, and consequently, the analysis is greatly expanded and more inclusive. And second, contingent concepts of social perception and power allow for autonomous combinations, with unpredictable results.

It also is fundamental that power be included when analyzing social perception. The different perspectives of power previously discussed have shown the vital role of power in social relations. However, power is activated for reasons beyond objective social relations. The subjective and group process of categorization already has been shown necessary for the formation of perception and interaction. But individuals and groups do not categorize information like a machine. A level of interest must exist on the part of individuals and groups before categorization takes place. This means interest is critical in the formation of social perception and interaction, and sets in motion the potential use of power on behalf of individual and/or group interests. While power may be exercised at the micro or macro level, may be realized or obscured, and may generate conflict or coordination, as long as interest exists, and others have some influence over that interest, a power relationship may be said to form. This is so whether or not that 'interest' matches social reality.

But what is the source of interests? de Sousa (1991) has argued that using the concept of interests is really just a way to avoid discussing emotions. Even material concerns cannot wholly explain material interests, especially since the level of interest varies so widely among individuals. And although individuals who exercise power, and those who receive it, view power as an internal subjective experience in relation to their shared culture (De Vos and Suarez-Orozco, 1992), what is the subjective foundation for interpreting that experience? Without emotions, then, interests have no source. Indeed, emotions must be connected to the development of social perception if, as it has been argued in this work, individuals are autonomous from both groups and macro structures. Without this connection, deconstruction, not contingency would necessarily result. This is so because subjective categorization would have no grounding. Individuals would simply emotionally absorb and categorize information in a haphazard way.

Consequently, the concept of emotional paradigms -- a combination of innate emotions mixing with social interaction -- has implications for comprehending power. The interest to exercise power now becomes the result of individual perceptions developed in relation to groups and wider social contexts. Moreover, interests will vary depending on the contingent relationship between the individual, groups, and macro structures. No purely psychological or objective analysis can sufficiently explain why or how power is exercised. Power is exercised because of more than a psychological need, and more than a predetermined social role. Rather, power is exercised because of the dynamic relationship among and between individuals and groups, and among and between micro and macro processes.

It is a mistake, therefore, to view interests within power relationships as solely expressed by those powerless or powerful who have some need or want fulfilled. Powerful individuals or groups may or may not develop perceptions, and may or may not act in interested ways to exercise power. Moreover, while powerful acts are social phenomena, and consequently, must be exercised through social interaction, power is not necessarily generalized to express a relationship between all powerful people and all powerless people. That is, power exercised within a particular field may not influence all, or even many, other people. Consequently, no correlation exists between the level of power and the number of powerless, nor the level of power and the number of powerful.

The reason why various possibilities emerge is because autonomous micro emotional and cognitive processes relate to macro processes. Thus contingency theory improves contemporary perspectives on power, where autonomy is eliminated as a possibility, and either micro power relationships are given ascendant status, or macro power relationships are granted descendent status, or as in the case of the realist position, the process becomes one of implosion. If the two processes are seen as autonomous, then power relations can be studied both at the micro and macro levels. It then becomes possible, for example, to see how a few powerful individuals and/or groups may have the interest to wield power over macro processes, and influence micro processes, yet escape the descendant trap of macro, universal explanations of all-powerful groups. As discussed in the next chapter, whether or not individuals and groups have an interest, and are able, to act in powerful ways within macro structures is contingent, not wholly defined by social role. Moreover, the opposite is also true. Since micro power relations may or may not be related to macro processes, no universal principle can claim power is so omnipresent that it necessarily leads to social integration, or is beyond change originated at the micro level. Whether or not individuals are interested in, and act on relations of power can be uncovered only through investigations of the micro/macro dynamic.

In sum, micro and macro levels of power may or may not be in concert, and as such, the potential for change or social cohesion is always present. Moreover, contingent results of power relations cannot be divorced from the process of social perception. This is so because without the emotions and categorizations that yield social interaction, the interest to exercise power becomes either objectified, deconstructed, or rationally determined to lead to social cohesion. Instead, contingency theory holds that autonomous micro and macro processes of power may or may not be recognized, and develop and relate in unpredictable ways.

Conclusions

Previously, the argument was made that any theory which predetermines outcomes must be rejected. This type of theory is not really a theory at all. Instead, it is usually an ideological set of assumptions about the nature of society. The advantage of a contingency perspective is that it allows for alternative possibilities. Contingency theory does not dictate findings, but rather provides an alternative to endless analytic debate about who has the best set of assumptions, and places the emphasis where it belongs: on empirical findings. The intent in developing a contingent theory of autonomous individual and group processes is to avoid preconceived mistakes and articulate postulates that would be inclusive of the important work done throughout the history of micro theories, but simultaneously encourage a non-assumptive search of social reality. These postulates would include:

1) Individual and group processes are not aimed solely at social order and integration. Contingency theory must allow for inconsistencies and conflict. The notion of inconsistency is not equal to conflict, however, as inconsistencies may be reordered within social perception or group perceptual systems to avoid conflict, or lead to non-rational disorder.

2) Emotional paradigms and the selection and categorization of social information are capabilities unique to human beings, and are necessary to avoid information overload. Without emotional paradigms, and selection and categorization, simple tasks would become impossibly difficult.

3) Emotions and the process of selection and categorization cannot be purely subjective because social interaction is required to obtain language, ideas, emotional paradigms, etc.

4) Survival needs also are a combination of subjective emotional paradigms and categorization, social interaction, and

wider social contexts. The form of survival, then, is necessarily contingent on the dynamic between them.

5) Given three and four, individual and group processes also must be considered a combination of individual processes, social interaction, and wider social contexts. This means that social perception and interaction may develop within groups, as well as within individuals. Consequently, individuals and groups are autonomous.

6) The social aspects of perception and interaction enables individuals to gain more social knowledge than would be possible on their own. Simultaneously, since external social objects are socially created, no macro process or object is irrevocably exterior to individuals.

7) Conversely to six, not all individuals and groups necessarily perceive or interact with all other individuals and groups. This means not all social reality may be available or comprehended by all social actors.

8) Nonetheless, and regardless of seven, the social aspects of perception and interaction within individuals, and within group dynamics allow for contingent relationships among and between individuals and groups to be examined.

9) As social actors perceive, belong to, and act within different groups the possibility exists that power differentials may emerge.

10) Power exists within and between individuals and groups, is generated by the interest to socially interact in a powerful manner, and therefore, power is related to the process of perception and interaction. Power may or may not be recognizable to all social actors, may or may not be accepted even when recognized, and may or may not be erected, maintained, and/or changed by large or small groups.

11) The social psychological processes of group dynamics includes the processes of conformity and obedience, but whether or not these prove to be an outcome is contingent

on whether inconsistencies and/or conflicts emerge among and between individuals and groups.

12) Inconsistencies and conflicts of social perceptions among and between individuals and groups, will generally be resisted. The more obvious and serious the inconsistency and conflict, the more likely it will need to be interpreted and acted on.

13) Following twelve, this helps explain why ethnic, racial and cultural differences are often used to explain away, and act upon, inconsistencies and conflicts. These explanations and actions often form the path of least resistance to already existing social perception systems.

14) Following thirteen, contingent changes within individual and/or group social perceptions and interactions will always be colored by the already existing perceptions and patterns of interaction.

15) None of the above requires the elimination of micro social theories. In fact, all of the above borrows heavily from these perspectives. Only those assumptions which preclude the autonomy between micro and macro, or the contingent nature of the relationship between the two levels, need be eliminated.

This chapter began with an important disclaimer: that the discussion would analytically be separated from macro processes. That disclaimer remains. Indeed, none of the postulates listed above may be adequately understood unless the relationship between micro and macro processes are uncovered. Chapter nine aims at making that relationship clear. However, before undertaking that discussion, Chapter Eight articulates the elements of contingent macro structures.

Chapter Eight

Contingent Social Structures

One day in my Sociological Theory class, after a heated discussion on the relationship between individuals and structures, a student asked a puzzling question. "I'm confused," she said, "as to what structures are exactly. How are they theoretically defined?" My response was to recite the various definitions covered in class. This diversity of structural definitions should be as unsettling to theorists, as it was to my student.

Micro theories consider structures as little more than amalgamations originating at the micro level, where structures become accumulated subjective thoughts and/or actions. The picture of structures is no more clear in structural theories. Although social structures obviously are of vital interest, macro theorists differ widely in their interpretation. Within classical sociological theory, Marx emphasized economic structures, and viewed control of these structures by the ruling class as influencing workers; Durkheim was concerned with how collective representations gained normative status and thus influenced individual behavior; and Weber argued structures are neither objective, nor scientifically recognizable, and concerned himself only in uncovering regularities created by social action. But what definition of structure can we garner from these efforts? Are structures economic or normative, and are they even comprehendible?

By the mid-twentieth century, macro structural theory was at its height, but definitions were still blurred. Parsons viewed structures as functional prerequisites for any society, and although micro elements gain some mention within his analysis, the structures of social system, culture, and personality were primary. All other aspects of society either do or do not have a functional role within the structures. Dahrendorf (1959) accepted functional prerequisites for the development of society, but emphasized the constraint needed to maintain development, and the conflict that would emerge in doing so. He believed society was made up of associations, where hierarchy and authority within associations were imperative if they were to remain consistent with functional structures. As such, conflict always has the potential to emerge. Finally, Peter Blau (1977) also accepts key functional assumptions, but without the emphasis on culture and norms. Blau views structures as social positions that emerge in relation to differentiation and the growing complexity of society. Thus, for Blau, structures become variables of social positions such as race, gender, or age.

Taken together, all three approaches highlight the flexibility of structural definitions. Culture, personality, associations, and social positions were each selected as defining characteristics of structures. It seems whatever the theorist chose to explain became the key to structural understanding. The reason for this variety of explanations is that functionally influenced theorists consider the growing complexity of society a process even more macro than social structures. However, since differentiation is viewed as a process, not a structure, and since it is an assumption equivalent to a social fact that needed no further explanation, functionalists of all stripes simply chose to define and explore structures within this factual context. Since the differentiation process was left unexplored, and the structures defined were seen as growing out of that process, significant variety and limits were placed on any articulation of structures.

Unsatisfied with the functional explanation of structures, a more recent effort was conducted by theorists of structuralism. Based on an interest in the structures of language, where language is perceived to follow universal laws, structuralism found a method that could avoid functionalist assumptions. In anthropology, Levi-Strauss argued structures exist at many levels, but most significantly in the unconscious mind. Here objective structures dominate not only language, but all forms of communication. Since the mind is inaccessible to investigation, unconscious structures become represented through human communication. Levi-Strauss examined a variety of divergent cultures to reveal the common universal structures within them (Ritzer, 1992). Thus Levi-Strauss was opposed to any method emphasizing human thought or action. Instead, he concentrated on social products to uncover their deep structures.

Structuralist Marxism attempts much the same, but from a more macro perspective. Althusser (1979), for example, accepts what he perceives as the later Marx's explanation of political economy, but argued structures are evident throughout all levels of society. Consequently, structures within structures within structures exist, each having their own logic and contradiction. Change is possible only when a confluence of changes within various structures at various levels become synchronized. Common to neo-Marxist structuralism (e.g. Poulantzas, 1978) is an absence of subjective thought or action. Society, at whatever level, is constituted by objective structures which reside outside the individual realm. Since structures are universal and objective, no room exists for the human creation, maintenance or change of structural determinants. Moreover, structures are often unobservable to human beings.

The limits of the structuralist approach led to, and were exploited by, poststructuralism, or what has been referred to in this work as postmodernism. As discussed previously (see Chapter Three), postmodernism is also concerned with language, but instead of underlying, universal structures, postmodernism suggests structures simply do not exist.

This brief review of how the concept of macro structures has been defined and used is of little help for a contingency theory. A critical area related to structures remains unexamined. That area is an explanation of how autonomous and contingent structural processes unfold. The failure to reveal structural processes rests, in part, in the distorted macro view of micro processes. Macro phenomena is traditionally seen as setting parameters for micro activity (e.g. Durkheim's anomie or Marx's alienation). Micro processes become adaptive, where micro activity and thought are subject to conditional developments, and individuals are often considered unaware of the structural conditions to which they must adapt (De Vos and Suarez-Orozco, 1992 p. 17-25). But as shown in the last chapter, this approach fails to emphasize both autonomous individual and group processes, and moreover assumes individuals or groups have little influence over the conditional processes. Simultaneously, it is equally wrong to assume from a micro perspective that all individuals actively create the macro conditions around them. This micro bias denies the importance of the autonomous level of macro phenomena, and the influence that it may have on micro processes. The two levels are autonomous and dynamically interrelate in a contingent way. These issues are discussed in the following section.

Creating and Maintaining Social Structures

The core of the micro critique of structural theories is the failure to explain how macro structures emerge, how they are maintained, and how they relate to micro processes. Is this a legitimate criticism? Macro theories have traditionally provided an explanation of structures, but it has been inadequate to ease micro concerns, and has little benefit for a contingency theory. After rejecting both theological and natural canon, classical macro theorists argued the relationship between micro and macro phenomena must be centered on social relations. And although widely divergent explanations emerged, social processes were considered the source of structural origination.

A contingency theory of structures begins on this same premise, but moves beyond traditional structural theories. As discussed in the last chapter, social interaction is a unifying force between individuals and groups. And since social interaction is both autonomous from, yet related to, subjective and group perception, not all individuals necessarily influence, or may even be aware of, all social interaction. Social interaction, then, enables and constrains micro and macro processes. First, social interaction allows for an expansion of human understanding and action beyond the limits of individuals, as other individual perceptions and actions become recognizable through social interaction. And second, since social interaction is the link between individuals and groups, and to the exercise of power, social structures can have no other source but this same social interaction process. Any alternative explanation for the existence of structures must be based on a set of faithful assumptions. This mistake was not made by the classical sociologists, who each gave macro developments a social source. Durkheim's collective representations, Marx's ruling class, and Weber's regularities of social action clearly, although differentially, posited people as the creators of social patterns and structures. Twentieth century social theory has lost sight of this important guidepost. The mechanical versions of theory exhibited in structural functionalism and orthodox Marxism gained dominance, then was attacked by micro theorists, and, in turn, have given way to the growing attraction of relativism. All of this was, and is, a colossal misstep in theory. It also is the reason why so few practical applications of macro theory have been advanced in the twentieth century. Once social interaction is removed from the equation of structural analysis, the separation of theory from practical applications is sure to follow. No wonder structural theories have been continually behind, not ahead, of the curve in recognizing many fundamental changes in structures throughout the century.

Structures, then, are not objective and separate from human activity. Instead, social interaction generates macro structures when, as the result of interactions of at least some people, macro processes are created and have an influence on the micro processes of large populations. This means that both micro and macro postulates about macro phenomena must be abandoned. Any micro theory that refuses to allow for the autonomous development of macro influences on micro processes misconstrues structures. Micro theorists are correct that structures cannot exists in a vacuum void of human action, but micro theorists are wrong when they insist that structures ascend from multiple micro activities. The micro belief that structures emanate from a kind of individual ballot selection eliminates the contingent possibility that actions by only some individuals is enough to create structures that influence many individuals and groups. Simultaneously, macro theorists are correct in arguing that structures may exist autonomously from, and exert an influence upon, micro processes, but are wrong to grant structures an objective status apart from the social interactions that create them. Similar errors have been committed in the last decade by the integrative theorists, who have attempted a micro-macro synthesis. Ascendant theorists have ignored autonomous macro influences, descendent theorists have ignored autonomous micro influences, and implosion theorists have ignored both.

The question of the origination of structures, then, is different than the traditional question about structures asked by twentieth century social theorists. The question is not whether macro structures are able to attain an objective status. Rather, the question is: What is the form of social interaction that both has enabled the development of macro structures and maintained and/or changed them? The answer to such a question must be contingent. No assumptions about the internal logic of structures, or about the primacy of a particular macro structure will aid in this search. Moreover, any assumption about social integration and order also must be rejected. While social integration, even at the international level, is always a contingent possibility, structural disintegration also must be considered. Nation-states, themselves, have recently disintegrated in the former Soviet Union and in eastern Europe, and earlier empires and regions of domination gave way to colonial powers, only to reemerge later in altered forms. Racial, ethnic, and cultural differences also may play a destabilizing role. And no one can guarantee ecological stability. Thus theoretical assumptions that determine the form of structures and their interrelationships will be of limited help in the search for social reality. Rather, the search must be an empirical one that attempts to uncover the autonomous macro structures of society that were created through forms of interaction.

In my view, the critical autonomous structures that have emerged in the contemporary era, and must be analyzed are economic, political, cultural and ecological. Further, the search for the forms of interaction that created, maintain and change these structures must include an analysis of power. As in micro processes, power is fundamental to macro developments. This does not mean that those who use power to develop, maintain or change structures do so within a purely rational context. Rational choice and unintended consequences, and even partial understanding of social reality may certainly play a role in the interaction to develop structures. The development of structures does imply, however, that those who have interactionally created them must have an interest in doing so.

While power and interest should not be defined solely within its economic or material context, economic interest is surely important in the development of economic structures. At the macro level, economic structures have been developed through social interaction of those who are powerful enough to create them. Monetary policies and practices, trade associations, trade unions, the power of management, the ability to influence forms of labor, and the free market itself, all have powerful influences on people and groups, and all have been developed through the social interaction of people with the interest and power to do so. The results of this interaction process is beyond theoretical prediction.

Political structures are similarly contingent and based on social interaction. Political structures emerge through social interaction and the interests and power of individuals who choose and are able to interactionally create them. Whether, democratic, socialist, fascist, communist, authoritarian etc., these political structures have an influence on micro processes and develop through the actions of powerful people. Cultural structures emerge for the same reasons. Forms of art, literature, architecture, popular culture, as well as symbolic interpretations of norms and values were developed by real people with enough interest and power to institute them. For their part, ecological structures are certainly partly natural, but develop, are altered, and interpreted contingently by those in a position and with the interest to do so.

Each of these processes are autonomous from the others. While the use of power may overlap, and while structures are interrelated, the development of each is distinct, and may or may not be consistent or encourage social integration. That is, while a powerful group may attempt, and even succeed, to exercise influence over the development of more than one structure, the result may be contradictory and conflictual. Moreover, power is rarely exercised in a vacuum, free from consequences, or from competition for power. Thus power must itself be considered contingent and may rest with the few or the many. Only

a contingent and empirical investigation of autonomous macro structures can uncover power relationships, and the formation and maintenance of structures.

As an illustration of how these macro processes may work, assume that a powerful group exists that attempts to influence social
structures. Their interests span economics, politics, culture and the
ecological environment. The group's interests are economic in that, as
business people, they hope to bring a product to market. Their interests
are political because they have strong views about government in-
volvement in the private sector. Their interests are cultural because of
their strong beliefs in family values, and also because they aim the
product for purchase by homemakers. And their interests are ecological
because the product they hope to market will have an environmental
impact, and because of their views about the relationship between economic growth and environmental balance. However, because the development of structures is autonomous, their power not only may be
contested, but the aims of the group may be inconsistent or conflictual.

For example, assume the group interacts with others to ensure that
economic structures maintain relatively low wages for employees. The
group raises the threat of leaving one area of high wages for another
with low wages, uses technological improvements to replace workers,
hires consultants to inhibit the formation of unions, etc. The aim of the
group is to lower the cost of production through lowering wages. Politically, the group uses their influence and power in ways that correspond to their economic efforts. The group exercises its power to
actively support lower taxes on businesses, fewer social welfare benefits to increase the pool of low wage workers, and a lower minimum
wage. Moreover, the group supports few government regulations, especially those related to environmental protection.

Culturally, the group extols the virtues of individualism, the free
market, and traditional religious and family values. The group chooses
to use their power to advertise their product only in mass media outlets
that correspond to these cultural beliefs. Finally, ecologically, the
group believes that technology can be used to both protect the environment and in the event of an environmental misstep, can correct any
errors.

This example highlights the consistencies and inconsistencies that
may arise through the use of power within the context of social structures. To begin with, while the product is aimed for use by homemakers, the contradictory economic need for low wages encourages
homemakers to seek employment in order to maintain current family
standards of living. Moreover, group cultural support for traditional

religious and family values also contradicts the economic interests for the same reason. The political aims of the group may contradict the goal of a growing economy, which is necessary if products are to be sold. And all three structures may conflict with ecological structures if damage to the ecological environment is severe enough to threaten human life.

The above illustration is only a limited example of the inconsistencies and conflicts that may emerge as any group attempts to exercise power within established social structures. Moreover, the effort to exercise power will be contested. In democratic, free market economies it is possible that the group's interest will be contested by workers, by environmental groups, by political movements, or by those groups with different cultural agendas. In authoritarian regimes, mass political or cultural movements may emerge that threaten existing powers. The result of these autonomous structural processes must be considered contingent, and thus beyond theoretical assumptions.

Another example of the interplay between micro and macro processes is the issue of family values, especially as it has spawned social conflict in the United States. In the U.S., right wing political conservatives have developed a definition of family and religious values which are proclaimed traditional, and are granted superiority over other values. These beliefs represent a combination of micro and macro processes. At the psychological and social psychological level, the individual and group come to perceive values through a process of categorization and in and out-groups. This micro phenomena is necessary to gain some sense of the world around the individual and group, and requires some level of social interaction. The result is various outlooks on how both families and values are defined, and an interest in taking social action.

But macro structures also play an important role, both in the perceptual systems of individuals and groups, and whether or not inconsistencies or conflicts emerge. Structures have an influence on micro perceptions because they provide the macro processes to which individuals dynamically relate. Nonetheless, the sheer size of contemporary society, and the corresponding development of various macro structures, provides an opportunity for groups to play a significant role. It also allows for divergent groups that may develop significant in and out-group characteristics.

In this light, divergent opinions about family values is a consequence of both autonomous micro and macro developments. Individuals and groups spend long periods interrelating and developing social perceptions and interests. Macro processes and developments that are inconsistent with that worldview are problematic, and will be resisted. This means individuals and groups who perceive 'traditional' families as religiously, morally, and culturally beneficial will react to inconsistent developments as an attack their world view. Similarly, dissonance will develop in any family that is not in the proscribed family mold. Such a family's world view is shaped by their own set of perceptions and experiences which certainly differ from that of the previous group. These divergent perceptions may create a dynamic of conflict.

However, to end the analysis here limits macro investigations into other phenomena. Autonomous structural processes have influenced the change from 'traditional' to a two-wage earner family. Technological structures and their development may influence whether or not jobs are available. Political structures and their development may or may not encourage politicians to exploit the issue in various ways for political gain. And cultural structures may or may not be inconsistent and/or in conflict with a particular form of family, and may or may not sanction the form of conflict which may develop. It is obvious, then, that both micro and macro processes must be included in the discussion. Moreover, since micro processes are autonomously developed among divergent groups, and macro structures, which interrelate with micro processes, also develop autonomously, the result must be contingent on the dynamic between and among them.

All of the contingent possibilities that exist within and between structures and micro processes are available for discovery when each structure is granted autonomy, when structures are collectively seen as autonomous from micro processes, when social interaction is seen as the source of macro development, and power is viewed as endemic to these processes. Taken together, these contingent principles of macro structural development avoid the theoretical mistakes exhibited in traditional micro and macro statements, and in the contemporary efforts at micro/macro synthesis. The autonomy of micro and macro processes, combined with the principles of social interaction and power, lead to an understanding of macro processes that avoids the purely macro and descendent mistakes of looking for laws of social order and integration, and granting structures an objective status. Autonomy, social interaction, and power also avoids the micro and ascendant failure to see the potential macro influence on micro processes. And finally, autonomy, social interaction, and power also avoids the implosion error which fails to see the inherent importance and influence of both micro and macro processes. In sum, the autonomous, social interactive nature of both macro and micro processes allows for contingent possibilities, where consistencies and inconsistencies, and social order or conflict may be uncovered in the realm of social reality, not in theoretical ideas.

The Scale of Structures and Their Interaction

An additional issue also must be discussed when considering structures. That is the issue of scale. Often, social theorists have posited society at the macro end of the micro/macro continuum. But society is, itself, a loose term. Some have tried to further delineate what is meant by society by making it equivalent with the nation-state. However, with the international interplay between cultural, political, economic, and ecological processes, the nation-state has certainly lost some of its definitional luster. The contemporary era has made the global frame of reference for structures appear inescapable.

Nevertheless, the globalization of structures implies neither that the world is becoming socially more integrated, nor that globalization is forever inevitable. The disintegration of the Soviet Union and its former east European satellites provides a useful example. While some believe that the disintegration is actually a step toward integration into a larger sphere of market based democratic societies, whether or not this occurs remains to be seen. Ethnic, political, and economic chaos seem, at present, to rule the macro process in various global regions. It is a mistake to assume that social integration and order is an inevitable, universal force in society. Rather, the macro cultural, political, economic and ecological processes must be considered autonomous, and as such, the possibility for inconsistencies and conflict must remain open, not only in the former Soviet Union, but in how that disintegration may influence the rest of the world.

The most well known theoretical application of globalization is world systems theory. Its founder, Immanuel Wallerstein (1974), argues that only two forms of world systems have existed: the ancient state and the modern market economy. The later is composed first of a core of nations which economically exploit other nations; second, a semi-periphery, where nations are neither wholly exploited or exploit other nations; and third, a periphery where nations are heavily exploited, especially for their raw materials. The development of these three forms of nations, beginning in the sixteenth century, has led to a corresponding international division of labor. The core nations are characterized by free labor, the semi-periphery developed sharecropping and peasantry, and the periphery developed forced forms of labor.

In the more contemporary era, these differences have been consolidated through the political use of the state (Wallerstein, 1980,
1989). While Wallerstein maintains the universality of the system and
the contemporary need for all nations to become incorporated within it,
the process is filled with conflict and power struggles. Thus the world
system may be seen as a zero sum game, where the advance of one
nation necessarily means the decline of another. Moreover, political,
cultural and economic changes and conflict within the world system
necessarily must reflect the global situation.

The emphasis of world system theory on the reactions to global,
structural processes has validity. Even at the level of micro processes,
the globalization of structures has important implications. However,
since macro phenomena interrelates with micro processes, the individual and group dynamic in the Third World necessarily differs from
similar processes in industrialized nations. Nation-states, themselves,
are relatively new in some parts of the world, where structures are not
fully developed. And these underdeveloped structures may not as directly influence perceptions and interactions, where, for example,
groups, not structures, may play the dominant role. Similarly, the development of individual perceptions may also differ from individuals in
core countries. Perceptual allegiance may be to families, clans, or
tribes, not the state (Elias, 1991 p. 178-79). In core nations, the emphasis on free labor more or less requires individuals to seek their own
fortune, and this allows for less constraint by groups and families etc.
Simultaneously, time space distanciation and compression in industrialized nations create the opportunity for new, albeit indirect, group relations.

Consequently, although global structures do influence micro
processes, it is important not to overstate the case. The root of the influence of macro structures lies in the autonomous interrelationship
with micro processes, not in macro determination. One mistake made
by world system theory is that it grants primacy to economic structures
over other macro phenomena. Rooted in a Marxist tradition, world
system theory sees economic processes as determining cultural and
political processes, while ecological processes are ignored altogether.
While it is possible that economics influence other structures, and
Wallerstein makes a strong case for this, other structures, nevertheless,
retain their autonomy, and are not determined. Like most contemporary
theories, the aim of world system theory is to establish a universal explanation for all of human society. As such, some structural component
must be assumed as primary and determining. In this case, economic
structures are chosen. The causal primacy of economics directs both

the global level of analysis in world system theory, and the interest it maintains in history. All that remains is to find facts that support the macro assumption. But other assumptions can be made to support other universal ideas. For example, Skocpol (1979) argues that it is politics, not economics, that is the primary force in the world system, and Anderson (1974a, 1974b) argues for consideration of 'extra-economic' factors, primarily political and cultural elements. The possibilities are endless.

Rather than making universal assumptions about global development of structures, a contingency theory must allow for autonomous global, national, regional, and micro processes. One effort toward that goal was conducted by Hall (1989), who suggested three important considerations when looking at global relations, especially as they relate to power differentials between colonial powers and regions that have not yet reached national status. First, how do powerful states affect changes in non-states; second, how does the structure of non-states affect the already existing states; and third, how are both states and non-states affected by various levels of interaction between them (Hall, 1989 p. 3). While Hall recognizes that modernization and social integration are not uniform throughout the world, nonetheless he also follows world system theory and asserts incorporation into the world system is omnipresent and only a matter of degree.

Another form of world system analysis is dependency theory (e.g. Amin, 1979; Frank, 1969). Here the emphasis in on conflict within the world system, where developed countries dominate the underdeveloped, first by force and later by economic domination. Both forms of domination allow advanced economic nations to purposively block and undermine development in the less developed. This is consciously done to maintain wealth and power in core countries.

A theoretical problem remains, however, no matter whether one views the world system as relative levels of incorporation, or as forcibly unequal. The macro elements attain primacy over micro processes, as if structures dominate all individual thought, action, and reaction. A macro influence is undeniable, but the interrelationship is contingent, and not predictable from a macro analysis alone. Empirical evidence supports this contention. Every historical period contains elements of social similarity and dissimilarity between nations. Even if it was conceded that twentieth century free market economies have developed into a world system (and to do so requires having a blind eye to the significant differences between socialist, fascist and authoritarian economic systems), the political, economic, cultural, and ecological differences between nations of the world system remain profound. One need

look no further than the three nations currently seen as leading capitalist countries. To generalize away the differences between the U.S.,
Germany, and Japan on the basis of a set of macro assumptions not
only underplays the significance that each autonomous structure brings
to that society, but ignores the micro processes which have helped
shape them. Once both macro and micro factors are accounted for, assumed macro generalizations loose their logic. In their place, the
autonomy between and within micro and macro processes lead to a
logic of contingency, where the processes are played out in the real
world with real consequences.

One of the more interesting ways in which macro and micro interrelate is through the expression of nationalism. Nationalism is as a consequence of both micro and macro processes. At the micro level,
individuals perceive in relation to the social perception systems of
groups. This requires social interaction and leads to a worldview that
both helps individuals materially survive, and emotionally and non-
materially generate values and interest in taking social action. This
process is intricately related to macro processes and the establishment
of the state. Although not always a smooth relationship, the nation-state
provides the outer boundaries from which most individuals and groups
are currently able to establish in and out-groups. Moreover, macro
structures, despite global encroachments, remain related, primarily, to
micro processes within the context of the nation-state.

To some extent, this is a matter of degree. For example, within
both developed and less developed societies, economic structures remain primarily national. This is not to ignore the globalization of economic well-being, the rise and importance of multi-national companies,
or how events in one part of the world have an impact on other regions.
Moreover, it is true that economic benefits, at least on a regional basis,
are evident within economic globalization. Core countries are advan-
taged when less developed economies simultaneously export raw materials to more developed nations, and become importers of low-
productivity machinery, technology, and pollution that benefit companies located in advanced nations. Core countries also gain an advantage
when markets on the semi-periphery are opened for their products.

Nonetheless, despite the various economic phases and transitions
of globalization in the twentieth century, a fundamental economic fact
has remained steadfast, especially within the advanced market economies: competition is omnipresent between economic structures. And
economic competition primarily has persisted between nation-states.
There is no evidence this has abated. On the contrary, as the twenty
first-century approaches, competition is accelerating once again.

Part of the reason for increased competition between states is due to autonomous economic structures. Free market economic structures are by their nature not limited to national boundaries. This was true almost from their beginning, as western European nations searched for raw materials and new markets. This era also saw a corresponding rise of new, powerful, national businesses that were able to concentrate their economic muscle within industrial sectors through the manufacture and marketing of critical products. It was on this economic basis that nations turned outward and attempted to control the production, raw materials, labor and trade routes necessary to sustain emerging industrial giants. The result was increasing levels of international competition, specifically over the control over geographic spheres of influence. At this point, little interpenetration of business across boarders took place.

The classical phase of free market economies has given way to the contemporary phase where multi-national companies often interpenetrate each other's markets. It is common for foreign investments to include entire sectors of industrial production. Multi-national companies need foreign markets, as do many national companies. The level and cost of technology, and the productive capacity that technology generates allow even relatively small companies to burst beyond any national or regional economic boundaries. In turn, businesses seek to maintain profits, in part, by finding lower wage regions of the world to manufacture their products, and this leads both to internationalization of production sites, and to a worldwide division of labor and immigration of people toward jobs.

However, these economic processes remain contingent. The globalization of economic structures could have, and can still take, many forms. For example, economic globalization could be expressed either through multinational companies from different nations dominating specific industries, or where many industries come under the control of a single nation. This process and its outcome is contingent, and moreover, may not be understood fully through an analysis of economic structures alone.

Thus one of the possibilities is that economic powers will be concentrated within a single nation. In fact, this was the case from the end of the second World War to approximately 1970, when U.S. companies gained a dominant position in the world. However, this too must seen as the result of a particular contingency: namely that all potential competition to the U.S. was destroyed by the war. Another possibility is that transnational economic structures develop to attempt to rationalize and direct the economic processes. These structures equally would rep-

resent and control economic interests in multiple countries. But, perhaps, the most likely development of contemporary economic structures will be the creation of regional structures. However, even regional
economic structures cannot be void of national interests. That is, if the
effort to create common economic structures in Europe is successful, it
will be dominated by the German economy; if a regional structure is
successfully created in North America, it will be dominated by the
U.S.; and if the Pacific rim successfully creates a regional structure, it
will be dominated by Japan. While any of these prospects are plausible,
neither the logic that pushes in a particular direction, nor universal assumptions about these developments can explain the contingency of the
results.

Moreover, the contingency of economic structures cannot be
comprehended apart from other autonomous structures. Political structures play an undeniably critical role in economic globalization. At
issue, then, is whether the political structures will develop in concert,
or in conflict, with economic structures. To discover this relationship
requires an understanding of the autonomous dynamics within and
between economic and political structures. This is an empirical question that needs analysis from theorists who are able to leave open the
possibility of contingent results.

While beyond the scope of this work, some ideas as to how this
process may proceed can be offered. Contradictory elements appear in
both economic and political structures, with some pushing toward tran-
snationalism, and others pushing toward a reaffirmation of national
interests. Within economic structures, a clear interest exists to push
beyond national boundaries. The productive capacity and ever increasing emphasis on technology demands this. However, this leads to an
endemic problem cited by economists of all stripes: the ability to sell
products. In brief, the more machinery and products that are introduced
into the marketplace, the more machinery and products must be sold.
At some point, markets become saturated. Keynesians call this a problem of underconsumption, and Marxists call this a crisis of overpro-
duction.

Moreover, no matter what traditional solution is offered, the
problem remains. Conservative economists argue for increased competition in the marketplace, along with the removal of government interference, especially taxes which are seen as a drag on the economy.
With more money available, conservatives argue, investments will increase and the economic process and growth would start anew. In contrast, Keynesians believe that in periods of economic slowdown, the
government should increase, not lower, spending to give the economy

a boost. At the international level, however it is difficult to see how the endemic problem of finding ever increasing markets can be solved using either approach, particularly when other nations also are searching for ways to expand. Marxists, of course, suggest that these problems are impossible to overcome, except by a social transformation of the political and economic structures.

The common denominator in each of these approaches is that they require political action of one form or another. But the autonomous political structures contain their own internal inconsistencies and contradictions. On the one hand, political structures in the contemporary era have developed a variety of mechanisms aimed at international relations. Even when limited to economic considerations, political structures related to the international arena are varied. These include monetary policy of currencies and interest rates, trade policies, level of budget surpluses and deficits, taxation, foreign relations, and the relative use of military power. In order for there to be a truly transnational economy, international political programs would need to be set on a transnational level. This prospect is a contingent possibility, but would require either a transnational political system dominated by one nation, or an international political consolidation of many nations.

Either of these two scenarios seems unlikely for at least three reasons. First, the nature of free market economies inhibit the development of a single dominant nation because it would require simultaneously both an economic dominance and a military dominance of world proportions. Empirical evidence of the twentieth century indicates that this is extraordinarily difficult to accomplish. Moreover, if a single nation made a political decision to institute free market economic structures by military force, it is difficult to see how the problem of too much economic capacity would be solved. Either that nation would have to place itself in a position to dominate economically, as well as militarily, or it would simply absorb the cost of creating and maintaining global political and economic structures, but run the risk of losing the economic competition to nations without global burdens of political and military rule.

Only the U.S., as the only remaining military superpower, is in a position to even attempt to institute unilateral and worldwide political structures. During the late 1980s, in Central America and culminating with the military conflict with Iraq, it is clear that the U.S. Government is not opposed to use force when it sees it as economically and politically useful. But the cost is enormous. So much so, that the U.S. government found itself soliciting contributions to pay for the conflict with Iraq from other nations. Moreover, with the U.S. Government consumed with controlling budget deficits, the money to establish and maintain even a skeletal transnational political and economic framework is unlikely.

However, a transnational system instituted by the U.S. remains a contingent possibility. One way to pay for cost of international political and economic control is to dramatically dismantle social spending and maintain, or even expand, military spending. To some extent, this has already been attempted, as U.S. programs benefiting the poor have been continually lowered in real terms for twenty years. However, since the U.S. already spends relatively little on poverty programs, even this will not solve the budget crisis. The only alternative is to slash other social programs that benefit the middle class, but not the rich. A corresponding pattern of economic growth would be essential to justify the economic harm placed on other segments of the population.

This raises the second reason why transnational political structures are unlikely to develop. Free market economies do not develop evenly within national boundaries, and especially at the international level. Always, winners and losers emerge. This creates enormous pressures for political responses at the national and local levels. While a multi-national company may have an interest in developing global economic and political structures, the power to do so does not rest solely with these companies. While economic interests certainly influence political decisions, the relationship is not determining. Few politicians, no matter how they are lobbied or financially coerced, are in a position to create an international economic policy that will result in local political condemnation. Instead, political reaction to uneven economic development is the tendency to protect emerging or already developed national sectors of the economy. And whether or not economic sectors are protected, winners and losers also emerge among those populations working within a economic structure, and between nations. All of these factors combine to encourage political structures to remain national in their focus. One of the serious problems facing unification in Europe, is the political pressure that can be brought by distinct segments of the population who fear transnational economic and political developments. Similarly, free trade agreements by the United States creates the potential for a political backlash by those who fear the loss of jobs.

At least three contingent scenarios may result from this complex web of economic and political factors. First, strict protectionist policies may be adopted, particularly in undeveloped economies to allow internal growth the chance to emerge. Second, protectionist policies may be avoided, particularly in developed countries, who see free trade as mutually beneficial in the long run, even if it means short term losses in particular sectors. Nations choosing the second option also may attempt to use political and, perhaps, military power to ensure all nations do relatively the same. A third option is to avoid trade wars by establishing multi-national production facilities, especially within nations with important markets that have trade barriers, assuming that such facilities are politically acceptable. It is also possible that some combination of the three will be employed. For example, Japan practices forms of all three options, while China tends to employ the first and third option, but allows location of foreign production within its boarders usually in the form of joint partnerships.

The contingent dynamic within national political structures, then, adds a great deal of flexibility to international trade. Nonetheless, empirical data shows most political structures in the late twentieth century are primarily national in emphasis, particularly in democratic states. This means national politics can influence economic structures. Only authoritarian rulers are in a position to avoid this, and this form of political power, whether capitalist, socialist, or fascist has been shown to be unstable. Consequently, political structures, by the nature of their support and sustenance, are geared toward the nation-state.

Even more than economic and political structures, cultural structures also are rooted in the nation-state. Part of the reason culture remains primarily a national process rests in its autonomy from economic and political structures. The notion of cultural autonomy has already been raised in this work (see Chapter Four). Nevertheless, in each case, cultural autonomy was given a weak form. Systems theory granted a level of autonomy, but only within the context of the growing complexity of society, and divorced from micro processes. Neo-Marxists isolate culture from economic domination, but have done so either by adopting a systems approach, a postmodern approach, a descendent approach, or by maintaining an assumption of social integration. And hermeneutic theory isolates the importance of symbolic understanding, but apart from macro considerations. None of these partial efforts at defining the autonomy of culture is adequate. Autonomy, as defined in this work, means that culture must be seen as containing its own micro and macro dynamic, and yet be related to other autonomous structures.

It is precisely this combined dynamic that places culture primarily within nations. In brief, autonomous micro and macro dynamics within cultural structures is difficult, though not impossible, to articulate at the international level. Like economic and political structures, cultural structures are socially developed and become structurally placed as a result of shared perception systems among groups. While common values are conceivable at the world level, the actual development of an international set of values seems unlikely at best. It is difficult enough for one nation to develop such values. Part of this difficulty is due, ironically, to the globalization of economic and political structures. While the expansion of communication systems and other technologies make international information easier to obtain, and has blurred group identity, time and space distanciation and compression also gives rise to new, global forms of out-groups. Much of the second half of the twentieth century has seen a division between the so called east and west blocks, pitting the former Soviet Union against the United States. Many countries, either willingly or coerced, took sides. This form of global in and out-group is inconceivable in a world less globalized. Consequently, globalized group formation remains primarily within the context of national interests.

However, national interests and values are not due solely to macro conditions. Here again, this is not to deny that cultures sometimes transcend nation-states. Entertainment, art, and patterns of consumption, have been extended to a global scale. To a somewhat less extent values and beliefs are exported. However, transnational culture is even less conceivable than transnational economics or politics. The reason for the relative lack of success in globalizing culture is that cultural interests are less direct than economic or political interests. That is, interest in exercising power over other cultures is less direct than interest in exercising economic and political power. Moreover, like in political and economic structures, cultural attitudes and beliefs are directly tied to micro processes, where individuals and group categorize and develop perceptual systems and interests. While it is at least plausible that a world-wide threat might lead to more global cultural values, perhaps the detection of a meteor on a collision course with earth, such a change would be possible only in conjunction with political and economic changes. The likelihood of this conflation of events is highly improbable. Moreover, even if autonomous structures could become internationally coordinated, they must additionally be related to micro processes in each of the structures, which in turn must develop new perceptions, again a highly improbable proposition. The complexities and conflicts of the dynamic between structural and micro processes will be discussed in more detail in the next chapter. The point here is that culture remains autonomous, and primarily national.

Like cultural structures, ecological structures also exist, primarily, at a scale smaller than the world. As defined in this work, ecological structures are those environments which influence and are influenced by micro processes. It is true that ecological environments, by their very nature, reach beyond the boundaries of any single nation. However, it is also true the earth's ecosystem is subject to a combination of macro and micro processes within its own structure, and in relation to other structures. Ecological structures are not a purely natural phenomena, or at least not a purely physical development. Ecology may be related to economic, political and cultural developments. In free market economic structures, the environment is perceived as the source of, and used to produce, socially constructed objects necessary for material survival. In turn, political structures take this fact into account. This means both political and economic structures are influenced by, and influence ecological structures.

Ecological structures also affect micro processes. While it may be true that beauty is in the eye of the beholder, it is nevertheless astounding how ecological familiarity breeds positive attitudes. While some would argue that all of earth's diverse regions contain beauty, individuals attach a special majesty to particular regions. For example, returning to where one was raised as a child often influences individuals. After moving from where I was raised, upon return, I have always felt that the Blue Mountains, a part of the Appalachian Chain in northeastern Pennsylvania, contain a special beauty. No matter how long the drive, even after days of travel, entering those mountains never failed to bring a smile and feeling of comfort. This is an example of how the ecological environment becomes embedded in the perception of individuals. This also explains why so many people enjoy their place of birth and growth above all others, whether it is urban or rural, in the mountains, on the plains, or at the ocean's edge. Once incorporated into the social perception system, specific ecological environments become attached to individuals and groups. Even when severe hazards are reported, individuals and groups are loathe to move from an area that has meaning for them (Preston, Taylor, and Hodge, 1983).

Thus a connection exists between ecological and micro processes, but the macro to micro process is not determinant. For example, aspects of psychological and group processes may encourage individuals or groups to dislike a particular ecosystem and avoid it. And more significantly, and more than any other species, human beings have developed the capacity to influence ecological environments. Pollution, acid rain, global warming, and the depletion of the ozone layer are primarily caused by human actions as they intersect with the environment.

How then should ecological structures be defined and used within a contingency theory. First, some limits need to be placed on how the term ecology is used. The structures of the ecological environment must not be seen as equivalent to the entire physical universe. The universe operates on principles and contingencies that human beings are unlikely to ever influence. The universe exists along a time and space path so autonomous from humans, that people are incapable of affecting universal contingencies. For example, the curvature of time and space will not be altered by humans. Even the earth, itself, is only relatively affected by human intervention. The earth existed for billions of years before human beings, and while human actions may alter the ability to maintain life on earth, the earth, itself, will remain. It is within this limitation that ecological structures are used in this work. The social ecosystem is defined here as those autonomous processes that influence and are influenced by individuals, groups and other social structures.

Thus, along with the micro processes of individual and group dynamics, and the generally accepted structures of culture, politics, and economics, it is critical to maintain the significance of the social ecosystem as an additional structure. Moreover, ecological structures are autonomous from other structures. That is, the ecological process cannot be determined by other structures. For example, culture may attempt to define the environment and this in turn may influence micro perceptions, but the culture cannot define the environment at whim. The environment may be culturally explained as controlled by humans, but polluted city air still affects the health of people living there. The reverse is also true. Ecological environments do not determine other macro processes. The environment does not, for example, dictate action by political structures.

For example, the 1992 International Conference on the Environment held in Brazil is illustrative of this point for at least two reasons. First, the rejection of the most important treaties emerging from the conference by the United States were not based on solely ecological grounds. President Bush and members of his Administration were abundantly clear on this issue. The reason for the rejection was their concern for a balance between environmental and economic concerns. Their fear, real or imagined, was that implementation of the treaties would hinder the economic growth and the creation of jobs. Secondly, implementation of the treaties put forth at the Brazil conference require large transfers of money from industrialized nations to those less developed. Whether or not this is feasible, and ignoring political and cultural considerations, depends on economic structures. A serious economic downturn within even some of the advanced economic nations would doom the prospects of any money transfer. The point here is not to argue the correctness of any particular stand, but merely to point out that ecological structures are autonomous, and yet integrally related to political and economic structures. While not denying the global affect of environmental developments, since political and economic structures remain primarily within the purview of national developments, so too must ecological structures.

A similar point can be made concerning the relationship between ecological and cultural structures. Here again, ecological structures are influenced by and influence the autonomous cultural structures. Cultural interpretations of the environment are not based solely on its physical nature. Cultural definitions, norms, and values are based on the dynamic that combines micro and macro political, economic, and ecological processes. The past and present variety of cultural beliefs about the environment are inexplicable in any other context. This explains why contemporary nations differ in ecological outlook from hunting and gathering or tribal societies, and why the Asian view of the environment differs from that of Europeans or North Americans.

Taken as a whole, the scale of structures currently remain at the national level. This is not to ignore the importance of international penetrations and influence of the globalization of structures. Nonetheless, the primary source of structures remains within the context of the nation-state. But this should be seen as a contingent development, not necessarily true for all time. Just as the nation-state, itself, was a contingent development from earlier forms, it remains possible that the current form could give way either to global integration or disintegration. The reality of what is to come, however, will not be dictated by a set of theoretical assumptions. Instead, the future of structures will be derived from the autonomous development of economic, political, cultural, and ecological structures, as they contingently relate to each other and to micro processes. In my view, this dynamic can most fruitfully be tracked by emphasizing the national level.

Conclusions

In sum, then, four autonomous and interrelated macro structures have been identified. They are: cultural, economic, political and ecological structures. No single universal set of assumptions (e.g. the growing complexity of society or social integration) can provide a logical imperative in which structures operate. Simultaneously, no single structure (e.g. economics) can be analyzed as a determinant of other structures for all times and places. Each structure contains its own dynamic, but it is also influenced by the other three. The fact that they are autonomous means that the dynamic between them must be contingent on the development of each.

The contingency of structures requires that assumptions concerning social integration and order be abandoned. Disintegration and conflict must be granted plausibility. While structures may emerge and develop into a coherent whole, they just as easily may fall apart. Ecological environments have the potential to become unbalanced and generate enormous hardships for human beings. Political systems can degenerate into ethnic, racial or class strife. Economic chaos can develop and create mutually experienced hardships. And cultural harmony may give rise to cultural conflicts. A contingent theory of structures must search for order, but also inconsistencies, and conflict. No set of assumptions can be accepted that predetermines that search.

While this chapter primarily explores the elements and dynamics within and between macro social structures, it does not fully explain the dynamic that exists between micro and macro processes. This interrelationship is critical because neither micro or macro processes may properly be understood in total isolation. The relationship between micro and macro processes is the subject of discussion of the next chapter.

Chapter Nine

Contingent Relationships Between Micro and Macro Processes

The last chapter closed with the reminder that macro and micro processes cannot be understood apart from each other. This chapter explores their relationship. Two additional concepts are considered within this discussion: emergence and social change.

Contingency theory leads to a fresh look at emergence. When macro theorists gran structures objective characteristics, it means that structures are assumed to have emerged from somewhere. And once structures stand independent from social actors, structures are usually explained through the birth of some process which gives rise to their distinct development. Yet despite this assumption, the concept of emergence has long remained implicit, not explicit, in social theory. The explanation of emergence becomes troubling for macro theorists when they try to explain how structures take a life of their own. Explaining where objective structures come from, and where they are going, requires a universal postulate of one form or another. Within contingency theory, viewing social structures as objective is a mistake because it denigrates the importance of micro processes in the emergence of structures. Conversely, when macro structures are seen as nothing more than amalgamated micro processes, social structures lose their autonomy and ability to influence micro processes. Moreover, it becomes impossible to fully explain power, an element critical to structural formation, maintenance, and change.

Similarly, social theory has continuously misconstrued social change. Social theorists regularly describe change, but only after the fact. Often, these descriptions aim at creating and collapsing social changes into previously held theoretical categories and assumptions.

The record of describing and explaining social change by social theorists and scientists is embarrassingly abysmal. A contingent theory of change will never be able to universally predict the form of social change. Nonetheless, investigations into autonomous micro and macro processes will elevate social change analysis from theory, and place it in the realm of social reality. Contingent theorists and practitioners would examine social change not to proclaim universal principles, but because change is inherent in the tangible relationship within and between micro and macro processes. Autonomy and contingency, then, place social change within theoretical and empirical reach.

Before a discussion of emergence and social change is possible, however, the interrelationship between micro and macro processes must first be investigated.

The Micro and Macro Interrelationship

It has been argued throughout this work that autonomy in micro and macro processes must be recognized. Neither can be determined by the other, and each proceeds on its own path. But autonomous micro and macro processes are not isolated; rather they are 'open' processes, characterized by varying levels of penetration at various times. The uncertain dynamic between them means the two levels are, theoretically and empirically, inextricably related.

One obvious example of this relationship is when structural processes are aimed at the very construction and/or protection of groups. A critical task of any nation-state is the protection of its members from external threats, and groups play their role by exercising power within macro structures to foster national in-groups. Macro structures also influence the formation of groups smaller in scale. In the contemporary era, groups acting within structures and in accord with their own interests have played a significant role in the rise of time/space distanciation and compression. The result is that older group formations are under pressure to give way to the new.

One instance of this micro/macro interplay is found within educational systems. In industrialized nations, education has transcended from a training ground for the clergy, and then upper classes, to an institution aimed at educating large masses of people. Political, economic, and cultural influences are endemic to the educational process and contemporary debate over its future. Determining appropriate levels of training necessary for job preparation, the political and cultural value content of curriculum, how many people should be educated and at what level, and how the educational system should be paid for, all have structural influences. Economic, political, and cultural structures, themselves contingent on powerful groups exercising power, encourage or discourage various forms of education.

Individual and group processes at the micro level, however, also play a distinct role and are never fully determined by macro structures. The micro processes, including the social necessity of categorization and classification, emotional paradigms, contingent and variable relationships between individuals and groups, power differentials between groups, inconsistencies and conflicts between groups, as well as order and integration between groups all autonomously must be taken into account. What emerges at the micro level is a social perception system that is both critical for the formation of structures such as educational institutions, and potentially penetrates those structures. Moreover, whether or not individuals or groups undergo change is not wholly due to structural processes. Various individuals and groups may or may not be consistent with macro developments, and this may or may not lead to change either at the individual, group or structural level.

The micro process, then, cannot be wholly manipulated by powerful groups who exercise power within structures. There are at least three reasons for this. First, unintended consequences are always contingent possibilities, and the ability of even the most powerful groups to directly influence macro structures is highly problematic. Structures are, themselves, potentially contradictory in their development, and like all groups, the powerful may experience internal conflicts, and less than a accurate perception of social reality. Second, the relationship between structures and autonomous micro processes may, themselves, be contradictory or conflictual. To establish what is in the powerful group's interest may lead to inconsistencies at the either the micro or macro levels. And third, power always may be contested if a competitor group, acting to influence individuals, groups or structures, perceives the action as inconsistent to its own social perception system, and, therefore resists change.

How, then, are structural changes successfully carried out? One approach to successful structural change is for change to be consistent with the dominant social perception system. That is, change must be perceived as consistent with group perception. For example, in the U.S., a dominant perception shared throughout much of the society is that individuals, or at a limit, families, are responsible for their own material well being. This is a perception of long standing and due to a variety of structural and micro processes. The particular history of the structural development in the U.S. encourages this perception. The

origin of the U.S. as a political outlet from other societies, the ecological expansion of its environment across the North American continent,
the emphasis on family farms and the cultural values derived from an
agrarian based economy and culture, and its political history of democracy all have influenced the micro social perception of the role of the
individual.

To be sure, these perceptions have been encouraged and exag-
gerated by powerful interests for their own perceived benefits, and ignore important inconsistencies. Not the least of which was the lack of
political enfranchisement of slaves and women at the time of the nation's birth, the existence of an apartheid system in southern states until
the middle of the twentieth century, and the de facto segregation of
large numbers of the population that exists today. Economically, the
perception of individual responsibility continues despite periods of
economic dislocation, discrimination of women and minorities, and a
growing gap between rich and poor. Despite all of these factors, the
perception of individualism and individual responsibility persists
among large segments of the population. Suggested change within
macro structures that is consistent with these perceptions has a greater
chance of being successfully accepted. For example, the call for equal
opportunity in the U.S. has always been perceptually received more
readily than a call for equality. This has been true no matter how well
the argument for equality is explained, or how favorable a change toward equality would be for even large percentages of the population.
Since an accurate and complete picture of social reality is beyond recognition for all groups, the success of structural change is due more to
the consistency within and between micro and macro processes than an
objectively accurate explanation of social reality.

Many examples could be cited for how the above process would
work. One can be found in the policies related to poverty in the U.S.
Government poverty programs have been continually cut back over the
last twenty years. The argument made to justify these cut-backs is that
the poor have developed a drug-like dependency on welfare payments
which have altered their individual drive to succeed and become self-
reliant (Gilder 1981; Murray 1984). According to this ideology, poverty policy should aim to change the character of the poor. But the
process of developing welfare policies is steeped in political and economic influences. Employers have a vital interest in opposing aid to the
poor (Piven and Cloward, 1987). Poverty programs not only distribute
income to the poor, they fortify the poor's bargaining position as workers. Those most vulnerable, such as the aged, disabled, single parents
and their children, are removed from the workforce as aid is made

available (Piven and Cloward 1987, p.6). This indirectly benefits other workers, particularly the working poor, by acting as a buoy for all wages, and by providing a safety net in case of dismissal.

Employers, then, view poverty programs as intrusions into the "free market," as economic meddling by the state, and a direct attack on their ability to obtain profits. Consequently, employers only reluctantly bow to political pressure in granting aid to the poor, and, if it is granted, strive to limit the amount of aid and its impact on business interests. Employers maintain that aid programs should be reduced and/or designed to propel recipients toward work activities. This is perceived as critical to an employer's ability to locate and hire workers at a wage that sustains profits. Who then benefits from a welfare to work program, where participants often are not adequately trained, are required to participate or risk being cut off from their portion of welfare payments, and often end up in low paying jobs with little hope of ending their poverty? The answer is obvious: employers (Itzkowitz, 1991).

In short, the characterization of the poor as 'dependent' has direct policy implications. If poverty is perceived as originating internally among the poor, it is incumbent on the federal government to end simple financial aid, and encourage the poor's transformation to self-sufficiency. In other words, let taxes collected from the general population fund the training of recipients for below poverty level jobs that will benefit employers (Itzkowitz, 1991).

This description of a powerful group having interests in influencing macro political structures points out that other structural developments, in this case primarily economic ones, also must be taken into account. But low-wage employers do not exercise power in isolation. Other groups competing for macro power may operate from a different perception and have different interests. For example, high technology employers may have little need for low wage workers, and see training programs for the poor as a waste of tax dollars. This may give rise to competition between two macro groups seeking to exercise structural influence. Finally, another group with potential to affect this process is the poor themselves. Throughout the history of the United States, the poor have made economic and social gains only when low-income people have become active politically (Piven and Cloward, 1987). To deflect this potential, employers champion a perception of the poor which is consistent with the social perception systems of many other groups. If the poor can be characterized as lazy and unwilling to accept individual responsibility, then the poor are easily made into an outgroup, and seen as inconsistent with the majority social perception system. The social reality of the poor matters little. The fact that the average length of time a family receives welfare payments in the U.S. is for two years, that many on welfare are old, sick or caring for someone who is, or that only 20% of the welfare population is able bodied, and the vast majority of the heads of these households are women with young children, matters little. If a group is able to exercise it's power within macro structures that is consistent with micro social perception systems, it has an increased chance of successfully carrying out the desired changes regardless of social facts.

Consistency between micro and macro processes is not always necessary to ensure macro change, however. Another contingent possibility is that a group becomes powerful enough to force change. The ability to forcibly alter macro structures is, itself, contingent on micro and macro processes. One form of this exercise of power is the domination of one nation over another. Part of the ability to dominate rests with macro structural developments. The political, economic, cultural and ecological structures must be such that one nation gains clear advantages in the tools necessary for domination. These tools may be used for military, technological, economic or political domination. In order to exercise such power, political and economic structures must also be consistent with cultural structures which internally interpret that domination positively, and with the ecological environment which is critical in the ability to give rise to tools of domination.

However, domination of one society over another does not rest on structural developments alone. If the dominated nation is not perceived as an important out-group, or the structural development of the tools necessary for domination are inconsistent with the social perception system, then individuals and group activity may halt the effort to dominate. Thus while the former Soviet Union, whose structural and perceptual systems were viewed as a legitimate out-group and even a threat by most nations and groups in the industrialized west, Viet Nam and the Vietnamese were not. This means that while the structures of the U.S. were developed in a way that encouraged the domination of Viet Nam, the social perception systems of growing numbers of individuals and groups both influenced the strategy of domination, and eventually even the attempt.

Autonomous micro processes, then, have important influences on macro structural developments. Moreover, micro processes may be initiators of efforts at national domination. History is filled with nationalist, as well as regional, ethnic, or racial attempts at domination. The rivalries reemerging with the dissolution of the Soviet Union and its sphere of influence in eastern Europe are acute examples of power at the micro level, especially in the formation of out-groups. While it is true that ethnic rivalries cannot be attributed wholly to micro processes, their importance is plain for all to see. Finally, the response of micro groups to macro changes is, itself, contingent on its own internal development. For example, while foreign domination may lead some groups to rebel, it may lead others to willingly accept change and adopt new perception systems.

The major emphasis in contingency theory, then, must be to establish the dynamic between micro and macro processes. Moreover, contingent analysis must establish whether these processes are consistent or inconsistent both internally and externally. To accomplish this requires that levels of influence internal to each process be accounted for, as well as the general level of influence each has on the other. This means that while autonomy is maintained, micro and macro levels are created and developed through the social interaction connecting the two processes. As such, the autonomy between levels is not total, for if autonomy meant total separation, the two levels and the elements within them would be separated from the social interaction which creates them both.

Maintaining the autonomous, yet related, nature of the elements within and between micro and macro processes has definite advantages over any theory that attempts to supply them with an objective status. Once a structure or micro process is seen as objective, it simultaneously is granted a determining status, and loses the ability for its own explanation. Explanations of change immediately become problematic. Differentiation has caused no end of troubles for functionalism, and similarly, the objective status granted to both economic structures and to social relations have been problematic for Marxists. The problem for both is that once objective structures or social relations are established, social change no longer is grounded in people. Instead, some additional force, itself objectively constructed, must be created in order to understand change. Differentiation was chosen by functionalists, contradictions between forces and relations of production were chosen by Marx and Marxists, and objective principles of unconscious and conscious forces were chosen by psychoanalytic and cognitive psychologists. All of these fail to understand the social nature of change.

In their place, contingency theory maintains the autonomous, yet related, dynamic between micro and macro levels is impossible to objectively determine. This must be so because the source of the dynamic is social interaction carried out by groups with real interests, not objectively placed groups with little or no choice but to carry out their predetermined roles according to objective categories. The construction,

maintenance or change within and between levels is due to social interaction, and since social interaction within both micro and macro processes is always in flux, and since this forms the basis for the dynamic
between levels, society has no choice but to be contingent on the result
of what social interaction creates. The lack of objectivity of micro and
macro processes does not imply that regularities of social action and/or
social structures are beyond detection. Social integration and order
remain contingent possibilities. However, contingency also implies that
whether or not micro and macro regularities exist may be uncovered
only through understanding social interaction within and between each
process, and that this dynamic relationship cannot be objectively determined.

The contingency of micro and macro processes also requires
structural development not be seen as the inevitable unfolding of history. History and social change has no predetermined logic. To see
history as objectively determined is to seek to unlock macro patterns
void of micro influences. Many macro choices have been wrongly selected on this very basis, ranging from Comte's positive phases of development and Hegel's absolute knowledge, to the more contemporary
selection of economics, or culture, or politics. History and social
change, however, are the result not of an overarching force, but of the
social interaction which creates the autonomous and dynamic relationship between micro and macro processes.

This suggests that contingency theory is at once both more narrowly focused and provides for a more expansive explanation than objectively based macro theories. Contingency theory is more narrowly
focused in that its emphasis, and future empirical studies, is not aimed
at participating in the endless search for objective universals of social
integration, but on the reality of social interaction and the dynamic
levels that it creates. Simultaneously, contingency allows for a more
broad consideration of social change. Social interaction and the dynamics of change within and between micro and macro levels result in variable developments within and between each process. During various
historical periods and places, micro processes may be the prime catalyst for change, while in other periods and places it may be structural
processes that dominate, or even a fairly equal influence by both. Thus
contingency theory allows for flexible social development, something
no objectively based theory can do.

Just as contingency theory corrects the deficiencies in macro
theories, so too does it add a necessary dimension to micro theories.
Theories based on the objective structures of language, for example,
repeat similar mistakes. Wittgenstein (1953, p. 199) and de Saussure

(1966) both saw the error in this approach and viewed language within a more social context. Contingency theory additionally suggests language must not only be viewed within the social context, but is, instead, essentially social. This takes Wittgenstein's and de Saussure's point one step further and places an indelible, yet autonomous, link between language and micro processes.

The critical issue is that words must be distinguished from the subjective conceptualization of the meanings of words, and the social act of talking. While individuals cannot conceptualize words without social context, speaking words is a social interaction. This means the act of speaking is distinct from either conceptualization by individuals, or social contexts. Instead, speaking, like all social acts, ties the two together through social interaction.

Similarly, subjective perceptions of attitudes and beliefs must be separated from both their social context and any social act based on them. The reason for the need for separation is that each is nonsensical without the autonomy of the other. Subjective conceptualization of words and meanings is impossible without an already established language, and so too, the development of a belief is impossible without a social basis. But the opposite is also true. Without subjective conceptualizations, at times based on emotional paradigms, social concepts become purely relativistic, if possible at all. Thus conceptualization and social concepts are mutually dependent, but they also must maintain autonomy because to do otherwise would supply an objective quality to one or the other. Without autonomy, either social concepts become immune to subjective influences and it becomes frivolous to investigate the social source of concepts, or subjective processes are shielded from social concepts and relativism is the result. Either choice ignores variations in the degree of social order existing in the tangible social world.

Moreover, the autonomous, yet related, dynamic between micro and macro processes leads to similar conclusions about general theories of social action. Social action is by definition always related to other social actors, and thus is more properly named social interaction. Purely subjective physical and psychological processes, such as conceptualizations of meanings or emotions, while related to external processes, do not become social acts until they are applied in relation to other people. But to act socially requires far more than subjective conceptualization. Social action also requires that acts take place relative to already-existing group and structural processes. Since neither may be seen as objective categories, when social actors interact they enter into a contingent and cumulative social world that is an expression of all previous micro/macro social interactions. This means social interaction may be neither determined by micro or macro processes, nor that inter-action is solely linked to either process. That is, social interaction is not limited to the constraints of macro categories, nor to the limitations imposed on action by micro theorists who believe all social action rests within the confines of individuals. Instead, once again, contingency theory suggests social action is both more narrow and more expansive than these traditional views. Contingency theory narrows social action because it ends the relentless search for universal principles that must be found in either micro or macro assumptions. At the same time, con-tingency theory expands the importance of social interaction by making it responsible both for the existence of, and link between, micro and macro processes.

The contingent nature of social action also avoids the entire theo-retical cul de sac created in debates between the rationality or irra-tionality of social action. The debate over whether or not a social action is rational necessarily implies some objective base exists to judge social actions from. One only can judge rationality in relation to objective political-economic structures, or functional prerequisites of structures, or psychological drives, or the structuration of routines, or existing social fields, etc. Thus rationality is debatable only within the context of an assumed objective reality or process. The problem, as previously discussed, is that this must be a false debate, since objective reality is itself a false concept. Objectively situating individuals as rational or irrational distorts and even ignores the critical role social interaction plays in the relationship between micro and macro processes. By ignor-ing contingency and replacing it with a set of objective assumptions, the question of rationality or irrationality of social action becomes little more than an elemental cog in the logic of some theory. Consequently, social interaction becomes rational or irrational only in light of theo-retical assumptions. This greatly diminishes the creative potential of social action, and averts attention from the link social interaction cre-ates between micro and macro processes.

Similarly, non-rational behavior, based on conscious or uncon-scious emotions, or the inability to articulate a rational response given the postmodern condition, suffers from similar theoretical problems. Non-rational behavior must be grounded in relation to the reality of social interaction. If non-rational behavior is due to undiscoverable emotions or a deconstructed reality, such behavior becomes void of social meaning. While this is what postmodernism argues for, such a principle also eliminates the verification that such behavior is decon-structed. While it is possible that such non-rational principles exist, they only may be accepted on a purely philosophical level, and must be selected from a myriad of possibilities. Even then, the principles and possibilities selected will be influenced by the particular development of society and the dynamic between micro and macro processes.

Rational, irrational, and non-rational subjective processes, then, must be connected to the current developments of the micro/macro processes. Only by comprehending micro and macro processes can social action be defined as rational, irrational, or non-rational. And since micro and macro processes may, themselves, be internally or externally developing in consistent or inconsistent ways, the dynamic within and between them can be connected and understood only through social interaction. That is, it is possible the dynamic process presents avenues for social interaction that may, or may not, lend itself to rational decision-making and interaction. The greater the consistency within and between micro and macro processes, the greater the availability for rational choices. The greater the degree of disorder, the more likely irrational choices will present themselves.

However, even consistency or inconsistency between micro and macro levels cannot wholly determine rational or irrational social interaction. Since micro and macro processes are autonomous and contingent, neither rationality or irrationality can be completely predicted, even when absolute consistency or inconsistency exists between the two levels. This is so because what might appear rational at one level may be irrational at another level. For example, maintaining strong outgroup feelings toward some group may be rational within a group process, but inconsistent and irrational at the macro level. Similarly, raising taxes to eliminate government debt may appear rational at the macro-economic level, but be inconsistent with other structures, or conflict with social perception systems. Finally, autonomy between levels ensures at least the possibility for either rational or irrational social interaction, even when order or disorder are consistent in both levels. Thus even if micro/macro levels were wholly consistent, the autonomous development of elements within and between levels always allows for social interaction to be irrationally based. Likewise, even if a state of total chaos were to exist within the dynamic of the two levels, autonomy would still allow for rational action to emerge. Within this framework, then, rationality or irrationality are secondary, and never objective or universal. Far more important than positing either of these choices as universal is the empirical discovery of the dynamic between micro and macro processes, and the social interaction that creates it.

Degrees of Certainty and Power

How, then, can any logic be formulated within the context of autonomy and contingency? This legitimate question arises because of the contingent nature of rationality, the lack of objective micro and macro categories, the contingent nature of social interaction, the contingency of social change, and the autonomy within and between micro and macro levels. Can contingency theory ever enable a degree of certainty so that reasonable discussions of society can ensue? The answer, I believe, is yes. The key to understanding how the complexities unfold is through an understanding of power. The concept of power relations is a root explanation for most social interaction. This does not imply that power is always gained or given up through force. Power may be granted willingly to the powerful. Moreover, power is not granted artificially through a perceived objective category or classification. Instead, power is always used, ignored, or remains hidden at various levels within the context of social interaction. When power is objectively defined, it becomes real only to the theoretician. Power as generated in social interaction is reflective of social reality. Dominant and dominated individuals and groups impose, challenge, reproduce, grant superiority to, and ignore power within social interaction. Social actors, then, create and define power; they are not merely subjected to it.

Various forms of social interaction may or may not create power differentials between people at both micro and macro levels. Once again, power differentials are not due to objective structural history. Rather, large and small groups have developed interests (rational or not) which they attempt to apply or choose not to apply through social action at micro and macro levels. The degree to which such groups are able to act on those interests and influence others is the degree to which that group may be considered powerful. Through social interaction, various groups have tried to enact their interests, and the result of those enactments represent an important element in the current dynamic within and between micro and macro levels. Thus the history of micro/macro processes must be accounted for not because it has an objective status, but because, in part, groups, through social interaction, have attempted to influence others, and in doing so, helped shape the current status of the dynamic.

The above description of power, however, should not leave the impression that power is a zero-sum game played out according to a pre-determined set of rational rules. On the contrary, power is contingent, ensuring no inevitable or universal winners or losers. Moreover, the exercise of power itself does not necessarily imply an intent to develop or maintain influence over others. While control is a contingent possibility, it is not a necessity. Part of the reason is that the powerful may or may not comprehend various amounts of social reality. An interest in gaining power does not ensure an accurate perception either of social reality, or that acts of power within that reality will be successful.

Conversely, the powerful may obtain power due to the inability of the non-powerful to comprehend social reality. That is, a group may obtain power and gain compliance because the dominated fail to understand both the micro/macro dynamic and the social interactions taken by the groups exercising power. Finally, another contingent possibility is that because social reality may not be totally comprehended, groups may act in ways opposed to their self-interest, or act in their self-interest, but create unintended consequences opposed to that self-interest. In short, all of this is contingent on the form of social interaction as it has developed the dynamic within and between the micro and macro processes.

It should also be recognized that power does not reside solely within either micro or macro levels. Too often power is perceived as a macro objective category. As postmodernism and feminists theorists have shown, power at the micro level is of critical importance. No matter the scale of interaction, a power relationship exists. If any individuals or groups have interest in taking a social action, power necessarily comes into play. Despite the fact that such actions may be accepted, rejected, changed, or ignored by others, or that the intent of the acting group has nothing to do with overt domination of others, the ability or lack of ability to act on interests, at whatever scale, implies a power relationship.

It follows that the form of social interaction which generates power within and between micro and macro levels can be instituted at both levels in various ways. There may be variability on the ability to form groups, express opinions, survive materially, become politically active, or form a relationship with ecological structures. It is also possible that power relationships have developed in such a way that the form of power relationships at the micro level is inconsistent with power relationships at the macro level, or that conflicts exist within the two levels.

Each of these possibilities require empirical analysis. No theory can, itself, uncover these relationships. For example, assume a society has been created through social interaction in such a way where perfect democracy exists. Of course, perfect democracy and power are not mutually exclusive. That is, democratically-originated power still leaves open the potential for inequality. Also assume that democratic inequalities, such as those created through the principle of equal opportunity, are accepted as justified. In a purely democratic society, groups would form freely, but because the micro processes are autonomous, one of the possibilities is that out-groups will develop in the process. Attitudes, beliefs, and emotions may well develop in opposite directions, with opposite goals. For example, groups may develop out-groups of such intensity that principles of democracy may be threatened. Simultaneously, power develops at the macro level in similar ways. Power groups within the structures of society may or may not have competing interests in relation to economic, political, cultural or ecological structures. These interests may be so intense that, once again, the principles of democracy may become a secondary concern.

In a fascist society a different set of contingent patterns would emerge. In a purely fascist society, the powerful hope to influence all that occurs within the two levels. The powerful attempt to control economic, political, cultural and ecological structures. And at the micro level, the powerful hope to manipulate the formation of groups, as well as attitudes and beliefs, and the formation of in- and out-groups. Once again, no guarantees for success exist for the powerful. Variable levels of acceptance, rejection, or ignorance will emerge at both micro and macro levels, and not necessarily in consistent ways.

The nuances that develop can only be uncovered empirically. In most cases, the exercise of power will not fall into neatly-ordered abstract or objective categories. It is possible, for instance, that a power grid-lock may emerge where power exercised autonomously at both micro or macro levels cancel each other. In such a situation, powerful groups within or between micro and macro levels may attempt to gain allies, manipulate the dynamic between levels, use structures for their own interests, or compromise. The contingent nature of power, based on the autonomous development between processes, assures any outcome of competition will not be permanent, cumulative or inevitable. Power is exercised contingently, not as if a stage play was being performed, or coming to its final curtain call. Such a Comtean view ignores the unique complexity that is contingent social interaction.

Once again, contingent complexity is not beyond understanding. Contingent processes become knowable because they are grounded in social reality through social action, and, therefore, are knowable. Powerful acts, like all social interaction, must be exercised in relation to existing micro and macro processes. At the micro level, the existing social perception system plays a significant role. If powerful groups apply their interests in ways inconsistent with social perception systems, the likelihood for compliance is diminished. For example, power-ful groups may have an interest in developing an area economically. However, if the area has a popular public use -- perhaps as an environmentally sensitive nature reserve -- no matter how consistent economic development is with the current political and cultural structures, the effort to exercise power may be resisted. If groups launch a social upheaval in reaction to the private development of a nature reserve, the political structures, once perceived as consistent to the suggested use of power, might react in ways inconsistent with economic development. In addition, a conflict might emerge within structures, even when micro processes ignore the structural change. For example, democratic political structures may conflict with economic development when the benefits are accrued only by a small percentage of the population.

To explore whether competition exists within micro groups, within macro groups, or between the two, requires considering social perception systems and structures. The tangible display of these processes makes the contingent dynamic comprehendible. Contingency is not haphazard. It is always borne from existing micro/macro relationships. And because micro and macro processes are autonomous, no amount of power can escape the reality of either. No powerful group, for example, can solicit change when it dramatically differs from existing social perception, or from structural developments. No matter how powerful, no group could convince large groups of people to move to Venus. It neither fits the social perception system, nor the current level of structural development. Acts of power will trend toward success when they are aligned to existing structures, are consistent with the social perception of reality unfolding within and between individuals and groups, and recognize the potential for competition at both micro and macro levels.

Power, then, is most easily exercised when it corresponds to both micro and macro processes. Powerful acts are least effective when they fail to concur with either. When inconsistent with both levels, defenders of either the existing social perception system, or social structures, likely will fend off attempts at fundamental change. The ability to deflect substantially new power arrangements is all the more likely when prevailing structures and social perception systems are, themselves, in concert. When in concert, corresponding micro/macro processes tend to create highly-stable societies, and these societies will resist change. Finally, when social perception systems and social structures conflict, but each remains internally stable, social acts for fundamental change may have even less flexibility. In this case, new power relationships must be instituted within both micro and macro levels, and the tendency for competition over power will arise in both. The intricacy inherent in such a scenario would render the imposition of new power relations more than a delicate operation.

A better chance for fundamental change arises when new power relations are consistent with at least one of the levels. A new group which enacts power in altered, but fundamentally the same structures has a greater chance for success than a group which tries to institute power in ways inconsistent with both macro and micro processes. For instance, new forms of technology are most easily instituted when they are adaptable to old structures, even when they are inconsistent with social perceptions systems. Of course the inverse is also true. A micro-oriented group vying for power over macro processes can still be successful in the face of inconsistency with macro structures, as long as its power is viewed as consistent with the current social perception system. For example, social movements that express commonly held perceptions may be successful even when they are in conflict with structures.

An additional avenue for fundamental change is when neither micro or macro processes are well established. In such periods, contingent developments are the most uncertain, and impossible to predict through theoretical categories. Finally, efforts to enact power that is inconsistent with both micro and macro processes is likely to be successful only when dominance is gained by force. However, no group can maintain such a position for long without a corresponding development in micro and macro processes generally consistent with their position.

While the various scenarios for the exercise of power requires empirical investigations, some preliminary ideas about modern societies can be offered. It would seem that contemporary, industrialized societies have developed a web of economic, political, cultural and ecological structures that are increasingly difficult to subjectively recognize. Even among macro power groups, attempts to act on interests often leads to consequences, both intended and unintended, that are difficult not only for subjective and group micro processes to fully detect, but difficult for macro groups as well. Consequently, the very complexity of modern macro structures makes it taxing for macro power groups to either fully comprehend macro processes and/or institute power in concert with them.

While micro power groups also have difficulty in complete macro comprehension, such a comprehension is not always necessary given their more provincial interests. That is, macro power groups aim at power over structures, while micro power groups often aim at consistency between structures and their social perception system. It is easier to articulate and act upon specific inconsistencies between structures and social perception systems than it is to enact power only at the structural level.

This complex web of contemporary structures, coupled with the relative ease for social action at the micro level, has given rise to a variety of micro group interests and actions in the contemporary era. The modern era is filled with groups contesting economic, political, cultural, or ecological structural developments. While both micro and macro inconsistencies and contradictions are always comprehendible, because they are created by people through social interaction, the current and contingent complexities of modern society may make micro social actions more likely, and more highly volatile. Ironically, the very entrenchment of macro power groups and structures means that extensive social action at the micro level cannot assure any change within structures. In most instances, grave inconsistencies between the two levels are necessary for fundamental change.

Rethinking Emergence and Social Change

Contingency theory suggests a different approach to emergence and social change. As far back as Simmel (1978), structures have been seen as emerging from micro processes with more or less objective characteristics. However, contingency theory views the emergence of structures as grounded in social interaction, both in structural formation, and in continuing structural development. Structures are not determined by objective positions, social roles, or theoretical assumptions. Nor is the sum of the structural whole larger than its parts, nor are structures an amalgamation of micro social acts. Rather, structures emerge because of real social interaction taken by at least a small number of people. The distinguishing feature of structures is their time and space path; the social interactions that create structures have developed over a longer time and over a wider space than social interaction at the micro level. People engaging in social interaction within structures often do so within macro processes that both outlive each individual and take actions that affects others. This is precisely why structures must be seen as autonomous from micro processes. While micro and macro processes share social interaction as their source, the form and issues concerning macro social interaction are distinct from micro social interaction.

The emergence of structures, then, is a tangible process, carried out by real people with real interests. In this light, structures are neither inevitably integrated or deconstructed, nor do all people necessarily share an equal influence over structural development. In short, macro structures and processes are contingent not only on the internal dynamic within each structure, but on the relationship between autonomous structural and micro developments. Once again, uncovering structural processes requires an empirical, not theoretical, examination.

Comprehending social change requires a similar theoretical framework and empirical methodology. Where emergence is usually aimed at an explanation of structures, social change conceptually, and more directly, involves both micro and macro levels. Social change, and for that matter stability, is at the heart of the relationship between micro and macro processes. Structural processes and change, and micro processes and change combine in the continual formation of society. Neither level is determined by objective categories, social roles, or individual acts. Rather, people individually perceive and take, or do not take, social actions based on their interests at the micro and/or macro level. The only possible way to comprehend social change and stability is to allow for autonomy and contingency within and between micro and macro processes. Moreover, the contingent result of the social interaction within these autonomous processes forms the relationship between micro and macro levels.

As an illustration of emergence and social change, consider the following. A peasant family has lived for generations in a remote area of South America. Each member of the family has thought about and absorbed their surroundings. Individually, they have fashioned impressions of peasant life. Their image of who they are encourage and discourage individual and family participation in groups, and each member is especially influenced by traditional, often religious groups and gatherings. Jealousies and minor family rivalries are the only factors upsetting an otherwise peaceful setting. Most people seem to have a sense of who they are and what their roles are.

The largest grouping in town revolves around the church. People are highly religious and the church is the cultural center, mixing traditional Catholicism with peasant values. The economic picture is simple, based on an agrarian pace and lifestyle. Very few are able to stockpile enough money to live beyond necessities of economic and social life. The traditional values and economic hurdles of the population encourages each family to support a combination of economically progressive, but socially conservative social policies and movements.

The social situation in the above example shows relatively consistent development between micro and macro processes. It is reasonable to assume stability would characterize social life. However, no matter how stable, circumstances far from the stability of this peasant town potentially generate fundamental social change. For example, in industrialized societies, the need for raw materials may become an ever increasing necessity to maintain productive capacity. Large multinational companies begin the search for suitable areas of the world for development and life for the peasant family will never be the same.

Through a series of international economic and political transformations, political structures undergo change, affecting the peasant family. That is, both nationally and internationally, individuals and groups act on their perceived interests and engage in macro social interaction. Where before support for the peasant economic and cultural life was consistent with older structures, the national government, and powerful economic groups, now encourage private development of rural lands by foreign companies. In short, macro development is no longer in tandem with peasant social perception systems.

Conflicts may be resolved in various ways. Depending on the micro process, including individual perceptions and group dynamics as they interrelate with more macro structures, the rural population may acquiesce, struggle against, or try to ignore social change. At the macro level, groups will act to carry out changes, including new forms of economic relationships within and between levels, new forms of political interaction to ensure support of change, and perhaps even attempts to undermine traditional culture if it is perceived as a hindrance to change. More than likely, macro competition will ensue between groups who view change as positive and those who do not.

This example illustrates how a stable society (one with consistent micro and macro processes and structures) can become unstable. The result may or may not be that new macro structures are easily adaptable to the old structures, and/or that the new changes may or may not be adaptable with social perception systems. What is certain is that social interaction at both micro and macro levels will be the source of both the effort for change, and the probability of resistance to that change. What occurs within and between each autonomous level will decide whether new structures and social perception systems emerge or remain the same.

Moreover, if we assume that new macro structures are instituted, and that the peasant family is removed from its historic position on the land, the family response to the change is also a contingent one. The family may move to the nearest major city, and like many in that situation, find economic opportunity lacking. The reaction of the family and others in similar positions is necessarily variable. The family or group response cannot be determined by objective category, social role, or rational choice. Rather, the response will be carried out according to the social interactions taking place at both micro and macro levels. At the micro level, new perceptions as they relate to old ones will be individually shaped. In turn, these new subjective perceptions will form a relationship with existing and new groups to form new social perception systems. Perhaps traditional cultural activities or the church may act as a source of acceptance or rebellion as individuals penetrate groups and groups influence individuals.

Simultaneously, but autonomously, macro structures also must go through their own process. Perhaps, new structures are not easily instituted, or competing groups engage in structural conflict. Whatever the case, the relationship between micro and macro processes must be established anew. Neither micro nor macro levels are determinate in this new interrelationship, nor is the degree of penetration by each process theoretically determined. Once again, this becomes an empirical question. Theory only can create better or worse models to examine social reality, it cannot foretell what will be found there.

Chapter Ten

Conclusions

Taken together, the previous chapters have made a series of arguments that may be collapsed into the following ideas and postulates.

1. The rise of modern science, especially discoveries leading to a vision of the mechanical universe, directly influenced philosophical inquires. Above all, early modern philosophers sought scientific laws applicable to human beings and human society. This search was based on the scientific belief that all micro and macro physical matter was inextricably and instantaneously related to each other. Philosophers hoped to apply the same principle to social events and society.

2. The classical sociologists sought to move beyond the philosophical legacy they inherited by replacing empiricism and rationalism with concepts of social interaction. However, the search for universal laws of social development and social integration remained, as did the belief that micro and macro social levels were contiguously linked.

3. Eventually, universal laws of social development and integration led to a fracture in sociological theory between established macro theories, (which explained social development as a result of objective structures) and micro theories, (which explained social development as a result of micro social thought and action).

4. The recent recognition that micro and macro levels must be linked has not led to a concurrent recognition that universal laws and social integration be abandoned. Instead, only flexible frame-

works have been abstracted to include more elements of the level previously ignored. The result is descendent theories which start from macro assumptions, but allow for more micro activity; ascendant theories which start from micro assumptions, but attempt an explanation of structures; and implosion theories which accept both micro and macro importance, but assume that each level mutually instantiates the other. These three contemporary approaches maintain the traditional belief in the contiguous relationship between micro and macro processes.

5.   Postmodernism, feminist theory, and ecological theory have shown the inadequacies of both fractured theories and contemporary efforts at micro/macro integration. While each indictment theory has shown the enormity of social reality missed by searching for universal laws of social development, none has articulated an adequate replacement.

6.   Twentieth-century science, itself, demonstrates the folly in maintaining a belief in either the contiguous relationship between micro and macro phenomena, or that the two inevitably mesh into a position of social integration. Instead, micro and macro levels develop along distinct time and space paths, and are more accurately described as autonomous. As such, the relationship between the two levels is necessarily contingent on the indefinite development of each.

7.   Since micro and macro levels are autonomous and contingent, each must be investigated independently. The relationship between the two is dynamic and may or may not be consistent, and may or may not be conflictual.

8.   At the micro level, individual and group processes are related, but autonomous. Each develops social perceptions based on the uniquely human capability of selection and categorization, and the development of emotional paradigms. While these capabilities are necessary for the survival and emotional well-being of individuals and groups, categorization and emotions are inconceivable apart from both social processes and social interaction. Moreover, as individual and group processes of emotional development and categorization are brought together through social interaction, the relationship within and between the two micro processes becomes knowable.

9. Not all social actors are aware of all social reality, as individuals interact with various groups. This opens the potential for power differentials, as actors exercise different interests within various groups. This also creates the potential for inconsistencies and/or conflicts between individuals and groups, and between groups.

10. At the macro level, four general structures are evident: political, economic, cultural, and ecological. Each is related, but is again individually autonomous and contingent. Structures are created, reformed, changed, and maintained by at least some social actors. Consequently, structures are neither necessarily objective, nor due to an amalgamation of micro social acts. Instead, social structures are autonomous, and created by social interaction at the macro level. Still, they remain related to the dynamic relationship of both levels.

11. Each structure may be consistent or inconsistent with other structures, as well as with individual and group processes. Social interaction and power is again inherent in structural development, and allows structures to be tangibly, rather than merely theoretically, understood.

12. The relationship between micro and macro processes, then, is defined by the dynamic that develops within and between each autonomous level. Neither process may be seen as determining or causing the other. The process of social interaction and the exercise of power makes each level unique and beyond universal laws of social development and integration. The two levels may penetrate each other to variable degrees, be consistent or inconsistent, may or may not be conflictual, and may or may not lead to fundamental social change. While the web of social development is beyond lawlike predictions, the social interactions evident within and between each level makes their autonomous developments observable. Social interaction is observable, however, only when the observer eliminates the desire to develop universal postulates, and instead, realizes the relationship within and between micro and macro levels is necessarily contingent.

13. Empirical investigations are required to establish the relationship within and between micro and macro levels. No theory is capable of predicting what will be found in the tangible social world prior to such investigations.

14. The need for empirical investigations at both micro and macro levels means that many of the concepts and methods developed by micro and macro theories and methodologies are useful, and even necessary, so long as those concepts and methods do not abstractly preclude autonomy and contingency.

References

Abercrombie, Nicholas, Stephen Hill and Bryan S. Turner. 1990. *Dominant Ideologies*. London: Unwin Hyman.

Adler, Alfred. 1931. *What Life Should Mean to You*. Boston: Little Brown.

Adorno, T. W., E. Frenkel-Brunswik, D. J. Levinson, and R. M. Sanford. 1950. *The Authoritarian Personality*. New York: Harper.

Alexander, Jeffrey C. 1987. "Action and Its Environments," in J. Alexander, et. al. (eds.) *The Micro-Macro Link*. Berkeley: University of California Press.

_____ 1988. *Actions and Its Environments: Toward a New Synthesis*. New York: Columbia University Press.

_____ 1991. "Sociological Theory and the Claim to Reason: Why the End is Not in Sight," in *Sociological Theory* 9:147-53.

Allport, G.W. 1968. "The Historical Background of Social Psychology," in *The Handbook of Social Psychology*. G. Lindzey and E. Aronson (eds.) Reading, Mass: Addison-Wesley.

Althusser, Louis. 1979. *For Marx*. London: Verso.

Alvarez, Walter and Frank Asaro. 1990. "What Caused the Mass Extinction?: An Extraterrestrial Impact," in *Scientific American* 263(4):78-84.

Amin, Samir. 1976. *Unequal Development*. New York: Monthly Review Press.

Anderson, Perry. 1984. *In the Tracks of Historical Materialism*. London: Verso.

_____. 1974a. *Lineages of the Absolutist State*. London: New Left Books.

_____. 1974b. *Passages from Antiquity to Feudalism*. London: New Left Books.

Antonio, Robert J. 1990. "The Decline of the Grand Narrative," in G. Ritzer (ed.) *Frontiers of Social Theory*. New York: Columbia University Press.

Archer, Margaret. 1988. *Culture and Agency: the Place of Culture in Social Theory*. Cambridge: Cambridge University Press.

Argyle, Michael. 1992. *The Social Psychology of Everyday Life*. London: Routledge.

Asante, Molefe Kete. 1980. *Afrocentricity*. Philadelphia: Temple University Press

Ashley, David. 1990. "Marx and the Excess of the Signifier." *Sociological Perspectives.* 33:129-46.

Ball, Richard. A, 1978. "Sociology and General Systems Theory." *American Sociologist.* 13:65-72.

Ball, Terrence. 1992. "New Faces of Power," in Thomas E. Wartenberg (ed.) *Rethinking Power.* Albany: State University of New York Press.

Bandura, A. 1976. *Social Learning Theory.* Englewoods Cliffs, NJ: Prentice-Hall.

Barbalet, J.M. 1992. "A Macro Sociology of Emotions." *Social Theory* 10:150-161.

Barnes. Barry. 1974. *Scientific Knowledge and Sociological Theory.* London: Routledge.

Bartusiak, Marcia. 1990. "Mapping the Universe. " *Discover* 11(8):60-63.

Beardsley, Tim. 1992. "Weird Wonders: Was the Cambrian Explosiona Big Bang or Whimper?" *Scientific American* 266(June 1992):30-34.

Bell. J.S. 1964. "On the Einstein-Podolsky-Rosen Paradox." *Physics* 1:195-200.

Bem, D. J. 1970. *Beliefs, Attitudes, and Human Affairs.* Belmont, California: Brooks/Cole.

Benhabib, Seyla. 1989. "Epistomologies of Postmodernism: A Rejoinder to Lyotard," in L. Nicholson *Feminism/postmodernism.* New York: Routledge.

Best, Steven. 1989. "The Commodification of Reality and the Reality of Commodification." *Current Perspectives in Social Theory* 9:23-51.

Bierly, M. M. 1985. "Prejudice Toward Outgroups as a Generalized Attitude." *Journal of Apllied Social Psychology* 15:189-99.

Blumer, Herbert. 1939. "Collective Behavior," in R. Park (ed.) *An Outline of the Principles of Sociology.* New York: Barnes and Noble.

Born, M. 1926. "Zur Quantenmechanik der Stossvorgange. *Zeitschrift fur Physik* 37:863-867.

Bourdieu, Pierre. 1977. *Outline of a Theory of Practice.* Cambridge: Cambridge University Press.

_____ 1989. "Social Space and Symbolic Power." *Sociological Theory* 7:14-25.

Boyne, Roy and Ali Rattansi. 1990. *Postmodernism and Society.* New York: St. Martin's Press.

Brown, Rupert J. 1988. *Group Processes.* Oxford: Blackwell.

Brown, R. J. and D. Abrams. 1986. "The Effects of Intergroup Similarity and Goal Interdependence on Intergroup Attitudes and Task Perfromance." *Journal of Experimental Social Psychology* 22:78-92.

Buckley, Walter. 1967. *Sociology and Modern Systems Theory.* Engelwood Cillfs NJ: Prentice-Hall.

Burt, Ronald. 1982. *Toward a Structural Theory of Action: Network Models of Social Structure, Perception, and Action.* New York: Academic Press.

Callincos, Alex. 1990. "Reactionary Postmodernism?" in Boyne and Rattansi (eds.) *Postmodernism and Society.* New York: St. Martin's Press.

Caspi, A. 1989. "On the Continuities and Consequences of Personality: A Life-course Perspective," in D. M. Buss and N. Cantor (eds.) *Personality Psychology: Recent Trends and Emerging Directions.* New York: Springer.

Chalmers, Alan. 1990. *Science and its Fabrication.* Minneapolis: University of Minnesota Press.

Chomsky, Noam. 1972. *Language and Mind.* New York: Harcourt.

Cohen, G.A. 1982. "Functional Explanation, Consequence Explanation and Marxism." *Inquiry* 25:124-147.

Coleman, James. 1990. *Foundations of Social Theory.* Cambridge: Belknap Press of Harvard University Press.

Collins, H. M. 1985. "Changing Order: Replication and Induction," in *Scientific Practice.* London: Sage.

Collins, Patricia Hill. 1992. "Transforming the Inner Circle: Dorothy Smith's Challenge to Sociological Theory." *Sociological Theory* 10:73-80.

Collins, Randall. 1987. "Interaction Ritual Chains, Power and Property," in J. Alexander et al. (eds.) *The Micro-Macro Link.* Berkeley: University of Calififornia.

Colomy, Paul. 1990a. "Introduction: The Neofunctionalist Movement," in P. Colomy (ed.) *Neofunctionalist Sociology.* Brookfield, VT.: Elgar.

_____ 1990b. "Revisions and Progress in Differentiation Theory," in J. Alexander and P. Colomy (eds.) *Differentian Theory and Social Change.* New York: Columbia University.

Comte, Aguste. 1975. "General View of Biology," in Gertrud Lenzer (ed.) *Auguste Comte and Positivism: The Essential Writings.* New York: Harper.

Condor, S. G. and R. J. Brown. 1986. "Psychological Processes in Intergroup Conflict," in W. Stroebe (ed) *The Social Psychology of Integroup and International Conflict.* New York: Springer.

Cook, Karen and Jodi Obrien and Peter Kollock. 1990. "Exchange Theory: A Blueprint for Structure and Process," in G. Ritzer *Frontiers of Social Theory.* New York: Columbia Univ Press.

Courtillot, Vincent E. 1990. "What Caused the Mass Extinction?: A Volcanic Eruption." *Scientific American* 263(4):85-92.

Craik, K. 1952. *The Nature of Explanation.* Cambridge: Cambridge University Press.

Cushing, James T. and Ernan McMullin. 1989. *Philosophical Consequences of Quantum Theory.* Notre Dame: Notre Dame Press.

Davidson, Donald. 1976. "Hempel on Explaining Action." *Erkenntnis* 10:239-54.

Davis. J. A. 1959. "A Formal Interpretation of the Theory of Relative Deprivation." *Sociometry,* 22:280-96.

Davis, Kingsley and Wilbert Moore. 1945. "Some Principles of Stratification." *American Sociological Review* 10:242-249.

De Bell, Garrett. 1970. *The Environmental Handbook.* New York: Ballantine.

de Certeau. M. 1984. *The Practice of Everyday Life.* Berkeley: University of California Press.

de Saussure, Ferdinand. 1966. *Course in General Linguistics.* New York: McGraw-Hill.

Derrida, Jacques. 1987. *The Post Card: From Socrates to Freud and Beyond.* Chicago: University of Chicago Press.

Deschamps, J. C. 1984. "Intergroup Relations and Categorical Indentification," in H. Taifel (ed.) *The Social Dimension: European Developments in Social Psychology,* Vol 2. Cambridge: Cambrige University Press.

de Sousa, Ronald. 1991. *The Rationality of Emotion.* Cambridge: MIT Press.

De Vos, Gerorge A. and Marcelo Suarez-Orozco. 1992. *Status Inequality: The Self in Culture.* Newbury Park: Sage.

Dewey, John. 1922. *Human Nature and Conduct.* New York: Holt.

Ditto, William L. and L.M. Pecora. 1993. "Matering Chaos." *Scientific American* 269(2):78-85.

Dollard, J., L. W. Doob, N.E. Miller, O.H. Mowrer, and R. R. Sears. 1939. *Frustration and Agression.* New Haven: Yale University Press.

Durkheim, Emile. 1964. *The Division of Labor in Society.* New York: Free Press.

_____. 1965. *The Elementary Forms of Religious Life.* New York: Free Press.

_____. 1973. "The Dualism of Human Nature and Its Social Condition," in R. Bella (ed.) *Emile Durkheim: On Morality and Society.* Chicago: University of Chicago Press.

Dyson, Michael E. 1993. *Reflecting Black: African-American Cultural Criticism.* Minneapolis: University of Minnesota Press.

Edey, Maitland A. and Donald C. Johanson. 1990. *Blueprints: Solving the Mystery of Evolution.* New York: Penguin.

Elder, G. H. and A. Caspi. 1988. "Human Development and Social Change: An Emerging Perspective on the Life Course," in N. Bolger, A. Caspi, G. Downey and M. Moorehouse (eds.) *Persons in Context.* Cambridge: Cambridge University Press.

Eley, Geoff. 1990. "Edward Thompson, Social History and Political Culture: The Making of a Working-class Public, 1780-1850" in Kaye and McClelland (eds.) *E.P. Thompson: Critical Perspectives.* Philadelphia: Temple University Press.

Elias, Norbert. 1991. *The Society of Individuals.* Oxford: Basil Blackwell.

Elliott, Anthony. 1992. *Social Theory and Psychoanalysis in Transition: Self and Society from Freud to Kristeva.* London: Blackwell.

Fanon, Frantz. 1963. *The Wretched of the Earth.* New York: Grove.

Feyerabend, P.K. 1975. *Against Method.* London: New Left Books.

Fine, Gary Alan. 1990. "Symbolic Interactionism in the Post-Blumerian Age," in G. Ritzer (ed.) *Frontiers of Social Theory.* New York: Columbia University Press.

Flax, Jane. 1990. "Postmodernism and Gender Relations in Feminist Theory," in L. Nicholson (ed.) *Feminism/Postmodernism.* New York: Routledge.

Foucault, Michel. 1965. *Madness and Civilization.* New York: Vintage.

_____ 1970. *The Order of Things.* London: Tavistock.

_____ 1972a. *The Archaeology of Knowledge and The Discourse on Language.* New York: Pantheon.

_____. 1977. *Discipline and Punish: The Birth of the Prison.* Harmondsworth: Penguin.

_____ 1978 *Power/Knowledge: Selected Interviews and Other Writings 1972-1977.* New York: Pantheon.

Frank, Andre Gunder. 1969. *Latin America: Underdevelopment and Revolution.* New York: Monthly Review Press.

Frank, Manfred. 1989. *What is Neostructuralism?* Minneapolis: University of Minnesota Press.

Fraser, Nancy and Linda Nicholson. 1990. "Social Criticism without Philosophy: An Encounter between Feminism and Postmodernism," in L. Nicholson (ed.) *Feminism/postmodernism.* New York: Routledge.

Freud, Sigmund. 1963. *A General Introduction to Psychoanalysis.* New York: Simon and Shuster.

Friedman, Debra and Michael Hechter. 1990. "The Comparative Advantages of Rational Choice Theory," in G. Ritzer (ed.) *Frontiers of Social Theory.* New York: Columbia University Press.

Fritsch, Albert J. 1979. *Environmental Ethics.* New York: Anchor.

Fromm, Erich. 1965. *Escape From Freedom.* New York: Holt, Rinehart, and Winston.

Gadamer, Hans-Georg. 1984. "The Hermeneutics of Suspicion," in Shapiro and Sica (eds.) *Hermeneutics: Questions and Prospects.* Amherst: University of Massachusetts Press.

Geisen, Bernhard. 1980. *Makrosoziologie.* Hamburg: Hoffmann und Campe.

_____ 1987. "Beyond Reductionism: Four Models Relating to Micro and Macro Levels," in J. Alexander, et. al. (eds.) *The Micro-Macro Link.* Berkeley: University of California Press.

Giddens, Anthony. 1984. *The Constitution of Society.* Berkeley: University of California Press.

_____ 1990. *The Consequences of Modernity.* Stanford: Stanford University Press.

Gilder, George. 1981. *Wealth and Poverty.* New York: Bantam Books.

Glass, Leon. 1988. *From Clocks to Chaos.* Princeton: Princeton University Press.

Gleick, James. 1987. *Chaos: Making a New Science.* New York: Penguin.

Goffman, Erving. 1974. *Frame Analysis:An Essay on the Organization of Experience.* New York: Harper Colophon.

Gould, Stephen Jay. 1989. *Wonderful Life: The Burgess Shale and the Nature of History.* New York: W.W. Norton.

Greenwood, John D. 1991. *Relations and Presentations.* London: Routledge.

Gurtzwiller, Martin. C. 1992. "Quantum Chaos." *Scientific American* 266(1):78-85.

Habermas, Jurgen. 1985. *The Philosophical Discourse of Modernity.* Cambridge, MA: MIT Press.

_____ 1989. *The Theory of Communicative Action: Volume Two.* Boston: Beacon.

Haferkamp, Hans. 1987. "Complexity and Behavior Structure, Planned Associations and Creation of Structure," in J. Alexander, et. al. (eds.) *The Micro-Macro Link.* Berkeley: University of California Press.

Hall, C.S. and G. Lindzey. 1978. *Theories of Personality.* New York: Wiley.

Hall, Thomas D. 1989. *Social Change in the Southwest: 1350-1880.* Lawrence: University Press of Kansas.

Haraway, Donna. 1991. *Simians, Cyborgs, and Women, The Reinvention of Nature.* London: Routledge.

Harvey, David. 1990. *The Condition of Postmodernity.* Oxford: Basil Blackwell.

Hawking, Stephen W. 1988. *A Brief Hisotry of Time: From the Big Bang to Black Holes.* New York: Bantam.

Hempel, Carl. 1966. *Philosophy of Natural Science.* Englewood Cliffs, NJ: Prentice-Hall.

Himmelweit, Hilde T. 1990. "Societal Psycholgy: Implications and Scope," in Himmelweit and Gaskell (eds.) *Societal Psychology.* Newbury Park: Sage.

Himmelweit, Hilde T. and George Gaskell. 1990. *Societal Psychology.* Newbury Park: Sage.

Hobsbawm, E.J. 1968. *Industry and Empire.* Hardmonsworth: Penguin.

Hogg, Michael A. and Dominic Abrams. 1988. *Social Indentifications.* London: Routledge.

Horgan, John. 1993. "An Eternally Self-Producing Cosmos?" *Scientific American.* 268:24.

_____. 1992. "Quantum Philosophy." *Scientific American* 267:94-104.

_____. 1990. "Universal Truths." *Scientific American* 263(4):108-117.

Hormuth, Stefan E. 1990. *The Ecology of the Self: Relocation and Self-Concept Change.* Cambridge: Cambridge University Press.

Itzkowitz, Gary. 1991. "Who Wins in Welfare Reform:? It's Business as Usual." *Humanity and Society.* 15:276-289.

Izard, C.E. 1977. *Human Emotions.* New York: Plenum.

James, William. 1890. *Principles of Psychology.* New York: Holt.

Jameson, F. 1984. "Postmodernism, or the Cultural Logic of Late Capitalism." *New Left Review* 146:53-92.

Jung, Carl C. 1972. *Psychological Reflections.* Princeton: Princeton University Press.

Kagan, Jerome, Ernest Havemann and Julius Segal. 1984. *Psychology: An Introduction.* New York: Harcourt Brace Jovanovich.

Kaye, Harvey J. and Keith McClelland. 1990. *E.P. Thompson: Critical Perspectives*. Philadelphia: Temple University Press.

Kern, Stephen. 1983. *The Culture of Time and Space: 1880-1918*. Cambridge: Harvard University Press.

Kitcher, Phillip and Wesley C. Salmon. 1989. *Scientific Explanation*. Minneapolis: University of Minnesota Press.

Klatsky, R. L. 1980. *Human Memory: Structures and Processes*. San Francisco: Freeman.

Kohler, Wolfgang. 1947. *Gestalt Psychology*. New York: Liveright.

Laclau, Ernesto. 1990. *New Reflections on the Revolution of Our Time*. London: Verso.

Laclau, Ernesto and Chantel Mouffe. 1985. *Hegemony and Socialist Strategy: Towards a Radical Democratic Politics*. London: Verso.

Lakatos, Imre. 1978. "Science and Pseudo-Science," in Worral and Currie (eds.) *Imre Lakatos: Philosophical Papers, Volume 1 and Vol. 2*. Cambridge: Cambridge University Press.

Lazarus. Richard S. 1991. *Emotion and Adaptation*. New York: Oxford University Press.

Lemert, Charles C. 1992. "Subjectivity's Limit: The Unsolved Riddle of the Standpoint." *Sociological Thoery* 10:63-72.

_____. 1990. "The Uses of French Structuralism in Sociology," in G. Ritzer (ed.) *Frontiers of Social Theory*. New York: Columbia University Press.

Lewin, Kurt. 1939. "Patterns of Agressive Behavior in Experimentally Created Social Climates." *Journal of Social Psychology*. 10:271-99.

Lovibond, Sabina. 1990. "Feminism and Postmodernism" in Boyne and Rattansi (eds.) *Postmodernism and Society*. New York: St. Martin's Press.

Luhmann, Niklas. 1982. *The Differentiation of Society*. New York: Columbia University Press.

_____ 1987. "The Evolutionary Differentiation between Society and Interaction," in J. Alexander et. al. (eds.) *The Micro-Macro Link*. Berkeley: University of California Press.

Lyotard, Jean-Francois. 1984. *The Postmodern Condition*. Minneapolis: University of Minnesota Press.

Manicas, Peter T. 1987. *A History and Philosophy of the Social Sciences*. Oxford: Basil Blackwell.

Magnusson, D. 1988. *Individual Development from an Interactional Perspective: A Longitudinal Study*. Hillsdale, NJ: L. Erlbaum.

Manis, Jerome G. and Bernard N. Meltzer. 1994. "Chance in Human Affairs." *Social Theory*. 12:45-56.

Marx, Karl. 1987. *Selected Writings*. Oxford: Oxford University Press.

Mead, Gerorge Herbert. 1962. *Mind, Self and Society*. Chicago: University of Chicago Press.

Mennell, Stephen. 1989. *Norbert Elias: Civilization and the Human Self-Image*. Oxford: Basil Blackwell.

Monod, Jacques. 1972. *Chance and Necessity*. New York: Vintage Books.

Murray, Charles. 1984. *Losing Ground: American Social Policy 1950-1980*. New York: Basic Books.

Murphy, J. Brendon and R. Nance. 1992. "Mountain Belts and the Supercontinent Cycle." *Scientific American* 266(4):84-91.

Muwakkil, Salim. 1992. "Dissecting Afrocentrism and its Growing Discontents," in *In These Times*. May, 6, 1992.

Nicholson, Linda. 1990. *Feminism/Postmodernism* New York: Routledge.

Offe, Claus. 1972. "Political Authority and Class Structures: An Analysis of Late Capitalist Societies." *International Journal of Sociology* (Spring, 1972):73-108.

_____ 1976. "Crises of Crisis Management: Elements of a Political Crisis Theory." *International Journal of Politics* (Fall, 1976):67.

O'Hear, Anthony. 1989. *An Introduction to the Philosophy of Science*. Oxford: Oxford University Press.

Panksepp, Jaak. 1982. "Toward a General Psychological Theory of Emotions." *The Behavioral and Brain Sciences* 5:407-476.

Parsons, Talcott. 1937. *The Structure of Social Action*. New York: Mcgraw Hill.

Peterson, Ivars. 1993a *Newton's Clock: Chaos in the Solar System*. New York: Freeman.

_____. 1993b. "Chaos in Spacetime." *Scientific News* 144(23):376-77.

Piel, Jonathan. 1991. "Science in the 20th Century." *Scientific American* 3:4-10.

Piven, Fracis Fox and Richard A. Cloward. 1987. "The Historical Sources of the Contemporary Relief Debate," and "The Contemporary Relief Debate," in Block, et al., *The Mean Season*. New York: Pantheon.

Popper, Karl R. 1966. *The Open Society and its Enemies, Volume 2*. London: Routledge, Keagan and Paul.

Porritt, Jonathan. 1985. *Seeing Green: The Politics of Ecology Explained*. Oxford: Basil Blackwell.

Poulantzas, Nicos. 1978. *Political Power and Social Classes*. London: Verso.

Preston, V., S. M. Taylor, and D.C. Hodge. 1983. "Adjustments to Natural and Technological Hazards." *Environment and Behavior* 15:143-64.

Prigogine, Ilya and Isabel Stengers. 1984. *Order Out of Chaos: Man's New Dialogue with Nature.* New York: Bantam.

Ranger-Moore, James. 1992. A Review of *Beyond Natural Selection* by Robert G. Wesson in *Contemporary Sociology* 21:220-21.

Richardson, Laurel. 1991. "Postmodern Social Theory: Representational Practices." *Sociological Theory* 9: 173-79.

Ricoeur, P. 1981. *Hermeneutics and the Human Sciences.* Cambridge: Cambridge University Press.

Rifkin, Jeremy. 1989. *Entropy: Into the Greenhouse World.* New York: Bantam.

Ritzer, George. 1992. *Sociological Theory.* New York: McGraw-Hill.

Rorty, R. 1980. *Philosophy and the Mirror of Nature.* Oxford: Blackwell.

Rose, Gillan. 1981. *Hegel Contra Sociology.* New Jersey: Humanities Press.

Ross, Lee and Richard Nisbett. 1991. *The Person and the Situation: Perspectives of social Psychology.* Philadelphia: Temple University Press.

Ruthen, Russell. 1992. "Catching the Wave" in *Scientific American* 226(3):90-99.

Salmon, Wesley C. 1989. *Four Decades of Scientific Explanation.* Minneapolis: University of Minnesota Press.

Sampson, E.E. 1988. "The Debate on Individualism: Indigenous Psychologies of the Individual and their Role in Personal and Societal Functioning." *American Psychologist* 43:15-22.

Sartre, Jean-Paul, 1948. *The Emotions: Outline of a Theory.* New York: Philosophical Library.

Schaffer, M.V. and M. Kot. 1986. "Chaos in Ecological Systems: The Goals that Newcastle Forgot." *Trends in Ecology and Evolution* 1(3):58-63.

Scheman, Naomi. 1983. "Individualism and the Objects of Psychology" in Harding and Hintikka (eds.) *Discovering Reality.* Dordrecht: Reidel.

Schwab, Martin. 1989. "Foreword" in Manfred Frank *What is Neostructuralism?* Minneapolis: University of Minnesota Press.

Seidman, Steven. 1991. "The End of Sociological Theory:The Postmodern Hope." *Sociological Theory* 9:131-46.

Senn, David J. 1989. "Myopic Social Psychology: An Overemphasis on Individualistic Explanations of Social Behavior," in Leary (ed.) *The State of Social Psychology*. Newbury Park: Sage.

Shapiro, Gary and Alan Sica. 1984. *Hermeneutics: Questions and Prospects*. Amherst: University of Massachusetts Press.

Sherif, Muzafer. 1935. "A Study of Some Social Factors in Perception *Archives of Psychology* 187:1-60.

_____. 1962. (ed.) *Intergroup Leadership and Relations*. New York: Wiley.

Simmel, Georg. 1978. *The Philosophy of Money*. London: Routledge.

Skinner, B.F. 1974. *About Behaviorism*. New York: Knopf.

Skocpol, Theda. 1979. *States and Social Revolutions*. Cambridge: Cambridge University Press.

Smith, Dorothy E. 1987. *The Everyday World as Problematic: A Feminist Sociology*. Boston: Northeastern University Press.

_____. 1990a. *The Conceptual Practices of Power: A Feminist Sociology of Knowledge*. Boston: Northeastern University Press.

_____. 1990b. *Texts, Facts, and Femininity: Exploring the Relations of Ruling*. New York: Routledge.

Smith, E.E. and D.L. Medin. 1981. *Categories and Concepts*. Cambridge: Harvard University Press.

Solomon, Robert C. 1976. *The Passions: The Myth and Nature of Human Emotions*. New York: Doubleday.

Spender, Dale. 1980. *Man-made Language*. London: Routledge, Keegan and Paul.

Spretnak, Charlene. 1991. *States of Grace*. New York: Harper Collins.

Stokols, Daniel. 1988. "Transformational Processes in People-Environment Relations," in McGrath (ed.) *The Psychology of Time*. Newbury Park: Sage.

Turner, Bryan S. 1990. "Conclusion: Peroration on Idoeology" in Abercrombie et al. (eds.) *Dominant Ideologies*. London: Unwin Hyman.

Vernonm M.D. 1971. *The Psychology of Perception*. Harmondsworth: Penguin.

Wacquant, Loïc j.d. 1989. "Towards a Reflexive Sociology." *Sociological Theory*. 7:26-63.

Wallerstein, Immanuel. 1974. *The Modern World System: Capitalist Agriculture and the Origins of the European World-Economy in the 16th Century*. New York: Academic Press.

_____. 1980. *The Modern World System II: Mercantilism and the Consolidation of the European World Economy*. New York: Academic Press.

_____. 1989. *The Modern World System III: The Second Era of Great Expansion of the Capitalist World-Economy.* New York: Academic Press.

Wartenberg, Thomas E. 1992. "Situated Social Power" in Wartenberg (ed.) *Rethinking Power.* Albany: State University of New York Press.

Watson, John B. 1930. *Behaviorism.* New York: Norton.

Weber, Max. 1949. *The Methodology of the Social Sciences.* Edward Shils and Henry Finch (eds.) New York: Free Press.

_____. 1964. *The Theory of Social and Economic Organization.* Talcott Parsons (ed.) New York: Free Press.

Werner, Carol M, Lois Haggard, Irwin Altman and Diana Oxley. 1988. "Temporal Qualities of Rituals and Celebrations in People-Environment Relations," in McGrath (ed.) *The Psychology of Time.* Newbury Park: Sage.

West, Cornel. 1993. *Race Matters.* Boston: Beacon Press.

Wheeler, L. 1978. *Interpersonal Influence.* Boston: Allyn and Bacon.

Wicklund, R. A. and J.W. Brehm. 1976. *Perspectives on Cognitive Dissonance.* Hilsdale, NJ: Erlbaum.

Wippler, Reinhard and Siegwart Lindenberg. 1987. "Collective Phenomena and Rational Choice," in J. Alexander et al. (eds.) *The Micro-Marcro Link.* Berkeley: University of California Press.

Wittgenstein, Ludwig. 1953. *Philosophical Investigations.* Oxford: Blackwell.

Wood, Ellen Meiksins. 1990. "Falling Through the Cracks: E.P. Thompson and the Debate on Base and Superstructure," in Kaye and McClelland (eds.) *E.P. Thompson: Critical Perspectives.* Philadelphia: Temple University Press.

INDEX